HISTORY LESSONS

for the

Modern Investor

Patrick Huey, CFP,® CAP®

LUMINARE PRESS

WWW.LUMINAREPRESS.COM

History Lessons for the Modern Investor
© 2018 Patrick Huey

Printed in the United States of America

Cover Design: Claire Flint Last

Luminare Press
438 Charnelton St., Suite 101
Eugene, OR 97401
www.luminarepress.com

LCCN: 2018941182
ISBN: 978-1-944733-46-9

For my clients. Thank you.
"What's past is prologue; what to come, In yours and my discharge."
—William Shakespeare, *The Tempest*, Act 2, Scene I

And for Dixie and Fletcher.
"There are no victories
In all our histories, without love."
Sting, *Mad About You (1991)*

TABLE OF CONTENTS

Introduction... 1

HISTORY 101
The Great Minds of Antiquity & Cognitive Biases 9

HISTORY 201
European Art, Science, War & Basic Economic Principles 93

HISTORY 301
The Building of America & Basic Investment Theory 201

HISTORY 401
Modern America, the New Normal & Financial Advice............... 295

Afterword 394

Notes & Sources 396

INTRODUCTION

"Write the book only you can write."

—UNKNOWN[1]

I have a confession to make. My head is a mess. Seriously, in there is an organized chaos of trivia, movie snippets, motivational quotes, tall tales, and hard data. It is the result of earning a bachelor's degree in history and liberal arts and then joining the Navy to fly airplanes; the product of years spent at sea with a personal library of Patrick O'Brian novels and a limited variety of VHS movies; the outcome fashioned by a Master's Degree in Business, most of another in education, and a professional designation in financial planning. I know some stuff. I've been a few places. So what?

---

1   I don't know to whom the opening quote should be attributed. As you'll see in the ensuing lessons, especially, the Extra Credit, I'm not afraid to delve the depths of the Internet, but my research here turned up very little. Most likely it is a paraphrased translation from the French author Andre Gide who cautioned authors to "Grow fond only of that which you can find nowhere but in yourself." Also, this is a good time to let you know that I rather like using footnotes and will continue to do so throughout the book.

"The wisdom of past civilizations, from Greece and India to the Middle East, is embodied in compelling narratives that modern audiences still find engrossing: the epics of Homer, the tragedies of the great Athenian playwrights… Humans have always instinctively understood that the key to conveying a message powerfully and unforgettably is to couch it in a story."

—MCCREA & WALKER, The Generosity Network

This is a book only I could write. I'm not bragging, but the fact is the mishmash of topics floating around in my brain was uniquely positioned to create this particular story. History, fiction, what passes for modern culture, investing, and planning: when you put it all together, you get a quirky collection of anecdotes stretching from antiquity to present day, which, like Aesop's Fables, will teach you a lesson if you aren't careful. And it is a lesson many of us desperately need. Amidst a retirement crisis, where few will have saved or invested enough to fund their post-career lives, we have simultaneously created the most amazing technology for broadcasting bad advice and money-losing strategies to the masses. Television, the Internet, and social media have created an unholy trinity bent on convincing you success is just a click or "simple trick" away. Of course, it takes more than that, but approaching people with the intent to teach is hard. You need to keep them entertained or lose out to whatever financial "advice" was advertised while screening cat videos on YouTube.

> *"All the math you need in the stock market you get in the fourth grade."*
>
> **—PETER LYNCH,**
> Fidelity Magellan Fund Manager 1977-1990

In this world of instant information, formula trading, and brilliant mathematicians running multi-billion-dollar hedge funds, what good can some stories about the past do? How about provide some perspective? You don't have to be brilliant or even good at math to be a successful investor. But you do need to know a few fundamentals about how markets and economies work. You also need to know that our brains are old technology not necessarily built for this task. Stories help illustrate these concepts in a way math never could.

> *"All the wisdom of the world is in stories."*
>
> **—PATRICK ROTHFUS,** The Wiseman's Fear

There are, believe it or not, other books like this one. Not many, but a few. Perhaps the first was by an Austrian poet and occasional biographer named Stefan Zweig. His *Decisive Moments in History (1927)*, was a series of vignettes that encapsulated how certain people at specific times tell much about humanity's ability to discover, create, and transcend their limitations. Like most Americans I didn't read it. Until, that is, I came across Simon Winchester's sweeping history, *Pacific (2016)*, a book about the ocean and the stories, from surfing to submarines, that best "tell in microcosm a larger truth." Winchester traced his idea to Zweig, whose "tumbling mélange of a book, quite charming and, even if perhaps lacking in academic rigor, one that quite transfixed me."[2]

In the following pages, I tell, in microcosm, a larger truth about who we are as humans *and* investors. I hope to tell stories that engage and entertain in a tumbling mélange of well-known characters such as:

- Julius Caesar tells a cautionary tale on the cognitive bias of believing that the future will be like our recent past.
- Benjamin Franklin, who for a while held the title as the most interesting man in the world, on the power of diversification.
- Jerry Seinfeld and his occasionally lovable creation George Constanza, on what it means to be a contrarian.

But history is more than famous people. We can also learn a lot from lesser known personalities like:

- Thomas Morton who was kicked out of the early colonies so often, he became their first export and can teach us something about international trade.
- W.B. Tegetmeier whose studies on the training of pigeons led to theories about adaptability for species, including humans at work.

2   See also *Caesar's Last Breath: Decoding the Secrets of the Air Around Us*, by Sam Kean, a "themed miscellany," as the Wall Street Journal calls it, of stories about the science behind the air we breathe. Basically, like Thanksgiving dinner with your unrefined uncle, these are a bunch of stories about gas. "Like gases themselves, *Caesar's Last Breath* holds together only loosely, and the reader must, as its author does, embrace the chaos."

Patrick Huey

- Patillo Higgins whose boom and bust career in the first Texas oil patch was a warning for investors in cyclical industries.

And yes, I have created or embellished the tales meant to illustrate these points, so parts of this work may lack strict academic rigor. Like a series of college courses, each building on the last, here is how I've organized my truths and embellishments:

History 101: The Great Minds of Antiquity & Cognitive Biases

After years of schlepping about Africa and Asia as hunter-gatherers, mankind coalesced into a more recognizable and modern form a few thousand years BC. Subsistence farming meant that instead of moving on as nomads, people settled and began cultivating grains for their daily bread. They banded together to keep beasts and rogues at bay. Their diets became more balanced and their health improved. Fewer predators ate them and life expectancies increased. Longer lives, safer conditions, and the ability to blend into a crowded city created the first opportunity in our history to be lazy. It also gave us the opportunity to sit and ponder a bit. Sometimes those two things look amazingly similar in action. An all-star lineup of thinkers including Aristotle, Socrates, Confucius, and Homer demonstrate the mental tricks our brains (built for big game hunting and survival) can play on a city dweller with too much free time.

History 201: European Art, Science, War, & Basic Economic Principles

The Renaissance emerged from the fall of Rome, and Western culture arguably became the dominant force in an ever-shrinking world. Exploration flourished and "new" worlds were discovered, in spite of the many indigenous people who would have preferred to pass on the discovery process, *thank you very much*. Humans progressed from developing their laws to imposing them on other people. Wonderful advancement, right? Thinkers and philosophers again found time to ply their trades after years of skulking through the Dark Ages. Sculptors, scientists, painters, and poets did likewise. We follow several of these characters as Europe emerges as a shining example of what ingenuity and incentives can produce after the slate is wiped clean and the stars align; when supply fulfills demand and technology advances; and when generalists become specialists and competition flourishes.

History 301: The Building of America & Basic Investment Theory

From the time of the American Revolution until the end of World War Two, the political and economic landscape shifted away from colonization and monarchy to independence and democracy, at least for some. Results, as they say, may vary. History 301 introduces us to the basics of capital markets, using the budding capitalist society in the New World to guide the narrative. Perhaps it was a coincidence George Washington took the first oath of office near Wall Street? Or maybe just historical karma. Following the famous, and sometimes merely notorious, citizens of the age, we trace the development of ever more complex financial transactions and discuss the basics of markets, speculation, and investment.

History 401: Modern America, the New Normal & Financial Advice

It would be tempting to look back over the preceding four millennia and award ourselves a participation trophy based on how far we've come. Not so fast my friend. In the conclusion to our lessons we examine modern music, movies, television, and sports to understand and overcome our persistent shortcomings by seeking professional help and advice. Where would athletes be without coaches, musicians without producers, and movie stars without publicists? They'd probably be schmucks like you and me. Good advice can be the difference between being a regular schmuck or an exceptional one. Hey, the choice is yours.

Each of the four courses contains ten to twelve individual lessons. And of course, because life isn't fair, there will be a test. But like a principal's nightmare, I'll teach to the exam, giving away the answers, and hopefully saving you from making life-altering investment mistakes. You are welcome.

Finally, each lesson will feature extra credit for you go-getters who want to take a deeper dive into related materials. Many resources are links to websites. So, to save you a fair amount of typing, you can go to the book's website at www.historylessonforthemoderninvestor.com for a comprehensive listing of previously published, updated, or new materials. You can also leave me your questions, comments, and smart remarks. I'll take all comers.

Well, there you have it. That is what is on my mind. I look forward to knowing what is on yours. Have fun, learn a few tales to impress your friends, and become a better investor, or at least a more informed one.

Patrick Huey

HISTORY 101

The Great Minds of Antiquity & Cognitive Biases

*"Mine is the first step and
therefore a small one..."*

—ARISTOTLE

*"Men in general are quick to believe
that which they wish to be true."*

—JULIUS CAESAR

*"Real knowledge is to know the
extent of one's ignorance."*

—CONFUCIUS

LESSON ONE: Living in Babble On
Hammurabi & Outcome Bias
C. 1750 BC

LESSON TWO: Every Dog Has His Day
Thutmose III & the Hot Hand Fallacy
C. 1457 BC

LESSON THREE: The Problem with Poets
Homer & the Rhyme as Reason Fallacy
C. 850 BC

LESSON FOUR: Questioning the Answers
Socrates & Anchoring Bias
469–399 BC

LESSON FIVE: The Ancient Chinese Secret
Kong Fuzi & Availability Bias
551–479 BC

LESSON SIX: Peripatetic Fits
Aristotle & Illusory Correlations
384–322 BC

LESSON SEVEN: To Be, or Knot to Be
Alexander the Great & Functional Fixedness
333 BC

LESSON EIGHT: Stuck in the Middle
Julius Caesar & Recency Bias
44 BC

LESSON NINE: With Friends Like These
Ovid, Augusts & Confirmation Bias
8AD

LESSON TEN: Where There's Smoke, There's Fire
Pliny & Risk Homeostasis Theory (RHT)
79AD

LESSON ELEVEN: Falling to Pieces
Hypatia & the Bandwagon Effect
451AD

Living in Babble On
Hammurabi & Outcome Bias

C. 1750 BC

T he Ancient Babylonians, who emerged as a regional power in present day Iraq around 1750 BC, literally cast their laws in stone, and occasionally, their accused into the river. The results were brutal, but predictable. Bad swimmers were to blame for everything, but good ones could get away with murder.

Stolid and stern, in a robe of white with a matching headscarf, the judge looked out over the crowd assembled in front of him, swatches of color on a uniformly brown background. The women wore cool shifts, while the men had the short, belted garments of the working class. The desert sands shifted in a midday breeze and a column of dust sprouted in the desert wind, a dust devil flittering toward the nearby river. The midday sun meant he had to squint to see all but the accused, who stood next to him sweating and sobbing.

On the wind were the various fragrances of the massive gardens in town. Cypress, olive, pomegranate, and fig brewed a pleasant mix of spicy, sweet, and musky scent. Palm trees rustled along the road into town, offering the only sound in the desert.[3]

Then the judge boomed, extending a finger, "Accused! How do you plead?"

The Ancient Babylonians were more than great gardeners, they were the first society to develop a written rule of law. Their king, Hammurabi, spoke plainly, laid out what was expected of his subjects, and inscribed it so everyone could see. Per the code, each of the two hundred and eighty-two laws was prefaced by the magic words: *Hammurabi says*. Today, Hammurabi's Code can be viewed in the Louvre Museum on a seven-foot-tall slab. If you can read the extinct Assyri-Babylonian language, the code will help you to establish the rights of contract, liability, divorce, and punishment. If you can't read Assyri-Babylonian, you will just have to trust me.[4]

"Not guilty," rasped the accused, a builder whose work, unlike Hammurabi's, had not stood the test of time. For that crime, as well as all major crimes in ancient Babylon, the penalty was death. A witness who testified falsely would be slain and there was no such thing as invoking the Fifth

---

3   The Hanging Gardens of Babylon, one of the Seven Wonders of the Ancient World, were a soaring work of tiered mud bricks creating vertical garden space for numerous species of plants, trees and shrubs. The site of the gardens was said to be in Babylon, though it is the only one of the Seven Wonders for which no exact location has ever been determined. It may have been a myth and never existed at all.

4   By comparison, the United States Code (2006 edition) is over 200,000 pages long with no catchy introductions. Your choice: Babylon or "Babble-On." Sometimes more is better, and sometimes it's just more.

Amendment. If a builder's work was shoddy and collapsed, the builder was killed and there was no union grievance. This particular builder could see the mist rising over the Euphrates where the river turned in a rocky curve of frothing rapids. He could even hear its roar. Perspiration flooded down his face and he felt his bladder let go.[5]

The judge arched an eyebrow. "Bind him up and let the God Marduk decide," he barked.[6]

There was no appeals process, with one exception: the accused could be thrown into the river and have his innocence or guilt decided by the waters. Wash ashore and you were innocent all along; drown and good riddance to the guilty.[7]

"For the love of Ishtar no!" A woman screamed then went limp in the arms of others gathered around her.[8]

The crowd swarmed about the prisoner, lashing together his hands, and dragging him toward the shore. The rapids got closer, and he felt the spray on his face and heard the thunder in his ears. Hands were on him, pushing him and feet kicked him further and further into the water. It rose around his waist, then his chest, and finally he breathed deeply and went under. Jagged rocks tore at his flesh and

---

5   One wonders if bad builders kept washing ashore downriver to start new settlements that collapsed into the desert. If so, the witnesses aren't telling.

6   Marduk was the god of judgment and the patron deity of Babylon.

7   Conducting physical trials of the accused persisted for thousands of years. Witches were persecuted using similar means up until the Enlightenment of the 17th Century AD.

8   Ishtar was the Babylonian Goddess of love. She is not to be confused with the 1987 movie Ishtar, starring Dustin Hoffman and Warren Beatty, which *no one* loved.

battered his bones. He bobbed once, surfaced spitting and gasping, and then went down again. The crowd watched for a long time. The man did not come up again. The river churned over his broken body and carried him down and away.

"I knew it all along," growled the judge. "Guilty! And Hammurabi says…the punishment is death." The judge spat into the dust and walked away shaking his head.

The crowd dispersed slowly, heading back to the temple in the shade of the great tower, the coolness of the gardens, or to work on the hot dusty plain. They left the woman alone, weeping silently, tears falling on the sand before being swallowed by the desert.

Sure, written laws are a nice advancement, but it wasn't all fun in the Babylonian sun and beach parties by the Euphrates. Hammurabi's Code could be rather harsh and was susceptible to **Outcome Bias**—focusing on the *outcome* of particular events, while neglecting potentially important contributing factors. After all, your ability to survive in the raging rapids is based on more than just your innocence or guilt. If you question that at all, please put this book down now and save us both some time and effort. Trust me, the rest won't help you.

How You'll Be Tested...

While it seems ludicrous to the modern ear, we still base many of our important decisions by looking at the outcome of previous events.

A friend has a hot stock tip and tells you how much money she made on her investment of lifetime. *Wonderful,* you think. *I need to get some of that.* You read no research. You peruse no periodicals. You don't even turn on the television. You just decide you will buy something based on the previous results of another person's investment. That is outcome bias.

Accused! How do you plead? Never mind, we know you are guilty. At least you'll only be figuratively swimming against the tide. Previous performance is never a guarantee of forthcoming results. A good investor will remember that the future, unlike the past, is never carved in stone.

EXTRA CREDIT

LOVE THE LOUVRE: The Louvre's "Closer Look" interactive tour of the code of Hammurabi will give you some idea of how rocking he was, what he said, and how he said it. http://musee.louvre.fr/oal/code/indexEN.html.

ROCK ON: How A Bill Becomes Law, a classic from Schoolhouse Rock. Note the nuanced differences between how modern American and ancient Babylonian laws are created. https://www.youtube.com/watch?v=FBpdxEMelR0.

GO FOR IT: 4th and 2 on your own 28-yard line, leading by six points with the game winding down. Convert for a first down and you win. Punt it away and you give your opponent time to beat you. What do you do? Well, the numbers convincingly say go for it. But when it doesn't work out, prepare to be crushed by sportswriters focused only on the results. https://fifthdown.blogs.nytimes.com/2009/11/16/defending-belichicks-fourth-down-decision/.

PLAY THE BLAME GAME: Researchers looked at how we judge people's ethics after the outcome of their actions are known. In a working paper published by Harvard Business School, they find "that individuals judge behaviors as less ethical, more blameworthy, and punish them more harshly, when such behaviors led to undesirable consequences, even if they saw those behaviors as acceptable before they knew its consequences." Not only can we find you guilty based on outcome bias, but we can determine that you were a lousy, unethical human being all along. Get the paper here: https://papers.ssrn.com/sol3/Data_Integrity_Notice.cfm?abid=1099464.

GET QUIZZED:

1. Three gamblers enter a casino with $1,000 apiece and spend some time at the roulette wheel. At the end of the night the first gambler has turned $1,000 into $5,000. The second gambler stayed flat, leaving with $1,000. The last gambler left with nothing, blowing all $1,000. Who was the best gambler?
2. The three gamblers are Dean Martin, Sammy Davis Jr., and Frank Sinatra. Frank Sinatra goes on to be nominated over thirty times for a Grammy and wins thirteen. Sammy wins four, and Dean just one for lifetime achievement. Who was the best singer?
3. Frank, Sammy, and Dean jump in their cars for a race down the strip. They arrive at the Sands in the following order: Dean, Sammy, Frank. Who was the fastest driver?

If you attempted to answer any of these questions you did it with incomplete information and probably based simply on the outcome. But other factors might have had effects on the results.

1. One night of gambling doesn't make you "good" or "bad." Lady luck has a say.
2. Sammy Davis was supremely talented in an era when his race kept him out of good clubs and recording contracts.

3. Dean Martin would often fake drinking whiskey, opting for apple juice to maintain his sobriety. Maybe he was the only one who could find his car keys or the other two stopped at the Rio for a belt?

Of course, if you said Frank was the best at everything because he was Frank frigging Sinatra, I'll give you a pass. See Part Four, Lesson Two.

Every Dog Has His Day
Thutmose III & The Hot Hand Fallacy

C. 1457 BC

Okay, deciding based merely on previous results is bad. But what if the results are the same over and over? What if things really seem to be going our way? What if we are on a monumental hot streak?

The column of horses, chariots, and soldiers ground noisily to a halt where the road forked. The sands of the Sinai desert blew in patches over the crossroads, but it was quiet save the low moaning of the pack animals and a few weary soldiers. On the horizon stretched a low series of dark scrubby hills rising above the washed-out desert around them all the way to Mount Carmel. The beloved of Ra and ruler of Egypt gazed south along the wide road that arched around the hills. He let his eyes trace northward to where the road again bent out of sight. He rested on his long staff and wiped sweat from under his headdress, feeling the heat of the desert rise in waves from his sandaled feet.

"What do you think?" he asked. He had waited for this day for over twenty floods of the Nile. Indeed, for twenty-two of them he had ruled Egypt along with his stepmother, causing many to view him as nothing more than a lap dog. He needed to show in his second year of sole power that his bite was more like Anubis himself. Before the day was over, he expected to make Anubis a very busy deified dog, readying his enemies for the afterlife.[9] [10]

His general shrugged. "It's a road." he said, stating the obvious to one so new to the ways of war. "It is wide and easily traveled. We can take it in either direction without dismounting and bring our chariots to bear on either of the rebel armies. We can defeat one and then turn on the other." He was having a hard time believing he was here with this new, weak, and incapable Pharaoh. During the entire reign of his stepmother the army hadn't fought a single battle. The army had been easy and safe duty, and the general had flourished. But now some Canaanite vassals thought their Pharaoh weak enough to challenge. And who could blame them?

Thutmose, the human son of the god Amun, seemed to focus on something off in the distance, and his voice was far

9 His stepmother was Hatshepsut, considered one of the first great women of history, though her co-regent might not have agreed. Various theories abound about their relationship—whether she usurped the throne from a two-year-old and shared power with him as he came of age, and if the boy king attempted to remove her from the historical record by defacing her monuments years after her death.

10 The Egyptian god Anubis, often depicted as human with the head of a dog, was associated with embalming and mummification, as well as the afterlife. By the period of the Middle Kingdom (2055–1650 BC) he had been replaced by Osiris as the chief deity of the underworld.

away. "You want me to take the easy way. It is good counsel."

"Thank you, Majesty." The general smiled. Perhaps this Pharaoh could understand after all.

Thutmose set his face and looked straight ahead, pointing to the looming mounds and rises ahead. His voice became clear and strong. "But if you expect me to go that way, so will *their* generals. We go straight ahead, over the hills instead." He had come to a fork in the road, and like a genius of another age, he decided to take it.[11]

"But Majesty…that way is much more difficult. We'll have to dismount and bring everything through the pass single file. It will take half the day. It is no way to fight."

"I don't expect to just fight…I expect to win. Come, you are an Egyptian. It is time to walk like one."

The general was right about one thing, the march was difficult and time consuming. The Pharaoh led the column through the eight-hour march, then paused and waited for several more as his men came through one by one. The rebel kings, who thought Thutmose III's force had been swallowed by the desert, awoke to find him in their rear gathering his men into line of battle. They fled toward the desert outpost of Megiddo with the Pharaoh's men in hot pursuit. Only the force's lack of discipline kept them from slaughtering the rebels. Instead, the inexperienced soldiers stopped to loot the abandoned camps. Thutmose was

---

11   "When you come to a fork in the road, take it." The saying is widely ascribed to baseball savant Yogi Berra who was describing to Joe Garagiola how to get to his home in Montclair, New Jersey. The saying, however, pre-dates him and can be found in print as early as 1913. As Berra admitted in the title of his 1998 book, "I Really Didn't Say Everything I Said." At least not originally.

enraged and forced to settle in for a long eight-month siege. But the army would have plenty of practice at military discipline in the ensuing years. As he had at the crossroads, the new Pharaoh continued to demonstrate both skill and a bit of luck in stringing together victory after victory. After defeating the rebels at Megiddo he returned to the Canaan Valley and modern-day Syria to put down another insurrection and collect tribute. Then he attacked Phoenician ports, settlements of the Jordan River Valley, and towns across the Euphrates expanding his empire campaign after campaign.[12]

By the fiftieth year of his reign, the Warrior King stood triumphant in a golden chariot as the enemy fled before him. The fourth waterfall of the Nile thundered nearby. The sand was pooled with blood, and the wounded called out for mercy as he dismounted ever so slowly. His knees ached and there was a knot in his back from riding chariots and smiting Nubians all day. He wasn't a twenty-year old pup anymore. But he had won sixteen consecutive campaigns since Megiddo and conquered more lands than any Pha-

---

12   He also demonstrated benevolence in pardoning some of the rebels at Megiddo and providing generous terms for surrender. Later, one of his most clever ideas was the transportation of a vanquished land's children back to Egypt to have them grow up there. When it came time to repatriate them, they were much friendlier to Egyptian dominance and further solidified Thutmose's hold on his subjects. To celebrate his mounting victories, Thutmose erected massive red granite pillars around the temples of Heliopolis. Cut from the quarries around Aswan at the first cataract of the Nile, each weighed over two hundred tons. The four-sided, tapering stone monoliths survive and you can visit them in New York's Central Park or Westminster in London. While known as Cleopatra's Needles, the reference to the Queen of the Nile is not historically accurate. The obelisks were created under Thutmose and already a thousand years old by the time of her reign.

raoh before or after including lands from the Nile in Nubia to the town of Niya in Northern Syria. He may not be the most famous of Egyptian Pharaohs, but he was the most successful Egyptian ruler in history.[13]

We will never know what might have happened had the great warrior fought a seventeenth campaign, but we can be forgiven for thinking he'd have been a heavy favorite to conquer and subjugate someone once again. That, however, is a dangerous assumption without any details or data on which to base a judgment. Psychologists have a name for this mental shortcut, calling it the **Hot Hand Fallacy**—just because something has happened several times in a row, or even sixteen times, doesn't alter the odds of it happening again. Human beings often forget or ignore how random and unpredictable life can be in order to avoid doing detailed analysis. But nothing lasts forever, not even a hot streak.

---

13   Thutmose III reigned for fifty-three years. Anubis came for the Warrior King at the age of fifty-five. Modern sources occasionally refer to him as the Egyptian Napoleon. The difference, of course, is that there was no Waterloo for Thutmose, who never lost a battle. When he died of natural causes he was buried in the Valley of the Kings and exhumed in 1881. His mummy remains at home in the Cairo Museum.
The title of most famous Pharaoh likely goes to Thutmose's successor much later in the 18th Dynasty, Tutankhamen known as King Tut. Tut is merely famous for being discovered with his riches. Like a Kardashian of Ancient Egypt, Tut is actually most famous *for being famous.*

How You'll Be Tested...

After a good run of a few months or years in the stock market, you just might feel like your investments have the hot hand or perhaps that the market itself does. Typically, cash flows in to markets or funds with the best winning streak, then reverses and flows out of the ones with negative returns.

Feel like letting your exposure to stocks ebb and flow like the Nile? A string of good results doesn't change the risks or long-term odds, and it shouldn't change your strategy any more than a string of bad years would. Believing otherwise is an undisciplined mistake for the incapable or foolish, pharaohs or not. Randomness and cyclicality, like Anubis and the afterlife, smite all of us eventually.

——— FLIPPED OFF REDUX ———

A coin flipped heads sixteen straight times doesn't change the probability of future flips turning up tails. The mathematical formula is still the same:

Number of events / Total number of possible outcomes

One flip and two outcomes (1/2) = .5 or a 50/50 chance. Of course, this assumes that the coin is fair and equally weighted. While you may get varying results with a few flips, the more times you flip the coin, the closer you get to the results being an even bet.

Patrick Huey

EXTRA CREDIT

FLIP OUT: NFL referee Phil Luckett created the only coin flip in history that wasn't even odds. During the Steelers vs. Lions Thanksgiving Day Game in 1998, he awarded the Lions the ball to start overtime after the Steelers chose tails and the coin turned up...tails. Apparently, there was no way for running back Jerome Bettis to win this one. View the evidence at: https://www.youtube.com/watch?v=1Nd9BM8ssYM.

VISIT YOUR MUMMY: Come face to face with what Thutmose III looks like today. Think you'll look better in 3,400 years? Face off at: www.awesomestories.com/asset/view/Tuthmosis-III-A-Mummy-s-Face. Then go back in time to see what he might have looked like during his rule: https://www.youtube.com/watch?v=dpQn5z8s-dg.

DO BATTLE: You know most of the story but feel free to dive deeper and see it all in living color and high definition on YouTube's National Geographic Channel. See Egypt's Napoleon at: www.youtube.com/watch?v=3dRD5UVC4rE.

FEEL THE FLOW: The Investment Company Institute publishes data on the flows into and out of mutual funds and exchange traded funds. You can view the weekly data here: https://www.ici.org/research/stats. Do stocks or bonds have the hot hand this week?

GET HEATED: See *The Hangover* (2009). Yes, you could watch a movie like *The Mummy* (1999 or 2017) for an Ancient Egyptian fix, but I prefer Todd Phillips' buddy flick about a night gone horribly wrong in Vegas courtesy of memory-erasing illicit drugs and the hot hand fallacy. Pay special attention to this scene:

SID: "Sweetie, it's Vegas. You lose track of time in casinos. There's no windows, there's no clocks. He's probably on a heater. And you never walk away from the table when you're on a heater."

TRACY: "You do if you're getting married."

Relying on a hot hand can lead to unplanned tooth extractions, stolen police cars, and nude mobsters in your trunk. Metaphorically, of course.

MAKE IT A DOUBLE FEATURE: So, you can't get enough of the Desert and still need your Vegas fix? Check out *The Big Short* (2015). The cameo by Selena Gomez and the hot hand fallacy are worth the price of admission. With a ten-million-dollar hand of blackjack on the table, Dr. Richard Thaler, professor of behavioral economics at the University of Chicago, interrupts her to point out that in basketball people assume you will make shots based on your previous ones going in, ergo the hot hand fallacy. This is now of some contention as researchers are finding that in sports, there may actually be a hot hand effect. But not so much in gambling as Selena finds out when her jack and eight are trumped by the dealers running seven, three, and king. Synthetic CDOs collapse, the housing market crumbles, and the world seems to end in a chorus of booing and four-letter words. Let's just hope there isn't a sequel in production.

The Problem with Poets
Homer & the Rhyme as Reason Fallacy

C. 850 BC

Before the invention of the written language, ancient poets relied on our ability to remember rhymes to pass on their stories. Well, thanks for the memories. But maybe it is time, we forget the rhyme.

"Wait," he said putting down his stylus. "Say that again?" The boy had an earnest expression and his sweat stained tunic showed he'd been working hard all morning.

The old man sighed. "Which part?"

"The part about them jumping out of the horse. I can fill in the rest about the pillaging and destruction. But I still don't understand the horse part." The younger man scribbled furiously to catch up.

"It wasn't *really* a horse. It was a fake and they brought it inside the walls of Troy as a trophy." The scribe stopped and looked at his elder like he was more than a little bit mad.

"Seriously? They built a fake horse? And the Trojans just

figured, sure that makes sense let's bring it inside?" His earnestness was gone, replaced with the easy sarcasm of youth. The old man threw up his hands. "Fine, you think you are so smart with your fancy symbols for words, tell the story however you want. But remember, Achilles gets shot with an arrow through his weak spot. On his *elbow*." He rose unsteadily and shuffled off, blind in his fury as well as in fact.[14]

The young boy watched him go for a moment shaking his head. Then he reconsidered. "Wait! Homer, I need that last part again!" He yelled after him. "Oh, why am I even bothering?" he said to himself. "No one is ever going to read this stuff."

Nothing is definitively known about the author we call Homer, whose grand stories of the Trojan Wars transformed early Greek culture. Indeed, there are various theories about whether he was one person or a combination of several authors whose works were standardized by oral traditions over the ensuing generations. Some historians believe that "Homer" may have been a generic name for storytellers who wandered the countryside telling their tall tales. Regardless, the Homeric epics remain literary standards for their scope and rich characters drawn from the gods, goddesses, and half-human characters of Greek mythology.[15]

---

14 The descriptions of the blind bard in the *Odyssey* have led some scholars to suppose that Homer himself was blind.

15 There is significant speculation that the *Iliad* and the *Odyssey* were written as much as a century apart. Perhaps Homer was the writer who finally collected the stories into a written form? It's not such a crazy thought.

Homer's poems, such as the *Iliad* and the *Odyssey*, are not only heroic in scale. They use a classic form of poetry known as the dactylic hexameter, which was the ancient standard for remembering heroes. "Dactylos" is Greek for finger. The dactyl imitates the pattern of the human digit (a long bone followed by two short ones) in phonetic sounds (a long syllable and two diminutive ones). Translated, dactylic hexameter means six fingers in a row. Actually, there are only five dactyls in a row, then a resolution.

The result is a pattern, or meter, of long and short syllables that was lyrical and poetic, at least in Ancient Greek. In English, it takes on a sing song quality that can distract from the serious nature of the story. Thus, when Alexander Pope translated the *Iliad* to English in the early eighteenth century, he did so in heroic couplets. Making it rhyme in English made it more memorable.[16]

As catchy as a great poet's verse can be in any language, it reveals a very real human folly: we like and remember things better if they have a certain rhythm or rhyme. How else could Homer's heroic hexameter have been handed down verbally through generations? It wasn't merely the memorable plot line. For, without poetry, the *Iliad* is just a rambling tale of boy meets girl; girl marries another boy; boy steals girl; thousands of Greek and Trojan warriors die. Without poetry, the *Odyssey* is a Mediterranean travel diary on acid. Neither of those would be remarkable enough to recall over twelve thousand lines in prose. But as poems

---

16   For English speakers, iambic pentameter is the most recognizable form of poetry, using stress on certain syllables to create rhythm. Isn't it just like the English-speaking world to create art out of stress?

or lyrical works, they became memorable for centuries of storytellers. Even today, who doesn't remember some bit of Shakespeare they were forced to learn in grade school? Or song lyrics from a one-hit wonder? How about a dirty limerick? [17]

Poems and rhymes seem harmless enough. Unless we remember incorrect information or ignore alternative information in favor of something merely because it rhymes. In other words, when you believe a misnomer, because of the likes of Homer, that is a mental shortcut known as the **Rhyme as Reason Fallacy.** As good as we all think we are, we still have weaknesses, including an "Achilles' *heel*" for rhymes.

── NOT AVERSE TO VERSE ──

Dr. Matthew McGlone of Lafayette College found that students not only remembered rhymes better, but supposed they were more accurate and truthful than mere prose. For example, "asked whether financial success makes people healthier, almost all McGlone's subjects disagreed, but 'wealth makes health' seemed much more plausible."

---

17   For those of you who have forgotten high school literature, the *Iliad* traces the story of Agamemnon and his quarrel with the Trojans and his sometime ally, Achilles. The quasi-sequel focuses on Odysseus and his travels home after the fall of Troy.

Patrick Huey

How You'll Be Tested…

As the calendar turns to spring and we look fondly toward the beaches and barbeques of summer, you may hear the old Wall Street adage to "sell in May and go away." Should you ditch your investments every spring and pick them up again in the fall to miss what have historically been more volatile months in the stock markets? Well, it sure sounds good and it is easy to remember. Yet, over the last fifty years the May–October return on US Stocks in the S&P 500 is 4.2%. Not as good as the other six-month rolling periods, but not the proverbial sacking of Troy either. And analysis by Oppenheimer Funds research showed that while a $1,000 investment held in stocks from January 1926–December 2015 would grow to $5.3 million dollars, the same $1,000 investment selling on May 1st and investing in T Bills until November 1st every year from 1926–2015 would be worth just $1.2 million. It turns out that missing the *summer* might just be a *bummer*. Adages are not to be confused with advice. Please don't do *anything* in *any month* based on seven syllables and a rhyme scheme.

EXTRA CREDIT

RHYME FOR ALL TIME: Go to this website: www.rhymezone. com and this one: http://www.investopedia.com/financial-edge/0511/the-top-17-investing-quotes-of-all-time.aspx. See if you can turn the top seventeen investing quotes of all time into more memorable rhymes. For instance, "An investment in knowledge pays the best interest" can become "To see the most gain, invest in your brain."

BE MEMORABLE: Which is more likely to be stamped on your memory?

Financial success leads to better physical wellbeing.		Wealth makes health.
Misfortune unites enemies.		Woes unite foes.
No matter how successful you are, there is always someone trying to knock you down.	OR	For every level, there is another devil.
You tend to be truthful when under the influence of alcohol.		What sobriety conceals, alcohol reveals.
People who are alike tend to associate with one another.		Birds of a feather flock together.
My client is not guilty.		If the glove doesn't fit, you must acquit.

HORSE AROUND: Watch *Troy* (2004). Wolfgang Peterson's mash up of Braveheart and Gladiator is based on the Iliad and at times seems almost as long as the source material. Still, Peter Travers of Rolling Stone calls it "the best crib sheet guide to Homer ever." Brad Pitt and Eric Bana wear sandals and loin cloths while fighting to the death as Hector and Achilles, while visual effects artists try to explain that whole Trojan horse thing. Yes, the dialogue is plodding and totally forgettable. Perhaps because David Benioff's screenplay doesn't rhyme?

Questioning the Answers
Socrates & Anchoring Bias

469–399 BC

For centuries, philosophers have struggled to unpack the true nature of what they call the Socratic Problem. Opinions on who Socrates was, and what he taught, usually reflect more about the observer than the subject. But it isn't just the deep thinkers who wind up in deep.

"Saphronicus, what are you doing?" The Athenian stoneworker, blessed by the gods with a healthy baby boy was ceremonially carrying him around the hearth, officially welcoming him to the family. His wife looked on nervously as he cradled the five-day-old boy. Yes, it was a local tradition, but seeing her beloved baby in those huge, rough hands made her uneasy.[18]

"Thank the gods, thank the gods," Saphronicus mumbled.

"Saphronicus, who are you talking to?" Her husband

---

18   In fairness, his wife deserved most of the blessing, but her name is lost to history.

had been annoyingly joyous about this birth. She wondered if he would have been quite so happy if it had been a girl. She thought not.

"Saphronicus, will you please give me the baby?" The big man stopped his mad dance and gently laid the baby in his mother's arm while continuing to coo. Then he stopped, turned on a heel and headed for the door.

"Saphronicus, where are you going?"

"Out," he sighed. "Someplace quiet...like the rock quarry. At least I won't hear any more questions." The door slammed behind him as his hulking form heaved out of sight.

Some days later, on the baby's tenth day, again in accordance with local custom, the craftsman and his wife finally gave the baby boy his name. They called him Socrates. Their home city of Athens had opened schools and gymnasiums to educate their youth around 500 BC, so the child grew up like most Athenians had for decades, well educated. Saphronicus's boy would frequent such places for most of his life and become a voracious reader and thinker. Throughout his life he came back to the places of his youth including the schools, gyms, and market places to discuss issues of interest. He was known to have attended various festivals in the city where he mixed and mingled with philosophers, traders, and visiting scholars from all over the known world. He was also known to ask a *lot* of questions.[19]

In his later life, Socrates was known as a particularly ugly man with bulging eyes and fleshy lips who went about

---

19 We don't know that the Socratic Method, his dialogue of argument, was inherited from his mother's side of the family. Then again, we don't know that it wasn't.

the city barefoot, unwashed, and wielding a walking stick. Perhaps sheer embarrassment was why his mother's name didn't make it into the historical record? Regardless, he continued to ask a lot of questions and became well known in local circles and amongst the philosophically inclined. He rarely transmitted knowledge or information. He was no traditional teacher. Instead, he would ask pointed questions, one after another, to guide his counterpart toward a conclusion. It must have been extraordinarily enlightening and exceedingly annoying. Like a five-year-old, he questioned virtually anyone, free or slave, man or woman, but claimed to know nothing of importance, gaining wisdom only by listening and actively guiding a conversation. Thus, we know a bit of historical background on Socrates, yet we know almost nothing about his actual philosophical teachings or thoughts. The great questioner was at best an indifferent chronicler. Indeed, there is no proof that Socrates ever *wrote* anything.

Most of this we know courtesy of Socrates' star pupil, Plato. It is clear from Plato's writings and later those of Aristophanes, that the way Socrates was viewed heavily affected the records about him. If you thought he was your mentor and a genius, you transferred to history a completely different picture than if you thought he was a ruffian and bad example for Athenian youth. First perceptions weighed heavily.[20]

As time has passed, just about every philosophical

20   Plato, Aristotle, Aristophanes, and Xenophon are the only sources we have for any of his thoughts or teachings, all second-hand information.

movement has claimed the funny looking, odd smelling man of questions as a founder or example of their order. With such a blank slate, it is relatively easy for anyone to claim that they know the *real* Socrates and what developed are a series of *interpretations* of who he was with no real definitive answer. It is as if the great questioner left one big question mark to posterity. While there have been several attempts to unravel the issue and discover the real Socrates, each bid to do so exposes how the author or philosopher already views him. The issue is so divisive and ubiquitous among scholars as to be known as the Socratic Problem. It is an ongoing example of **Anchoring Bias.**[21]

It's an ugly fact, but our brains are trained to take what we "know" and apply it to save time. Brain cells have other things to do like algebra, rocket science, and developing snarky comebacks for curious spouses. A good, efficient, evolved brain doesn't want to start from the beginning every time it tries to solve a problem. If I ask you how long it will take to drive home from work, you don't do the mileage computation from scratch. You simply use experience as a guide and adjust a few minutes either way for traffic. In short, you use an **anchoring bias.** Socrates believed that an unexamined or unquestioned life was essentially not worth living. So, let me drive this home, you need to be extremely curious and brutally honest with yourself.

---

21   The Socratic problem is even more baffling since the philosopher himself supposedly encouraged people to do their own thinking without regard to reverence or emulation.

Anchoring bias occurs in a variety of situations from philosophical to numerical. To demonstrate, researchers get Socratic and start asking questions. Like these:

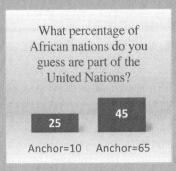

What percentage of African nations do you guess are part of the United Nations?

In the seminal work on anchoring in 1974, Amos Tversky and Daniel Kahneman asked participants to guess how many African nations were part of the U.N. after spinning a wheel of numbers rigged to either land on 10 or 65. Higher anchors guessed a larger percentage than lower anchors.

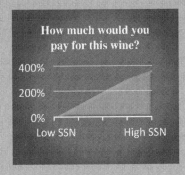

Dan Ariely of MIT conducted several experiments for his book *Predictably Irrational.* After asking each student to write down the last two digits of their social security number, an auction was held for a bottle of wine. Students with high numbers bid up to 346% more than those with low numbers.

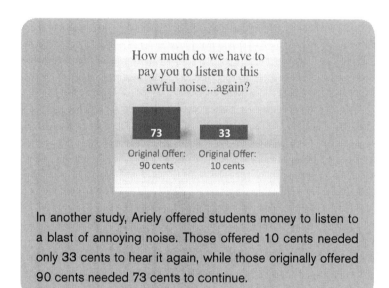

How much do we have to pay you to listen to this awful noise...again?

73 — Original Offer: 90 cents

33 — Original Offer: 10 cents

In another study, Ariely offered students money to listen to a blast of annoying noise. Those offered 10 cents needed only 33 cents to hear it again, while those originally offered 90 cents needed 73 cents to continue.

How You'll Be Tested...

The news can be vicious and unexpected. The value of one of your investments is plummeting upon reports that the company is looting the rain forest to plant tobacco while using child labor in an off-the-books accounting scheme. But you, stone faced like a warrior of Sparta decide to wait and see what happens. You'll sell when it gets back close to what you paid for it.[22]

Investors, you see, are especially prone to **anchoring**. A stock bought at $100 will always have an intrinsic value of

22   When he came of age at eighteen, Socrates served his time in the Athenian militia and there distinguished himself as soldier in an undistinguished army moving toward war with neighboring Sparta. He participated in three military campaigns during the twenty-seven year Peloponnesian War, which the Athenians finally lost in 403BC.

$100 to the buyer. But when the facts have changed, why wouldn't the true value of the investment as well? Time to ask yourself, are the decisions you are making based on today's information or on old anchors to previous data? Are you relying on mental shortcuts? Have you called your Mom lately? Hey, are you asking enough questions?

EXTRA CREDIT

ANCHORS AWEIGH: There is another side to anchoring, using it for advantage. Think car salesman who wants to make sure you know the manufacturer's suggested retail price. Author Blair Enns offers a disciplined process to selling without pitching, including using anchoring bias to guide the negotiations. Drop an anchor at: http://www.winwithoutpitching.com/always-be-anchoring/. But buyer beware.

DO SOME MATH: Solve the following equations by estimating an answer in less than five seconds:

1 X 2 X 3 X 4 X 5 X 6 X 7 X 8 =?

8 X 7 X 6 X 5 X 4 X 3 X 2 X 1 =?

Then...

BE HUMBLED: https://www.youtube.com/watch?v=NFiDdbquWJY. Laurie Santos, a psychology teacher at Yale, will help you understand why you were a) wrong and b) came up with different answers to the same question framed in a different way. Here's a hint, you anchored on a small number first and a larger number second.

ANCHOR ARTFULLY: In a 2009 edition of the *American Economic Review*, researchers Alan Beggs and Kathryn Gradyy tested the extent to which current art auction prices are anchored by previous sales. Don't know your Manet from your Monet? That's okay, just concentrate on how the study seemed to confirm a higher rate of bias with Impressionist works versus Contemporary art. Why? We still don't know, but how recent the anchor was produced and how steady it is appeared to be contributing factors. Download it at: http://people.brandeis.edu/~kgraddy/published%20papers/ BeggsAGraddyKAER2009.pdf.

BRIDGE THE GAP: Peruse *The Behavior Gap* (2012) by Carl Richards. For visual learners, the book is full of stories told through pictures drawn with a sharpie and cocktail napkins instead of historical anecdotes. Now that is art!

The Ancient Chinese Secret
Kong Fuzi & Availability Bias

551 BC–479BC

The life, death, and eternal fame of a man named Kong Fuzi is used to disseminate easily memorable information of dubious quality. With his purported sayings, we have a way to pass down any kind of information through repetition. But we shouldn't, and not just because he deserves better.

A team of horses was approaching at a trot; hoofs beating rhythmic time. The master, sitting cross-legged at his writing desk, heard the team stop outside and the rider dismount. The silence of the day was gone, his reverie broken. *News*, he thought. *And based on previous history, probably not good.*

Boards creaked, and a squat man appeared at his door in a red, straight collared tunic with coiled buttons that he fidgeted with nervously. "Master Kong," the man said, giving a cursory bow. He was courtly and polite, but there was a hint of tension in his voice.

Kong arched an eyebrow and stroked his pointed black chin whiskers. "Eh?" He knew this man, a counselor to the king. Through years of experience he knew what was coming and prepared himself for the inevitable.

"I regret in the extreme to inform you that your services will no longer be required." The fidgeting stopped. The voice firmed. "You're fired."

Kong Fuzi placidly set his face, determined to take it well and remain dignified. The master of antiquity and expert on court manners merely nodded. He packed his writing instruments and meager belongings; then plunged into the blinding daylight and choking dust of the road leading into and out of the capital of Luoyang. As was often the case, he had nowhere in particular to go.

It had happened before, and he would not despair over such things. But it seemed to him as if he were constantly moving on from one place to another. As a *shi* or lordless itinerant counselor to petty kings and occasional despots, what could he expect? By his own personal philosophy people ought to treat each other better, but in a China torn apart by invasions and the fall of the Zhou Dynasty, compassion was often a luxury few took the time to think much about. What could one say, except that, occasionally *shi* happens?

The philosopher known as Kong Fuzi or "Master Kong" had his name Romanized by missionaries into the western

version, Confucius. We know relatively little about Confucius's early years. There is some controversy over whether he grew up in a royal household or, due to family misfortune, found himself poor and destitute before reaching his fame. Modern historians believe that the royal lineage of Confucius was mythology, created after the fact to reinforce the wisdom of the ruling dynasties. This was much more palatable than adopting the philosophy of a former herder and accountant who endured a humiliating path to prominence. With mythology, religious dogma, or political slogans, the longer and more often it is repeated and made available, the easier it is to believe. We'll come back to that concept in a moment. [23]

Confucianism's principles are relatively straightforward—an ancient humanistic set of beliefs, including worship of the ancestors and respect for ancient writings. Born into a period of upheaval in what would become China, Master Kong stressed compassion and self-discipline to leaders whom he thought should set proper precedents. Some listened, some didn't. So, he, or one of his disciples, wrote his teachings down and they were compiled into four books. The *Book of Odes*, the *Book of Documents*, *Lunyu and Spring*, and *Autumn Annals* are translated for English speakers in *The Analects of Confucius*.

The Master died thinking that he had contributed relatively little and had failed to make much of an impact. His successes were few, his failures seemingly many. He can be forgiven for remembering mostly the latter. But people kept

---

23   Despite his potential royal lineage, at no time did Master Kong become King Kong.

talking about the philosopher from Qufu and within two centuries of his death, Confucianism would become part of the official philosophy of Imperial China until the twentieth century. And yet, today, in western cultures, Master Kong is probably more famous for jokes using his name in vain. For instance, "Confucius says, shotgun wedding is a case of wife versus death." Seriously, is nothing sacred anymore? There are literally thousands of them available on the Internet today, many of them bawdy, which I'm sure his descendants find incredibly hilarious. For a man who prided himself on developing concepts of self-discipline and providing a positive example, it is an eternal insult. But at least he isn't forgotten.[24]

For all that, it is a handy example of how easy it is to despoil the memory of the greats, or any memory for that matter, due to repetition. We've heard the words "Confucius says" so many times that we expect something witty, funny, or dirty to come next. Repetition sticks with us and lets us create a mental shortcut known as the **Availability Bias**.

Availability of information impacts how we assign probabilities and determine, seemingly, what is and what is not important. When a story you can easily recall plays too large of a part in how you reach a decision, that is a hazardous mental shortcut. Even if we just hear about some topics incessantly, like the musing of a certain Chinese philosopher, we will assign them more meaning.

---

24   Indeed, allow me to pile on. I wrote, for instance, after the Gulf Oil spill in 2011 "Confucius says…Oil well in deep water is not really *well* at all."

SHARK!

Availability Bias causes us to think that the possibility of an event is increased if we can remember it happening previously. Shark attacks are horrific, receive a lot of media attention, and are turned into movies and TV shows. Thus, they are extremely memorable despite being extremely rare.

Is it safe to go back in the water? The television show Myth Busters found that ten times more people were killed by falling coconuts in a year than by shark attacks. Confucius says, beware of that next Pina Colada!

The veracity of information has little relation to how easy it is to be recalled or remembered. Confucius says, judging by what is available sometimes means availing yourself of bull. Okay, Confucius said no such thing. But I'm sure he would agree that instead of judging information by its availability, you should judge it on its merits, using Confucian self-discipline.

How You'll Be Tested...

Someday, approaching the proverbial watercooler you may hear something like the following: "The stock market is for suckers. My 401k became a $200^{1/2}$k in about eleven months! I'm not doing that again, I pulled it all out and put it in cash." You too remember being curled up in the fetal position while stock markets plummeted. And that memory is powerfully negative. So, you do the sensible thing and alter your strategy, figuring that a similar decline is imminent.

You went for water only to hear someone yell, *shark!*

Please, get your *shi* together. Your goals haven't changed. The investment world hasn't suddenly become riskier. Yet you *perceive* more risk because negative information is readily available and psychologically painful, meaning more memorable. It bears repeating that investment decisions should be made on the *best* available data, not just the *most* available data.

EXTRA CREDIT

HAVE A COOKIE: Someone else wants to protect the memory of Master Kong and it is the guy who writes the fortunes you read after polishing off your General Tso's chicken and cracking into the cookie. "Confucius is the best-known philosopher, respected, a good person. Making a joke of him is not right," he says. Read *Why Confucius Quit the Cookie Business* at: http://theweek.com/articles/516149/last-word-why-confucius-quit-cookie-business.

PLAY THE GAME: *Confucius* (2008) is a sort of combination of Monopoly, Clue, and Axis and Allies. The focus seems to be on developing relationships to build power and influence in the government. Play it more for the period design than to learn much about Confucian philosophy. It gets a 6.9 out of 10 from Board Game Geek but is out of stock on Amazon so you'll probably have to go garage sale hunting for this one.

BE A LOSER: Buy a lottery ticket. There is no better way to participate directly in an activity where the small number of winners are hyped endlessly so you remember them and ignore the astronomical odds. Call me if you win and there is anything left to invest after taxes and that fleet of sport cars you've always wanted.

GET SOME SHI TO READ: A five volume translation of *The Analects* and other Confucian works is available here: http://www.sacred-texts.com/cfu/cfu.htm. Order Chinese take-out and settle in if you intend to read the whole thing.

THINK FAST: Author Daniel Kahneman, whose research work we introduced earlier, wrote a book called Thinking Fast and Slow (2011). Reading it tends to be the latter, but you can get the abridged version by watching part of a series on books with big ideas by FightMediocrity: https://www.youtube.com/watch?v=uqXVAo7dVRU.

GET BACK IN THE WATER: Don't worry, it is safe despite the simple ostinato of two bass notes, F to F Sharp echoing in your ears. Watch the movie *Jaws* (1975). One of the most chilling moments in Spielberg's film comes when Quint, captain of the Orca, relates to his new shipmates the horrors he experienced during the sinking of the USS Indianapolis during WWII. "Over 1,000 men went into the water, 316 survivors came out, and the sharks got the rest". Terrifying? Yes. Historically accurate? Not so much. Indianapolis was indeed sunk by the Japanese in the summer of 1945 (Quint incorrectly says it was June 29th, it was July 29th). But, it is believed that a few hundred of the casualties died in the initial torpedo attack and that many more perished due to dehydration after five days floating at sea without fresh water. This didn't stop the incident from being dubbed "the biggest shark attack in history." Hollywood rule #1: never let the facts get in the way of a good story. Investing rule #1: always let the facts get in the way of a good story.

Peripatetic Fits

Aristotle & Illusory Correlations

384 BC

The fact that ancient philosophers needed to develop a system to keep us from assuming that any time two variables move in tandem there isn't necessarily a relationship, tells us a lot. The fact that we still get it wrong most of the time after thousands of years tells us even more.

It was a quiet morning in Stagira, the sun rising from behind the Aegean Sea. The Doctor had a house away from the stink of the fishermen hauling in their catch; far enough up the hill to catch the soft shore breeze and cool his home. Usually, one could hear the birds screeching overhead, looking for easy food in the harbor. But today, there came a different kind of screeching, washing away the solitude of the northern Greek outpost and creating a heat that no breeze could carry way.

"No son of mine will be running around in a toga spouting nonsense on the streets," bellowed the Doctor.

"But Dad, that's not fair! All the other kids are going to study with Plato." Like many kids, his dad wanted him to follow in his footsteps and was miffed to be shelling out tuition to study philosophy.

"Listen boy and heed me. Over my dead body!"

Nicomachus of Macedon might have regretted that bit of theatrics, dying while his son was still a boy. It was the boy's brother-in-law, turned guardian, Proxenus who encouraged him, at the age of eighteen, to travel to Athens and attend the academy of Plato. And so, young Aristotle, finally got his way, and he proved his father wrong. It turns out that three centuries before Christianity, there were actual jobs available for philosophy majors. He would go on to contribute more to the physical sciences, ethics, and rhetoric than anyone else before, or since. He basically wrote a complete encyclopedia of Greek knowledge, and it wasn't the abridged version. It was rumored that while discussing and thinking at his school called the Lyceum, he walked/moved constantly. The Greek word for walking (perpatima) led the followers of his school to be called the Peripatetics.[25]

It was in the field of logic where Aristotle walked the tallest and had perhaps the most pervasive effect on western ideas. He introduced a system of thought based on deduction and inference, called syllogism. In a syllogism, two inferences that are assumed to be true are combined to reach a categorical conclusion. In all, there are two hun-

25 Were it not for Aristotle's perseverance we might not even have subjects such as philosophy, mathematics, or history (*gasp*), as he was the first to classify knowledge by topic or discipline. Some of his classifications are still in use today.

dred and fifty-six distinct types of syllogisms, produced by altering the forms and using universal affirmatives (all), universal negatives (none), and particular affirmatives or negatives (some). It was an early effort to address a common fault in human reasoning—our tendency to find meaning in **Illusory Correlations**. We see random data that *appear* meaningful together, but whose connections aren't valid or don't exist. But syllogism was not a perfect solution. Of all the combinations, only twenty-four, or less than ten percent, are valid. The rest lead us to conclusions that are false.[26]

SYLLOGISTIC REASONING

Major Premise	Minor Premise	Conclusion
B is Part of A	C is part of B	C is part of A
Philosophers are Human	Humans are mortal	Philosophers are mortal

---

26 A prolific mind, Aristotle likely wrote more than two hundred works in his lifetime on a variety of subjects, most of which are lost to us. Though a student of Plato, his ideas diverged enough from his mentor to cause controversy. Where Plato, according to his theory of forms, saw the properties of an object to be abstract and independent, Aristotle argues they were intrinsic and objects could not exist without them. It was Mr. Outside versus Mr. Inside. It was also the philosophical equivalent of a long-time Boston Red Sox player signing with the Yankees. As a historian and not much of a philosopher, I have no idea who is right. Most likely because I don't know what they are talking about. But the difference was enough to keep Aristotle from succeeding his mentor as leader of the Platonic school in 347 BC. Luckily, like any good entrepreneur he went on to lead his own ventures in Macedon and founded his own academy. Eventually he would teach his own star pupil, Alexander the Great, at the Royal Academy of Macedon. More on him in the next lesson.

Patrick Huey

The major premise comes first. It is a general statement and will form the predicate of the conclusion. The second term, or minor premise, is more specific and will form the subject of the conclusion. For instance, "all philosophers are human" is a major premise. "All humans are mortal" is a minor premise. The conclusion, therefore, based on this simple structure is that "all philosophers are mortal." Aristotle proved this case, not merely by syllogism, but also by dying in 322 BC of natural causes. Considered an immortal mind, he was all too mortal in body.

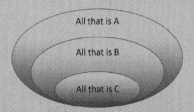

While a powerful step forward in logical thought, syllogism, like any other tool is subject to misuse. Incorrect conclusions are easy to form. Using two particulars and eliminating the universal term "all" from the major premise will completely break down the structure. If "some poodles are black" and "some black things are cats," then it does not follow that "some poodles are cats." You may think that poodles are pretty cat-like based on their size and failure to play fetch, but *logically* you are barking up the wrong tree.

Ignoring how terms are distributed or accounted for between major and minor premises will also lead to syllogistic folly. "All historians are smart. No politicians are historians. Therefore, no politicians are smart." While it sounds true, the syllogism isn't valid, which happens quite often. But don't worry, there are plenty of other ways to prove that politicians aren't that smart. That is what the non-stop election season is for!

If all of this is Greek to you, or gives you fits, you aren't alone. Aristotle had to invent a way of reasoning, imperfect as it is, because our natural thought process seeks out clear-cut conclusions with minimal and often conflicting data. **Illusory correlations** help us reach quick conclusions, but not correct ones. For humans, an abridged version of making decisions saves us valuable time at a subconscious level at the cost of often being wrong. It's a poor tradeoff, and one *we* should walk away from whenever possible.

How You'll Be Tested...

Nothing makes an investor salivate more than a sure thing. So, when you find one, you will want to act on it. I mean, who are you to go against the tide of human nature? You note that oil prices are spiking. Oil prices are positively correlated to stock prices. Oil goes up, stocks go up. Simple, right? Which means when crude is climbing, halcyon days are ahead and it's time to buy more stocks! Now, you aren't just acting on gut feelings, you have data to back up your mistake. And it *is* a mistake. Because the idea that if x occurs, y will follow is just as dumb today as it was when Aristotle was strolling the Acropolis.

Yes, the two variables are correlated mathematically. But beyond that? Oil prices were soaring in 2008, stocks not so much. Post-recession the opposite happened, and stocks rebounded sharply while oil pretty much crashed. So much for a sure thing based on correlations! If the variables, oil and stocks, are correlated until they aren't... then *that* is an **illusory correlation**. Time to put someone's philosophy degree, if not yours, to good use. Heed this: stick with your plan and don't be tempted by your own misconceptions. Wouldn't that make dear old Dad proud?

EXTRA CREDIT

DON'T WAIT, CORRELATE: If you need to be reminded of how bad you are at math and statistics, here is the site for you; http://guessthecorrelation.com/. Based on scatterplot charts of two variables, guess the correlation coefficient for the two. Look for username historylessons on the scoreboard, but don't be surprised if I'm not there. Math is hard.

SPARE A MINUTE: Okay, you may need to spare almost four minutes for Three Minute Philosophy: Aristotle. Part of a series on great thinkers, this piece stretches a bit longer because Aristotle basically did and knew just about everything. Mr. S. Peter Davis goes really fast to try and get it all in. See it here: https://www.youtube.com/watch?v=tbgHbzrL3d0.

SUSPEND JUDGMENT: Dr. L. Kip Wheeler of Carson-Newman University provides the following syllogism worksheet on his website: https://web.cn.edu/kwheeler/documents/Syllogisms.pdf. Give it a try and see how you do. Hint: many times, a conclusion may seem false based on your particular knowledge or outlook. Ignore your judgments and focus solely on the logic of the argument and the structure of the syllogism.

LINK YOUR LIES: Create your own questionable connections at home with fun variables like causes of death and worldwide staple sales: http://www.tylervigen.com/spurious-correlations. Did you know that the more money we spend on science and technology in America, the more people die by suffocation and strangulation? Are the added taxes choking the life out of us or is the correlation illusory? You decide.

GIVE THIS A SHOT: Read *You Are Not So Smart* (2011). David McRaney's look at all the ways we deceive ourselves is worth a read on its own and is a good primer for the rest of our lessons. For now, focus in on Chapter Five and the Texas Sharpshooter fallacy, a bias where the randomness of information is ignored, and patterns deduced that seem to make sense. Kind of like shooting at a barn and painting a target around where the bullets holes cluster. Hence the name.

SHOOT FASTER: Check out a video synopsis of McRaney's chapter on the Texas Sharpshooter Fallacy if you don't want to read a whole book before moving on to the next lesson: https://youarenotsosmart.com/2016/03/23/yanss-071-the-texas-sharpshooter-fallacy/.

To Be, or Knot to Be

Alexander the Great & Functional Fixation

333 BC

Throughout history, humans have tended to use objects only in their traditional manner because our brains form habits to avoid continually recalling how common things are used. But one man would be called Great for how he conquered objects and subjects alike.

From the bow of his boat, Alexander of Macedon watched the shoreline of Asia Minor as it loomed large on the horizon. You may know the Macedonian king as Alexander the Great, military genius, student of Aristotle, alleged practitioner of patricide, and terminator of independence movements in his late father's kingdoms of Thrace, Greece, and Illyria.[27]

---

27 Alexander allegedly figured in the demise of his late father Phillip in 336 BC. Phillip's murder by one of his bodyguards has spawned conspiracy theories for ages. The soldier, Pausanias, had a grudge against his King for not punishing a man who took advantage of him in more ways than one.

As the dark smudge of land resolved itself into details of sand and rock he hefted his war spear and waited. When his boat came aground with a thud, he sent the projectile arcing skyward to strike the continent he had come to conquer. Leaping into the surf, he strode slowly to the weapon and yanked it free of the earth with a short battle cry. Then he lifted it overhead for his host of invaders to see.

"This spear!" he bellowed. "This spear will soon conquer all of Asia!" The men in the boats roared their approval, but as the bellowing voices died away there was a strange sound. It was the tinkling of laughter.

Alexander looked and saw a Persian horseman, perhaps forty or fifty yards distant. He was grinning; eyes gleaming like polished dark stones above his black beard. He pointed to the spear and shouted derisively, "You may want to bring more than just one." With that he waved merrily, turned his horse, and galloped off toward the forces of his own king, Darius III.[28]

The horseman was not wrong, but in a few days, he wouldn't be laughing. It had taken Alexander three years to consolidate his power after his late father Philip's assassination, but with the Macedonian kingdom subdued, his mind wandered toward a showdown with the Persians. Now his armies wandered that way. In days, an army of nearly twenty

---

But it is also surmised that he was doing the bidding of Alexander and his mother, Olympias, in their campaign to make Alexander great.

28   Darius, to his regret, dismissed the upstart Alexander, about whom he had heard so little. He chose to send local commanders to keep an eye on the boy king, though none of them thought much of him either. Indeed, Alexander found that in this battle, at least, the Persians did not fear him because they did not know him. This would be the last time he'd be at such an advantage for the rest of his life.

thousand with their horses, shields, and spears would fall on Darius's army of nearly the same size near the river Granicus and the ancient city of Troy. Soon, resistance in Western Asia Minor was at an end, and Darius was on the run. Alexander followed. Seeking ultimate conquest and a definitive showdown with the Persians, he continued eastward, reaching the town of Gordium in 333 BC.[29]

Pursuing the retreating Persians, he came to Gordium, straddling the Sangarius River and linking the western world with the Persian Empire and the Asian continent. The town's name emerged from a legend that an oracle decreed the area, in need of a king, would be ruled by the first man to come through with an ox cart. Gordias drove through and, problem solved, became king. His son Midas then tied up the old ox cart as an offering to the gods. For a few hundred years, the cart stood still, tied to the palace with an intricate knot, and perhaps a whole host of parking tickets, though one suspects Midas, of all people, could afford the fines. According to tradition, the future King of Asia would be the only one capable of undoing the knot. Alexander was heading for Asia anyway, and figured he might as well prove his bona fides before getting there. In fact, what better way to prove to everyone his destiny than to solve the ancient

29   Seizing the initiative, Alexander marched and found his adversaries, including five thousand Greeks who had joined the Persians to avenge their subjugation by Phillip and Alexander. Urged by his commanders to wait until morning to attack, Alexander ignored the advice and went forward. The Persians were poorly arrayed for battle, their cavalry and chariots all but useless along the banks of the muddy river. Alexander's army sliced through them and routed the entire Persian force in a little over an hour. The Greeks surrendered and begged for mercy, which they did not get. He was Alexander the Great after all, not Alexander the merciful.

riddle of the Gordian Knot?[30]

When he arrived, he bent before the rope and the cart for a long, quiet moment. The silence stretched uncomfortably, and his bodyguards began to fidget. "Quiet," he whispered distractedly, deep in thought. Abruptly, he straightened to his full kingly height.

"Give me my spear," he demanded. When the weapon was brought forward, he brought the point end down once in a decisive thrust at the line just before the knot. It snapped with a twang, cords of the rope exploding and unraveling. Alexander gave back the spear and stepped forward, working the now loose end through the loop, untying the Gordian Knot and becoming the presumptive king of the continent.

Turning to his men, he grinned. "I told you this spear would conquer all of Asia."[31]

The legend of the Gordian Knot is said to represent bold action or "outside the box" thinking to solve a difficult problem. The fact that the knot sat for generations demonstrates the psychological concept of **Functional Fixation**.

30 One of the three kings named Midas is remembered in Greek mythology for being able to turn everything he touched into gold, ergo the "Midas touch." For obvious reasons, he remains a favorite historical character of financial advisors.

31 The traditional story has Alexander cutting the strands with his sword, not his spear. His contemporary biographers missed a golden opportunity to have things come full circle. Regardless, when faced with an intractable problem, the greatest ruler of the ancient world found a creative way around it. You might say, he cheated; though no one would have dared to at the time. It's easier to say it now with Alexander dead and gone for a few millennia.

If we perceive the correct way to undo a knot is to untie it, we will continue to try even if a simpler fix is apparent. **Functional fixation** is what keeps us from finding creative or novel solutions to problems. It is the grumpy old man of cognitive biases, wearing black knee-high socks with white tennis shoes and saying things like "back in my day, we never did it that way." Seizing the initiative and using a little creativity from time to time can be good for us, even if you aren't trying to conquer an entire subcontinent.

- YOU ARE BEING SO TACKY -

Psychologist Karl Duncker pioneered the study of functional fixation in 1945. Participants were presented with the following items: 1) a candle, 2) a box of tacks, and 3) some matches. They were then asked to attach the candle to an adjacent wall without using any other materials.

There are some creative ways to do it, but the easiest is to use the tacks to attach the box to the wall and then put the candle in it. But most participants only see the box as a container for the tacks. Their minds reject using familiar items in unfamiliar ways.

Researchers have since replicated similar results with only 23% of Stanford students able to solve the problem in a 2003 study. Other researchers have noted the effect of priming or pre-utilization on test subjects. When the box was presented empty, more of the participants could imagine it used for something other than toting tacks.

How You'll Be Tested…

Alexander was great because he avoided a classic military blunder, confusing strategy and tactics. But a less confident investor might make that mistake from time to time. Your overall strategy, be it world domination or moderate growth of your portfolio shouldn't change much over the years. But your tactics, using a wedge or phalanx, buying individual stocks or mutual funds, probably will…if you aren't functionally fixated.

That is what keeps investors from allocating their portfolios internationally or using alternative investments to reduce risk. Functional fixation will keep us in CDs for income, when they provide next to none and Treasury bonds for safety when there may be better choices. When faced with a challenge, free your inner conqueror and look for options. You might follow in the footsteps of Alexander and prove to have the Midas touch.

EXTRA CREDIT

MONKEY AROUND: Do apes have culture? From the *Sydney Morning Herald* comes the answer, sort of, as it turns out to be complicated: http://www.smh.com.au/national/do-apes-have-culture-20160525-gp3qz7.html. Certain apes may be a part of a conservative tribe where innovation is scant and traditional ways of doing things are rarely supplanted. This is clearly cultural mores at work, unless it is functional fixedness instead. It is difficult to understand the motive of creatures who can't explain themselves. Regardless, I like this definition of fixedness: "an innate inability to do things differently." Perhaps it is also a primate inability to do things differently?

GET GRUMPY: To properly channel your inner curmudgeon, get a few pointers from *Saturday Night Live* comedian Dana Carvey's Grumpy Old Man: http://www.hulu.com/watch/271497. Progress? Flibbity floo!

THINK LIKE A STONE: *Alexander* (2004). Oliver Stone's one hundred and fifty-five-million-dollar epic about the conqueror of ninety percent of the world, was skipped at the theatre by ninety percent of movie goers. The few who did see it didn't think it was so great, calling the movie ambitious and risky but unfinished, unwieldy and flawed. Historians hated it because it was inaccurate and directed by Oliver Stone, which is often redundant. Luckily for you none of the endless stream of names, places or dates narrated by Anthony Hopkins as Ptolemy will be on the final exam. Stone created the film as a historical opus to explain Alexander's kinder, gentler side but you don't have to use it that way. Instead, utilize it purely for its visual entertainment value and to ask yourself if any ruler with flowing locks as bad as Colin Farrell's could truly conquer the world?

Stuck in the Middle
Julius Caesar & Recency Bias

44 BC

W e like to use the very recent past as a predictor of
the future, overestimating the probability of current events continuing. Gaius Julius Caesar suffered
from such shortsightedness, a poor selection of friends, and
ultimately many stab wounds.

The cool of an early spring morning stretched out across
Rome, the sun seeping in the shining stone of the great
monuments and the filth of the back alleys alike. From the
tenements and ramshackle housing along the Tiber, the
commoners emerged to celebrate the Idus, a Latin word
roughly equating to *the middle*. It was a time to kick off your
sandals, if you had any, and slide casually into the days of
drudgery for the rest of the month. There would be drinking and speeches, even gladiatorial games. It would, most
thought, be a grand day. But no one knew that it would
change the world and the course of history. For this was

the Ides of March, 44 BC.[32]

Commoners spilled onto the streets and plazas, flowing through the capital drunk on wine and the achievement of living through another month. From the unwashed masses emerged their hero in a crisp white toga wandering the city, pondering his next move and receiving the adoration and well wishes of the plebs.[33]

"Hail," they cried. "Hail!"

And after a sleepless night and a morning full of portentous rumors, their hero must have looked around and thought, "Hey, what the heck do I care, the gangs all here." He'd slept poorly, awoken numerous times by his wife who had awful dreams and feared for his safety. She didn't want to nag, but could he stay home with her and the kids? He was up, dressed, and out the door in no time. Now messengers approached him with tales and gossip of plots against him. He thought seriously of calling in to work with a case of the pox. It wasn't too late to turn around and head for home.

Instead, Gaius Julius Caesar headed off to kill some animals and have their entrails read for any omens. I don't recommend this next time *you* consider calling in sick to work. It is an awkward conversation to have with most HR departments. But the haruspex, or seer, named Spurrina had told him weeks earlier that his life would be in danger for a period of thirty days, which would expire on the 15th

---

32 In Ancient Rome, there was no such thing as our modern "Hump Day." The conquerors of most of the Mediterranean had a wider perspective and eschewed a mid-week celebration for one at mid-month.

33 Hey, when you are unwashed and your average life expectancy is somewhere just shy of forty years old, you celebrate all the months you can.

of March. Now they met again, and he chided the "sooth-sayer" that his prophecies weren't worth much considering the Ides had come and nothing had happened. Spurrina muttered something that roughly translates into modern English as, "Day ain't over yet." Caesar turned stone faced and ashen. Chastised and worried, he returned to the streets headed for home.

From the crowds emerged a young friend, another clean toga below an earnest face beaming with a combination of delight and disapproval. "Not going to work? Are you a barbarian or a Roman? Did you conquer the Gauls or become one of them?" He swept an arm around the Forum. "Cast aside the forebodings of all these people and come," he demanded.

The advisor was named Brutus. And it was the worst possible advice for his advisee, Julius Caesar, dictator of the Roman Empire. Upon arriving at work, he was stabbed to death, his enemies inflicting over twenty puncture wounds while he stood, and then fell, in the Senate House. His last words may have been "You too child?" referencing Brutus's treachery. They ought to have been, "My wife was right! I should have stayed in bed."[34]

---

34 In 49 BC Caesar crossed the River Rubicon from Gaul with his legions to attack the forces of Pompey, his rival for power. Though Romans were averse to having an outright king, Caesar's victory effectively made him their sole ruler. Yet he was always careful never to be called a sovereign for fear of alienating the common people who supported him. Murdered for his ambition, if not his actions, sources differ on Caesar's last words. They certainly were not the oft quoted invention of Shakespeare, "Et tu, Brute?" Many historians think it likely Caesar said nothing at all given all the puncturing of vital organs and whatnot.

It is common to engage in **Recency Bias**—extrapolating recent trends into the future. And to believe, despite rumors and intuition, or even research and historical precedent, that what is happening right now will continue to happen. Caesar was tempting fate by counting his proverbial chickens before they had hatched. Prematurely celebrating the inefficacy of his fortune teller indicates that he was overconfident his current condition, that of being alive, would not or could not change, with little regard to randomness, circumstance, or knife wielding Senators. Take my advice and develop a wider perspective. Live for the moment, but don't get trapped thinking that moment will last forever.

- STOP BEING SUCH A BABY -

If you thought your recency bias was, well, recent...think again. A study by researchers from Stanford and the University of Rochester reveals that you've been partial toward the most recent option since you were still in diapers.

Children age 2-3 exhibit a "robust recency bias" when responding to questions in a two-alternative choice scenario. That means, if you let them choose between blue and red as their favorite color, they will choose red most often because it is the most current in their memory. Think about that before you paint the bedroom.

How You'll Be Tested...

Unless *you* have resentful, knife-wielding friends there is a good chance you have a life expectancy longer than next March. And during your (long) life, at some point markets will be down, perhaps dramatically. Protracted market downturns convince many that negative returns are the new norm. You'll become gloomy, morose, and sullen. You'll begin to believe that this really is the time where things don't bounce back. Ever. In other words, you believe that the downturn will continue simply because it is most recent in your memory.

Take a walk. Visit some friends. Clear your mind. Try to remember 2008 and 2009 when the oracles said the end was nigh and turned out to be dead wrong. When markets are down it doesn't mean they will stay there forever, though the masses will be quick to assume the end of the world. For that matter, when everything seems to be going right, that too shall pass despite the seemingly non-stop bacchanalia. Establishing a strong rule over your future doesn't mean you should know when the good and bad days will appear, just that you must endure both from time to time. Which is a good thing, because our wives and soothsayers are nowhere near as good as the Romans when predicting the future.

EXTRA CREDIT

MAKE A LIST: On a spreadsheet, catalogue your top one hundred favorite movies, songs, or books *of all time*. Now look up and enter the date each was released. Sort by that date and look at how many of your choices were recent, say the last five or ten years, versus in the distant past. Has literature, movie making, or songwriting gotten so much better recently? Hardly. But remembering is hard and recency bias is easy.

SHARPEN YOUR KNIVES: *Julius Caesar*, by William Shakespeare, is available on Google Play as an e book with voice output. I find it especially fun to read during the month of March. Et tu?

ROME IF YOU WANT TO: Tune in for *Rome, Season 1* (2005). Before HBO had an over-sexed, blood-drenched mini-series with dragons, they had an over-sexed, blood-drenched mini-series with legions. Watch Caesar cross the Rubicon and descend on Rome while intrigues play out amongst the nobility and plebs alike. Spoiler alert: It doesn't end well for Caesar.

RUN AWAY: Train for a marathon. At the end, you will discover that the race had a fanfare beginning, a long torturous middle, and a merciful end. But you won't remember much except the thrill of finishing. At least, so I have heard. Race promoters can thank the recency effect for filling fun runs and long-distance races nationwide. If it weren't for this mental bias, the hours of pain would overshadow the achievement, and no one would ever run more than one.

HAVE A WINNING FANTASY: Less of a go getter? Perhaps you are one of the dozen or so people in America who still isn't playing fantasy sports? Sign up and start drafting your team. Keep a tally counting the number of times you engage in recency bias while evaluating a player. Are you letting last year's stats determine much of the rating instead of the overall prospect? Player age, coaching, and type of system matter just as much if not more. Perhaps it is recency bias that has kept you from hoisting the league trophy all these long years.

With Friends Like These

Ovid, Augustus & Confirmation Bias

8AD

P oets wouldn't exist if humans were not lovers as well as fighters. And we love no one more than ourselves. Enamored with our own theories, we search for information that confirms them, giving less consideration to those that don't. It's really rather obscene.

"Publius Ovidius, the seller of smut and peddler of pornography, thank you for coming to see me on such short notice," grumbled the old man. He sat rigidly on a dais in a shady courtyard. A hard wind was blowing in and the billowing clouds would soon bring rain.

His friend the poet smirked and shrugged. "That has a nice ring to it I suppose. And it does differentiate me from all the other 'most famous poets in the world.'" Publius Ovidius Naso, better known as Ovid, wondered what he was doing here, why he had been summoned so abruptly to this meeting and escorted by a chiseled soldier who smelled of new sweat and old wine. "But if I might offer an alternative title, Ovid the Obscene and Erotic?"

"I'm glad *you* think it is funny." The elder man slumped a bit. "Come and sit down. I need you to tell me a story Ovid. Tell me about Narcissus." The old man, his blond curly hair streaked with gray wafting in the stiffening breeze, eyed the poet coolly and waited.

"Narcissus?" Ovid began hesitantly, then laid out his poetic story of the beautiful young man who fell in love with himself. Ovid *was* the most famous man in Rome, known far and wide for his ability to tell an epic story and this material was fresh in his mind, having been part of his most recent collection of poems.[35]

When he finished, the old man smiled wanly. "Would you say that this man from your poem fell in love with himself at the expense of the rest of the world? Would you say that his flaw was to value himself too much?"

Suddenly wary, Ovid looked sideways at his escort, or was it his guard? "I would say that he had the common affliction of believing himself to be better than the rest of us."

---

35   Narcissus was an extraordinarily proud and good looking lad. One day, the forest nymph Echo saw him hunting deer and fell madly in love. But Echo, not being human didn't really communicate well. She had a habit of repeating words that were just spoken as if they were wholly new; which they likely were to her. He would have none of it. He much preferred to hear his words in his own voice. How could he love her, little nymph that she was, when he was way too busy loving himself? Echo withered and died from the rejection, living on as an echo in the voices of human beings. Narcissus was so weary from all this rebuffing he sat down by a pool for a drink of water. He immediately fell for his reflection and could not bring himself to leave it for any reason. He died of hunger leaving nothing but a flower, the narcissus. Like many contemporary young egotists, he ultimately expired poolside due to an overdose. An overdose of himself.

The old man's voice hardened. "I think you have the same flaw my old friend. You've fallen in love with your own words and ignored their effect on Rome and on Romans. But I have not. Many think you write your filth to make me look foolish and then come here and laugh in my face. I expelled my own daughter for adultery, yet you write about it as if it is the most natural thing in the world."[36]

"That was years ago Caesar Augustus. I've written in a style more suitable to you in my new collection."

Augustus, Emperor of Rome, sighed. "It is too late. You are very popular, and you have been my friend for a long time. Neither fact will do you much good now."

"But Caesar Augustus, you forget that I've written kindly about your uncle, uh father, uh about Julius Caesar. You forget that I wrote of you, as his successor, as the deified ruler of mother Rome. You ignore my years of friendship."[37]

The Emperor flicked a hand dismissively. "I forget nothing. Your pleas are irrelevant. Its time you had a change...a metamorphosis as it were." The Emperor then brought himself to his full height, glaring at the poet as if he was considering what to say next. He pointed out of the arcade and his next words came out in a whisper. "Go my friend. Go north. You are banished from this city to Tomis in the Kingdom of Thrace."

"Tomis? What the hell is in Tomis?"

36   Julia the Elder was exiled to the tiny island of Pandateria in 2 AD for adultery while married to her stepbrother and future Emperor, Tiberius.
37   In Ovid's *Metamorphoses* Julius Caesar ascended to the heavens as a divine being to be followed by his heir, Augustus. Born Gaius Octavius, Augustus was the son of Julius Caesar's niece Atia. In his will, Uncle Julius adopted young Octavius and made him his heir. Thus, their relationship status remained "it's complicated" for all of history.

"Interesting question. For you, what is in Tomis *is* hell. There, no one will understand your foul writing, because no one speaks Latin. It's the only place I can think of where you can keep your pen *and* your head."

"Caesar Augustus, my Emperor, my friend. I hope you will reconsider?"

But the old man just shook his head. "It is done," he said simply.

The legionnaire took Ovid's arm and led him from the royal presence. For once, the poet with the silver tongue was speechless, cast out of the only home he had ever known by his erstwhile friend. As he passed under the arch of the arcade and out into the streets of Rome for a final time, a cold stinging rain began to fall. He wouldn't give up, he thought. He'd keep trying to convince Augustus to relent. "My hopes are not always realized, but I always hope," he whispered to no one in particular. [38]

In expelling Ovid from Rome, Caesar Augustus focused on Ovid's salacious poems, while discounting the bulk of his work, an example of **Confirmation Bias**. At a subconscious level, this bias entails listening to only that which validates

---

38   Banished in 8 AD, Ovid continued to write in exile for ten years, occasionally pleading with Augustus, and later his heir, to rescind the ban. It never happened and he died in exile. Why exactly was Ovid banished? We don't really know, but he mentions the reasons being a poem and a mistake. The poem was likely the *Ars Amorata* written in 2 AD, but the mistake is another of history's mysteries. Theories abound, including one of a romantic tryst with Julia. Some historians even question if he was banished or if he, though it seems a stretch, merely used it as a literary device in his writing.

what you already believe to be true. It is the tendency, like Narcissus, to fall in love with yourself, or with your theories and ideas, which can get even the best looking, most popular, or most intelligent of us into deep trouble. If you only look for confirming data, this information will echo endlessly in your head at the expense of an open mind.

APPRECIATING THE NUMBERS

Researcher Peter Cathcart Wason began the experiment for his 1960 paper on Confirmation Bias by showing participants the following numbers: **2 4 6**

They were told that the numbers satisfy a rule that the researchers had created. To determine what that rule was, the subjects should develop a hypothesis and test it with their own three numbers. The scholars would give them a yes or no answer about whether their figures satisfied the rule. They could do this as many times as they liked.

Most participants quickly deduced that the rule was a series of even numbers and set about testing it with series like 4-8-10, 6-8-12, etc. They often went a few rounds giving strings of even numbers to confirm their hypothesis and then stopped because they figured they had discovered the rule. They hadn't. It was: *each number must be larger than the one before.* This could have easily been determined had participants tried to *disprove* rather than *prove* their theory, but few did. Most people do not try to critically evaluate their suppositions, they merely look for confirming evidence.

How You'll Be Tested...

As an investor, eventually a friend or acquaintance will ask you the following question: *are you bullish or bearish?* As if it weren't hard enough to avoid confirmation bias, investors have created terminology and a binary choice to reinforce their predisposition. If you believe markets are generally trending upward, you are bullish. If you believe the bottom will fall out any day, you are bearish. And once you have labeled yourself as one or the other you will find all kinds of corroborating evidence to back your stance. Bulls will put their money anywhere and hope for the best. Bears never find the right time to invest much at all.

Reconsider who your friends are and choose a different path. Be both bearish *and* bullish. Analyze the pros and cons. Read different viewpoints. Recognize that while the general trend in most investment markets has been upward over meaningful periods of time, there are panics, crashes, and bear markets aplenty. And one just may be waiting for you around the next archway. Will you be able to keep your head? Silence that silver tongue of yours and prepare yourself mentally for whatever might happen next. Hope alone isn't much of an investment strategy. But neither is fear. Indeed, the story that the world is about to collapse is older than the myth of Narcissus.

EXTRA CREDIT

ROME SOME MORE: Rent, buy or stream *Rome, Season 2* (2007). Originally there were more than two seasons planned, with season three through five covering Augustus's consolidation of the Roman Empire and perhaps his booting of Ovid. But the show was cancelled due to budget constraints. Fans must content themselves with two measly seasons and an ongoing rumor about a film version.

GET OVID IT: Listen to Ovid's *Metamorphoses* recited in several parts. Don't worry, it's in English and easily available on YouTube: https://www.youtube.com/watch?v=4xSf1yBQx5c.

GO BACK TO ELEMENTARY: Read *A Few Lessons from Sherlock Holmes* (2013) by Peter Bevelin. Want to avoid the mental errors of Emperors and mere mortals? Learn from the great detective on Baker Street. Be sure to highlight this paragraph: "The fatal mistake which the ordinary policeman make is this: He gets his theory first, and then makes the facts fit it, instead of getting his facts first and making all his little observations and deductions until he is driven irresistibly by them into an elucidation in a direction he may never have originally contemplated."

GO BOHEMIAN: Or pick up *A Scandal in Bohemia* (1891). The first of Sir Arthur Conan Doyle's Sherlock Holmes escapades makes the point on which the whole series turns: "It is a capital mistake to theorize before one has data. Insensibly one begins to twist facts to suit theories, instead of theories to suit facts."

GO TO BAKER STREET: Discover Sherlock (2012), the BBC's excellent reboot of Sir Arthur Conan Doyle's sleuth features Benedict Cumberbatch dispensing wisdom and deconstructing the mental follies of criminals, friends, and his local police force alike. If it seems authentic, there is good reason. Benedict Cumberbatch is distantly related to Sir Arthur Conan Doyle, the author of the original Sherlock Holmes books. They are 16th cousins twice removed.

GET SCHOOLED: Professor David Nystrom of Biola University in California provides a one-hour primer on the life and times of Ovid. With a background in New Testament theology, Roman social history, agronomy, and plant pathology his background is admirably eclectic. Not unlike your humble author. See him here: https://www.youtube.com/watch?v=FQaykZo_TuU.

READ THE PAPER: Buy a newspaper with an editorial bent with which you tend to disagree. Read the editorial page for one week highlighting any information or opinions you don't like. Do some research on one or two of the highlighted areas. Change your mind, or don't. At least you've approached the topic from an alternate viewpoint.

Where There's Smoke, There's Fire

Pliny & Risk Homeostasis Theory (RHT)

79AD

Our opinions on risk are constantly altered by our environments and our behavior changes based on those, sometimes faulty, perceptions. The adventures of one man, his teenaged nephew and their neighbors throughout the centuries, demonstrate how sensing lower levels of danger leads to riskier activities.

The seaside sun beat down while cooling breezes wafted through the olive orchard carrying the scent of thyme and basil that thrived on the hillside leading away from the water. "My gods, this is the life," sighed the man stretched out in the sun around his villa, lazily popping figs into his mouth and sipping on a mildly tannic red wine mixed with water. It was summertime, and the living was easy on the Italian peninsula.

"Uncle?" The summons echoed through the house. "Uncle!"

"What now," moaned the Admiral, Pliny the Elder. Could the leader of the Roman fleet get no rest, even at home?

Gaius Plinius Caecilius Secundus, known as Pliny the Younger, barreled into the courtyard, his sandaled footsteps echoing behind him. His face was ashen. "Uncle, you have to see this."

At the front of the house both Pliny the Elder and Younger joined their sister and mother at the edge of the crescent shaped bay. To the west, they watched a large, oddly shaped cloud forming on the horizon. A vertical column of black and gray shot upward from the opposite coast, flattening into an anvil shape at its apex high overhead.[39]

The Elder turned to a nearby servant. "Make a galley ready, we'll depart immediately," he ordered.

The boy took a slight step backward hoping to blend in to the orchards or perhaps be mercifully swallowed by the earth. "*We?*" he thought warily.

"Pliny my boy, will you come with me?"

"Gosh, uncle, sounds great and all, but I've got a few things to catch up on, and I probably shouldn't leave mother alone." The seventeen-year-old demurred, opting to stay behind and read. At least, that was what he recalled later. One suspects he thought better of charging into strange clouds on otherwise sunny days. Well, teenagers know everything, just ask them.

The uncle arched an eyebrow, about to say something

---

39   Pliny the Younger used the Stone Pine tree with its narrow trunk and mushroom shaped plumage to describe the shape.

about Roman manhood. His sister gave him a hard look that said, *Don't. Just let him be.* He merely sighed with resignation. "Very well. I'll be back soon."

As the boat pulled out into the surf, the bow pointed at danger, the young scholar waved goodbye. "Fortune helps the brave," he said reassuringly to his mother. But that was easy to say on a beach with others heading toward harm's way.

Alas, Pliny the Elder would never return, perishing with about 12,000 others in the eruption of Mt. Vesuvius in August of 79 AD. Volcanic dust and rock rained down on the cities of Pompeii and Herculaneum, followed by clouds of toxic gas and a landslide of volcanic mud. Pliny the Elder's asphyxiated body was discovered under the ash when the cloud finally dispersed . Ironically, this volcanic detritus from previous eruptions formed the base of the soil around Pompeii, which was rich and fertile and supported local vineyards and orchards making the area wealthy and more populated.

———

Risk is always present. We merely perceive more or less of it and act accordingly. Today, the area wiped out by the eruption in 79AD is again wealthy and popular. Over 700,000 people now live in the "death zone" around Mt. Vesuvius. Clearly the painful lessons of history are no match for the allure of wine, olives, and ocean-front property. **Risk Homeostasis Theory** holds that we self-regulate the amount of risk we take on by checking the amount of danger we feel exposed to and comparing it to the amount we are willing to assume.

Believing you are safe and your subjective risk is low can lead you to take on riskier behaviors, sometimes with catastrophic consequences. With no major eruption of Vesuvius since 1944, and none of the explosive variety since 1779, it is easy to downplay any danger at all. So, more elaborate homes have been built in the shadow of places like Vesuvius *adding* to the potential hazard. Thus, *when* an eruption *does* occur, things end up likely worse than if there were more frequent eruptions and no illusion of safety.[40]

Risk Homeostasis
Target risk =
subjective risk +/- behavioral modifications

While what risk we are willing to accept is relatively static, how we perceive risk is highly subject to our environment and other mental biases. When subjective risk and target risk are balanced, there is no behavior triggered. But when we perceive less risk than our target, we will engage in some behavior to balance the equation.

---

40   Do a Google search for villas near Vesuvius or price land in the Amalfi Coast to test the theory. You'll find tens of millions of dollars at risk in a single property well within the "death zone."

> ### ── DON'T GO CHANGIN'... ──
>
> Richard Thaler, who we met in Lesson Two, isn't just a mere movie star. In a 1999 study, *Risk Aversion or Myopia? Choices in Repeated Gambles and Retirement Investments*, he and Shlomo Benartzi found that investors in retirement accounts changed their investing behavior depending on their perception of risk.
>
> Investors who looked at short term, more volatile returns chose lower proportions of stock for their portfolios than those who looked at longer term returns where losses were less common. With a higher perceived risk, investors changed their behavior and allocated just 40% to stocks. But when shown 30-year returns, with less volatility, perceived risk was lower, and they allocated up to 90% to stocks.

How You'll Be Tested...

All investors, not just those in tony Italian real estate, engage in similar behavior. For you, it may come when you notice a fund in your 401k or other investment account is doing so well that you decide not to take money from a strong performer and rebalance the account to reflect your strategic risk tolerance. Lulled by recency bias into perceiving less risk because of current positive returns, you change your behavior, accumulating more volatile assets.

Guess what happens next? When volatility erupts, you get burned. Instead, act like an adult and base your proportion of risky assets on factors such as your personal time horizon and future needs, not a perceived risk level that blows with the proverbial wind. It's the only way to make sure your own plans don't go up in flames.

EXTRA CREDIT

GET A HELMET: Grab a paddle and check out *Risk Homeostasis in Kayaking*: https://tsunamirangers.com/2014/04/07/sea-kayaking-risk-homeostasis/. Though lives have been lost on calm waters, it is only when perceived risk rises that a change in behavior occurs. When finding themselves up a creek or confronted by higher subjective risk, as in a Class III river instead of a placid lake setting, kayakers change their behavior and don a helmet.

SURF THIS SITE: Not into kayaking? How about surfing? Check out the website: http://riskhomeostasis.org/. Gerald Wilde, PhD Professor Emeritus of Psychology at Queen's University in Kingston, Ontario, Canada was the original researcher in Risk Homeostasis Theory. Often the original is the best, so spend some time here. You can even drop him a line and ask him questions via e mail. No risk in that.

WATCH THE RADIO: The *Radio Wammo Show* broadcasts on Kiwi FM, New Zealand and this time they had cameras rolling to talk about mental biases. Yes, they get the name of the Space Shuttle Challenger wrong, but this isn't supposed to be rocket science: Enjoy here: https://www.youtube.com/watch?v=nqMQ7yAVNSg.

CONTEMPLATE THIS:

- Would you drive more or less carefully if we took away your anti-lock braking system? What if we

removed the seatbelts from your car?
- Would you choose a different route on your bicycle if you weren't wearing a helmet, versus the one you would take with one on?
- What would you do if you were asked to drive a boat without personal flotation devices in it? Stick closer to shore? Drive slower?

TAKE A STUDY BREAK: Russian River Brewery makes a triple IPA called Pliny the Younger. But this is no beverage for a teenager. At 10.25% alcohol, even the most experienced connoisseur will want to take some safety precautions to balance their risk before cracking open a second one, like locking yourself in the house. See the suds at: http://www. beeradvocate.com/beer/profile/863/21690/.

DITCH THAT HELMET: What goes better with beer than football? If you can find it on one of the lesser used channels in your cable or satellite package, tune in for a bit of rugby. Then compare what you see with college or professional football while ensconced in your couch for the weekend. Notice anything? Rugby players have developed specific techniques to take down a ball carrier, while bigger pads and helmet technologies have led many football players to throw their bodies around with all the grace of a jackknifing tractor trailer. Doctors and researchers worry about Chronic Traumatic Encephalopathy or CTE due to repeated head trauma. Perhaps a culprit is also RHT?

Falling to Pieces
Hypatia & the Bandwagon Effect

415AD

M aking decisions based on what others are doing can be used as a cognitive shortcut in lieu of developing one's own information or opinions. But it's a bad idea, and not just because it's the type of thing that led to mayhem, murder, and the end of the Classical Age.

The salt air of the Mediterranean lay heavy around them, and the moon hung high above, ducking periodically behind thin clouds. The looming figure of the great stone Lighthouse of Alexandria rose out of the shadows overhead. Waves crashed nearby, and torchlight flickered in the court-yard where a crowd was starting to gather.[41]

"She is a witch," a man called Peter was shouting. "A

---

41 The lighthouse was one of the Seven Wonders of the Ancient World, a stone work rising up some four hundred feet. It was the tallest man-made structure in the world for centuries and the third longest lasting of the Ancient Wonders. Constructed around 280 BC it was destroyed by a series of earthquakes between 959 and 1323 AD.

pagan witch who is dividing the Christian community with her sorcery," he screamed, spittle landing among the closest of the crowd before him. The governor of Alexandria, Orestes, and the Christian Bishop, Cyril, weren't on speaking terms, instead keeping a steady stream of messengers running to the Emperor in Rome to undermine the other's authority. Local Christians like Peter were confused, divided, and angry.[42]

"Come now Peter, Theon's daughter is a beautiful and brilliant woman. Who can fear such a creature?" The only child of a philosopher and the last member of the Museum at Alexandria, the daughter of Theon was so well educated in mathematics and science that she is thought to have ghost written some of her father's early works. She was also said to be arrestingly beautiful, though that was never of much importance to her. Her intelligence and dedication to a chaste life, befitting a disciple of the neo-Platonic philosophy, allowed her into the circle of learned men and politicians at the center of Alexandrian society. Some approved and some did not. [43]

---

42   Orestes had been dealing with public demonstrations from Jews and Christians alike, and they were getting out of hand. Violence had erupted and the bishop expelled all Jewish subjects from the city without Orestes' consent. Because both were Christians, it was difficult for church followers to openly oppose either.

43   Fairly little is known about Hypatia's birth and life, at least in comparison to her death. Her father was perhaps the last overseer of a severely depleted museum and library at Alexandria. Clashes between Christians, Jews, and non-believers were becoming more and more fiery in those days and the collections, seen as a hot bed of paganism or non-conforming thought, had been burned several times. Flames destroyed numerous books and scrolls from the ancient philosophers and historians. For all the gifts of science to come out of Alexandrian society, fire safety clearly wasn't one of them.

"Yes, if she is a witch, I'm sure spellbound," said another man with a wink at his neighbor. His leering smirk disappeared abruptly when the magistrate named Peter turned on them.

"Oh, grow up," Peter snarled. He was in danger of losing the crowd and he knew it. He continued to glare, letting his eyes move sullenly across the throng. "Do you all approve of a pagan woman consorting with the Roman Christian governor?" There was a rumble amongst the more traditionally minded men. "What kind of Christian would approve of such thing?"

"But Orestes *seeks* her council," someone countered from the press of men.

"Yes, and look what it has wrought! Should he heed the counsel of a pagan instead of meeting with a Christian brother?" Peter asked.

"No," came the collective answer. No one joked now, the early dissenters silenced by the building fury.

Peter put on a grave face. "Obviously, she has bewitched the governor in order to sow strife. She may be a beautiful, brilliant pagan. But she is still a pagan."

"And a witch! We all know it!" someone yelled. And suddenly the crowd seemed to scream assent with one voice. Everyone now understood that Hypatia was keeping the feud alive and without her Cyril and Orestes would reconcile. Soon they were moving through the colonnades of the ancient city looking for the wise woman who was causing their woes.

Several blocks away the woman named Hypatia walked with her head high and shoulders back, an air of easy authority about her and heads turned to follow her as she made her way. Neither the world's, nor Egypt's first feminist, she was at least antiquity's first, and for many years last, female *scholar*. Tonight, she was on her way to teach mathematics, astronomy, and philosophy to pupils from many walks of life, including Christians, pagans, and foreigners.[44]

She had much on her mind that night, thinking through several new philosophical problems and perhaps considering a mathematical formula or two. With her mind elsewhere, she neglected the sounds of men running heavily on cobblestones and the flickering of torchlight off of the stone facades around her. And when someone broke into her reverie yelling "There she is!" It took precious seconds for her to realize, they meant her.

She knew she needed to run but found herself frozen. A circle formed and closed around her, hot breath and the smell of wine in her face. Then they came from behind and hands were on her, lifting and carrying but some were landing blows on her shoulders and head while others began tearing at her clothes. A door opened, and she smelled burning incense, felt a cool draft across her now naked body. She knew they had taken her into the nearby church. Perhaps she'd find sanctuary here? Then there was a cracking sound of pottery breaking on the stone floor. The crowd around her surged again, voices welling in anger and rage and she knew there would be no refuge. Instead she felt her skin jabbed and torn by the clay pottery shards and the hands that had beaten and stripped her were now stabbing her

---

44 She surpassed Theon as an intellectual and took to teaching all comers, which is where much of the controversy began.

again and again. She saw her blood run onto the stone floor and saw her life draining away. She must have wondered if all she'd done was for naught. Unfortunately, for many generations, the answer would appear to be yes. None of her original works survived the coming conflagration and her name was lost to history for generations. Many scholars now mark this single murder as the end of classical antiquity; a dark end to a millennium of enlightened thought and scientific advance.[45]

It was certainly the end of Hypatia.[46]

Hypatia's story shows how easy it can be for the loudest voices to drown out the logical ones and the tragedy that can ensue. It is a particularly violent example of the madness of crowds, also known as groupthink or the **Bandwagon Effect.** Peter spread the word that Hypatia was the problem separating the local leadership and the idea caught on. In fact, as the proportion of people adopt a line of thinking it becomes more likely that the belief will spread to new adopters. Like a fire in an ancient collection of dusty manuscripts, groupthink spreads quickly and seems to feed on itself.[47]

---

45   Not all historians agree with this timeline, noting that the teachings of Aristotle and Plato remained popular long after Hypatia's death and into the 6th century.

46   Hypatia's body was brutally dismembered and her remains burned. It was a macabre metaphor for the enlightened teachings and thought of the classical era, much of which, was going up in smoke. Alexandria declined rapidly after 415 AD with many scholars fleeing for their safety. The town was conquered by the Persians in 619 AD and Arab Muslims in 649 AD.

47   Not much is known about Peter the Magistrate, but he does appear in the historical record and is not a fictional character.

Joining the **bandwagon** typically fulfills two psychological needs: comfort and information. Conformists derive a certain amount of relief in being one of the crowd, usually adopting the idea early and waiting for others to join before becoming too vocal. Information seekers are looking for a cognitive shortcut, avoiding the heavy lifting of developing their own thesis by adopting someone else's. These are later adopters who are swept along with the tide.

Symptoms of Groupthink & the Bandwagon Effect

	Alexandrians	Investors
Rationalization	People don't agree with us because they are under an evil pagan influence.	People don't agree with me because they haven't done as much research or aren't as savvy.
Peer Pressure	If you don't like what we are doing you may not be a good Christian.	If you aren't invested like we are, you will probably lose money.
Complacency	Well, Peter has been right before and has become a magistrate, so he must be right now.	Well, others have bought this fund and tell me it has worked so I am probably going to be fine.
Stereotyping	She's a pagan, therefore she must be working against us.	They work for a financial company and must be working against us.
Moral High Ground	We've been taught by the church what is right, so this must be right.	We've been taught by the financial media what is right, so this must be right.
Self-Censorship	If everyone says she is a witch, maybe I am the one who is wrong.	If everyone says it is time to get out of the market, maybe this time I am wrong.
Illusion of Unanimity	Clearly, we all agree, so it is decided. Let's go get her.	Clearly everyone is selling. Let's go to cash.

Patrick Huey

How You'll Be Tested...

As an investor, you've probably said something like "we all know the market is due for a pullback." And you may find yourself in the future muttering things like, "everyone is saying, stay out of bonds until rates rise." Whatever the context, the next time you find yourself using such universal axioms, consider whether you are forming your own logical ideas or *con*forming to those that are presented by the loudest voices.

Television, the Internet, and social media are powerful platforms, the likes of which people like Peter the Magistrate could only dream. While not likely to lead to *your* ultimate demise, groupthink is dangerous for investors and can lead to underperformance, missed opportunity, and dark days in general. You don't need to be a brilliant classical intellectual to avoid it, just possess a shard of self-restraint.

EXTRA CREDIT

HITCH UP YOUR WAGON: Read the article, *Network Externalities: Bandwagon Effect and Snob Effect* at http://www.economicsdiscussion.net/essays/economics/network-externalities-bandwagon-effect-and-snob-effect-with-diagram/934. Learn how the demand curve for a good will shift when demand creates more demand via the bandwagon effect. Don't worry, there are pictures to help explain it.

GO TO DINNER: To make it a good one personally taste-test each of your options. No time? Check out ratings from places like Zagats or Yelp. Sure, you've engaged in groupthink and followed the crowd, but that isn't always a bad thing or a life and death decision. Unless, of course, you are looking for a raw bar or sushi.

MAKE IT DINNER AND A MOVIE: Rent or stream *Agora* (2009). How do you make a Hollywood film out of a chaste, neo-platonic philosopher? Insert a romantic interest of course! Slaves and governors fawn over Rachel Weisz but she proves elusive to the last. Alejandro Amenábar's film was con-troversial for painting early Christians in a negative light, though frankly, the historical record already does much of the same. Tolerance is a tough sell during the stampede of the runaway bandwagon.

LOVE A LEMMING: Think the lemming, known for mindlessly following the herd during mass migrations including leap-ing over cliffs to its death, would be the best mascot for groupthink? Think again. Humans merely bought in to the story after a 1950s documentary set the stage; literally, as in they staged the whole thing. Instead of proving that Arctic rodents have a death wish, it proves we will believe anything if enough others do too.

See the original clip here: https://www.youtube.com/watch?v=AOOs8MaR1YM.

Animal Planet debunks the myth here: https://www.youtube.com/watch?v=HsFVzywPNEc.

The best animal mascot for the bandwagon effect still looks a lot like you and me.

HISTORY 201

European Art, Science, War & Basic Economic Principles

"The greater danger for most of us lies not in setting our aim too high and falling short; but in setting our aim too low and achieving our mark."

–MICHELANGELO

"And Chaos ancestors of Nature hold, Eternal anarchy amidst the noise, Of endless wars and by confusion stand."

–MILTON, PARADISE LOST

"The greatest deception men suffer is from their own opinions."

–LEONARDO DAVINCI

"For God's sake let us sit upon the ground And tell sad stories about the deaths of kings"

–SHAKESPEARE, RICHARD II, A3,S2

LESSON ONE: Exceptions to the Rule

The Fall of Rome & Creative Destruction

235–1453 AD

LESSON TWO: All the Kings Men

King John vs. The Barons & Property Rights

1215 AD

LESSON THREE: Building Blocks

Santa Maria al Fiore & Competition

1296–1418 AD

LESSON FOUR: Ratted Out

The Great Plague & Equilibrium Pricing

1347 AD

LESSON FIVE: Crowd Control

The Battle of Agincourt & Technology

1415 AD

LESSON SIX: King Me

The War of the Roses & Cost Benefit Analysis

1483 AD

LESSON SEVEN: The Italian Job

Michelangelo & Opportunity Cost

1497 AD

LESSON EIGHT: Upward Facing Dogma

Copernicus & Inflation

1514 AD

LESSON NINE: Brave New World

Thomas Morton & Trade and Exchange
1624 AD

LESSON TEN: Going Around in Ellipses

Edmund Halley & Business Cycles
1682 AD

LESSON ELEVEN: Fowl Play

W.B. Tegetmeir &
Division of Labor and Specialization
1882 AD

LESSON TWELVE: A House of Cards

World War I & Unintended Consequences
1914 AD

Exceptions to the Rule
The Decline of the Roman Empire & Creative Destruction

312AD–TBD AD

Historians debate when the Roman Empire actually fell because, well, that is what historians do. But there is no arguing what came after the collapse was a tragedy, except when it became a triumph.

The peasants rubbed red eyes, choked, and coughed as the dirt cloud drifted down from the mountain pass leaving Gaul, plunging into Northern Italy. Red oval shields clattered against chain mail shirts as the footsore soldiers ascended the high path with muttered curses in a number of different languages. Forty-thousand Roman soldiers were on the road and the local rustics watched them pass with pinched faces of disdain.

"Going back to Italy, eh. C'est normal," said one.

"Oui, back to Italy where they belong. Hail Caesar." The other spat and made an obscene gesture.

"Eh, plus ça change, plus c'est la même chose."[48]

Indeed, the more things change, the more they stay the same. But while history repeats itself often, it usually does so with echoes of nuance. This was *a* Caesar and not *the* Caesar returning from Gaul to plunge the Italian peninsula into civil war. This was 312 AD and four hundred years since Julius Caesar crossed the Rubicon and established an Empire that would last for…well, let's just say a long time and come back to that later. Flavius Valerius Constantinus, or just Constantine in his less formal moments, held the *title* of Caesar, one of four in command of the complex political division of the late Roman Empire known as the tetrarchy. He desired to consolidate that power into a single Caesar Augustus, found himself worthy and willing, and was about to attack his rival in Rome when a funny thing once again happened on the way to the Forum.

The march from Gaul was long, and Constantine arrived in camp weary and fell into a deep sleep. That night he dreamt of winning the crown beneath the banner of a white cross, and he became a visionary in the most literal sense. The God of the Christians, a vocal and growing religious sect, would lead his men to victory over the superior force led by Maxentius if he painted the sign of the cross on his legions' shields. It was a pretty sweet deal. Constantine painted and Maxentius attacked. Constantine drove his rival and his troops into the Tiber and became ruler of the Western Empire. He would soon successfully consolidate the east as well, establishing the city of Constantinople and credit Christianity for his success, though

---

48   "The more it changes the more it's the same thing" attributed to Jean-Baptiste Alphonse Karr. French, a Romance Language, is a descendent of the dialects of Northern Gaul.

not enough to be baptized and fully adopt the religion.[49]

What followed was a complex story of tolerance and trouble. The Edict of Milan in 313AD made religious freedom the law of the land, but Christians still struggled to fit their deified leader into a monotheistic religion with strict commandments against worshipping idols. When Constantine fell ill in 337AD, he was at last baptized on his death bed. It then became official, a Roman Emperor had recognized and validated a religion that minimized his power and doubted his divinity. It was the end for the Roman Emperors and the Empire itself.

Except that it wasn't. After Constantine, the empire fragmented again as his sons battled it out for supremacy. Yet Roman Emperors, east and west, continued on until the fifth century when barbarian tribes, like millions of future travelers, decided life would be better in Italy. Along came Alaric, leader of a band who appears on the scene around 400AD in the Eastern Empire attacking westward and eventually negotiating a Roman title and payments in return for peace. But by August of 410AD, payments were lagging, and Alaric was frustrated with the bad faith of the Roman negotiators. His forces entered the city of Rome and plundered it. For nearly a thousand years, Rome had remained untouched except by Romans. Now, it was burning. Thus, with the sack of Rome and the rise of the barbarian tribes, Rome fell and passed into history. [50]

---

49   Nor did Constantine make Christianity the official religion of Rome as many mistakenly believe. That historical origination was due to Theodosius I and the Edict of Thessalonica in 380 AD.

50   For years, tribes such as the Goths and Visigoths had spilled over the borders into Rome, most of them fleeing invaders to their north such as Attila the Hun. Roman policy toward them veered from outright hostility to exasperated tolerance, sometimes buying their loyalty and sometimes fighting them outright.

Except that it didn't. Alaric left the city after a mere three days of looting and pillaging. The succession of Emperors, chaotic as ever, was reestablished. They came and went, rarely even recognized by their counterparts in Constantinople as true sovereigns. Meanwhile the Huns pressured the eastern border, the Germanic tribes flowed across the Rhine and the Vandals carved off the African provinces from the Empire. While the Empire may not have fallen, the foundation was in sad repair. What was left of the Roman Army was in shambles, much of it consisting of barbarian mercenaries like the German Odacer. He launched his own attack in 476 and captured the Emperor and his crown at Ravenna. And so, it was that a Germanic king took the throne of Italy, ending the four-century empire in the place where it started, near the river Rubicon. With a barbarian ruling in Italy, the empire had well and truly crumbled.[51]

Except that it hadn't. Part of the Roman Empire was thriving to the east; its capital in Constantinople, its religion Eastern Orthodox, and its language Greek. If new Rome was flourishing had Rome ever really folded? Regardless, history came full circle in 1453 when another Constantine, this one the XI, watched Constantinople fall to the Ottoman Turks before dying in battle. With the fall of the Byzantine Empire, it could well and truly be said that the Roman Empire was gone forever... seriously. [52]

---

51   Odacer's revolt was against his commander Orestes, who had ambitiously proclaimed his own son Emperor naming him Romulus Augustus.
52   It was Constantine who founded the Byzantine Empire, named for the ancient Greek colony around the Bosporus Straight. And when he founded the city bearing his name, his intention was to make a new Rome. That creation would last for nearly a full millennium after the West fell. In his excellent series of lectures on the History of the Ancient World, professor Gregory Aldrete notes that some scholars even go so far as to claim Rome

Whenever you date its fall, the Italian scholar Petrarch would note that the light of Roman art, literature, and engineering was extinguished, leading to what he called The Dark Ages. Cultural advancement in Europe seemed to have ended and then reversed. Aqueducts crumbled; roads deteriorated; literature, art, and science stagnated. It was the end of the world. *Except that*…well, you get the point. From that cultural vacuum of Roman decline would spring a rebirth across Europe. The lights would be turned back on and the arts and sciences would flourish again. But the continent needed to go backward to go forward, in one giant example of **Creative Destruction**.[53]

How You'll Be Tested…

The Austrian economist Joseph Schumpeter described a "perennial gale of **creative destruction**" whereby whole industries and individual jobs vanish to be replaced when something new topples the old order. It was a succinct label for the complete mess that economies and markets often make on their way to progress and prosperity. As

---

the Republic was recreated in eighteenth century America and so it exists to this day. A lovely sentiment, but not one I can get behind. We must draw the line somewhere.

53 Scholars today shy away from terminology such as the Dark Ages and prefer less definitive terms such as the Middle Ages. To be sure, there was some progress during this period and it was not a total loss depending on your geography. But I prefer Petrarchs's euro-centric, less politically correct terminology.

an investor, you will hear pundits bemoan the perception that "we don't make anything *here* anymore" indicating that investing in America is about as timely as buying stock in Roman toga makers. True, these days manufacturing jobs are often replaced by information technology and service work. Your test will be to determine if that is bad or good.

IT'S NOT ALWAYS KIND TO REWIND

The decade of the 1980s brought about awesome technological advances like the VCR. Indeed, by the mid-80s the Bureau of Labor Statistics (BLS) was tracking how many workers were engaged in the video tape and disc rental industry.

In 1985, there were about 87,000 seasonally adjusted jobs in an average month. The numbers climbed steadily, it was a growth business! By the late 90s there were over 168,000 positions.

Then, some genius invented the Internet. Today there are less than 12,000 such jobs thanks to streaming services like NetFlix. The pimply faced kid who used to check you out at Blockbuster had to find other work. But the hundreds of millions streaming worldwide don't complain much while watching *House of Cards.*

Was it progress when we transitioned from a nineteenth century agrarian economy to an industrialized society? In retrospect, it is hard not to call this advancement, unless *you* want to wake up early to feed the hogs. **Creative destruction** is an uncomfortable part of life and it is going on somewhere around you right now. Indeed, c'est normal! To be sure, it is an untidy way to progress, pain traded for gain with the potential for whole classes of people to be left worse off, perhaps forever. But you shouldn't sack your investment plans for fear of inspired demolition. True believers realize when you aren't certain if something is progress, it may be a good sign that it is. The Romans were pretty sure there was little upside to the loss of their empire. And for a long time, they were right, *except that they weren't*. What was destroyed would later be recreated and bettered during a little thing we've come to call The Renaissance.

Extra Credit

GET SOME PERSPECTIVE: Sign up for T*he Great Courses, History of the Ancient World, A Global Perspective*. Lecture 41 discusses the problem of dating the end of the Roman Empire. Check out the first forty in your spare time for a good review of many of the previous course's historical topics as well. Choose your medium at http://www.thegreatcourses.com/courses/history-of-the-ancient-world-a-global-perspective.html.

GET THE APP: Roman Emperors with sporadic ties to Christianity? Sure, there is an app for that! The Edict of Milan for Android devices features the original text of the decree along with other articles about Constantine the Great and his birthplace in modern day Serbia. Download it here or search on Google Play: https://play.google.com/store/apps/details?id=com.edictofmilan.whitecircleepub.AOUJVESDVNTBTKBIX&hl=en.

TAKE A TAXI: Call a surly dispatcher and then wait for a dingy yellow cab with a broken credit card reader that might never come. If it does, take a ride and ponder the mobile ride sharing revolution and the impending destruction of the cab business. Feeling bad? Then relive the glory days of the industry by watching *Taxi*, the hit 1970s TV show. Its available on Hulu. While viewing, try not to think about all the cable TV operators you are putting out of business. http://www.hulu.com/taxi.

LISTEN TO THE BOSS: No music encapsulates the feelings of loss when an economy leaves people behind like the early works of Bruce Springsteen. Give a listen to 1975's *Born to Run* in its entirety and revel in the desperation and dark quasi-enthusiasm for the middle-class way of life at the dawning of the "me generation."

RIDE A HORSE, READ SOME ECONOMICS, MAKE A LITTLE LOVE: Joseph Schumpeter supposedly set out to be the eminent economist in the world, the greatest horseman in Austria, and the paramount paramour in Vienna. You can read *Prophet of Innovation, Joseph Schumpeter and Creative Destruction* (2007) by Thomas K. McCraw to figure out which two of the three he felt he achieved. McCraw's book is the definitive tome regarding the angel of economic demolition. If you can't get through all 719 pages without destructing yourself, feel free to create some efficiencies and read this summary by Thomas Leonard of Princeton: https://www.princeton.edu/~tleonard/papers/McCraw.pdf.

HAVE A SLICE OF ORANGE: For an idea of the relationship between Gaul and Rome, visit the Provencal city of Orange in southern France. The city houses two relics of the Roman occupation. First the Triumphal Arch, built to honor Caesar's legions, who conquered and settled the area. Second, the statue of Emperor Augustus inside of the magnificent amphitheater with his boot being kissed by a Gallic slave. The symbolism isn't terribly subtle, and you will note that the slave, like the rest of Rome's subjects, has since disappeared. If you are looking for subtlety, the local wines from Chateuaneuf du Pape fit the bill and pair well with contemplating crumbling empires.

All the King's Men

King John vs. The Barons & Property Rights

1215 AD

W hen you are naughty and get caught, it is generally recommended that you show some remorse, especially when your prosecutors are heavily armed. One such meeting, a run in at Runnymede, created a "great charter" establishing limits on the power of monarchs and allowing nobles, and one day all of us, to save our own assets.

"I am sure in for it this time," thought Little Johnny. He sat turning crimson from chastisement and shame, the high grass of the meadow slapped against him in reprimand as the late day summer sun set over London and the River Thames.

He'd gotten into trouble in church, gone wandering out of the neighborhood, and taken money that wasn't his. Golly, what a mess. He'd admitted he was wrong, and now he'd have to promise never to do it again. Gosh it was sure humiliating! His big brother had never been embarrassed like this. Then again, his big brother had been Richard the Lionheart, a military mastermind and hero of the Third Crusade. Little Johnny, after Richard's death now King John of England, was the hero of nowhere and the mastermind of nothing. And it made him *really* mad.

Little Johnny had lost territory to the French King, who was a nasty bully and made a bunch of demands Johnny knew someone like his big brother wouldn't have liked. So, he ignored that king and kept trying to take his lands. When things went bad, Little Johnny didn't give up and quit, no sir! He kept right on trying. And trying. And trying.[54]

Of course, to finance his tries and overseas misadventures he raised taxes and ruthlessly wrung every penny he could from his barons, his nobles, and the church. When they grumbled, Johnny didn't learn his lesson. And so, they had come for him with many more soldiers than he had, then forced him to meet and sign something at this place called Runnymede. He signed and put his seal on the Articles of the Barons, later known as the Magna Carta, voluntarily limiting his royal powers. Or so everyone thought. You see, Little Johnny had his fingers crossed!

The preamble and sixty-three clauses of the Magna Carta dealt primarily with specific feudal grievances from the point of the English Barons. One specifically addressed the growing national scourge of fish weirs, or traps, on the

---

54 War with France was renewed in some part due to John's marriage to an heiress named Isabella who was already betrothed to a French nobleman. When the French rebelled, he lost holdings in Normandy, Maine, Anjou, and part of Poitou. He spent the better part of a decade trying to recover the lost lands and prestige without much success.

Thames. In retrospect, it seems a quaint document with little to recommend it to modern readers. Yet it is often mentioned in the same breath as the Declaration of Independence or the US Constitution when discussing influences on democratic thought.[55]

Those seeking mentions of democracy or a government giving voice to the common people are invariably disappointed by the Great Charter. But the document is a precursor to democratic constitutions because it puts limits on executive power and claims rights of property that are inviolable even by government force. Indeed, the fish weir prohibition merely seems out of date, specifically prohibiting the government from taking fish from private lands without paying for it. If you replace fish with gold or oil you have a modern-day version of what those Barons were fighting against. And it all worked out, until King John chose to ignore every promise made within the Magna Carta and enter a not so civil war. Little Johnny just couldn't be good.

While an immediate and spectacular failure, the Magna Carta turned into a long-term success after it was reissued and reworked several times by King John's heir Henry III. Only after Henry's defeat of the rebels and his *voluntary* reissue of the document did the concepts of limited government and **Property Rights** really take hold; this time, with no take-backs. The beginnings of representative government and parliamentary elections would come much, much later. But they would come, turning a somewhat backward island

---

55   The Charter celebrated its eight hundredth anniversary in 2015. In February of that year, all four remaining copies of the document were brought together for the first time.

Patrick Huey

into the center of European political life in just a few hundred years. English parliaments would control the purse and thus place important checks on centuries of their monarchs.

So, once upon a time, a failed government of overtaxed, indebted, and under-represented citizens reformed itself to become a cornerstone of European representative government. And everyone lived happily ever after. Well, happier than they were before anyway. Like your stuff? Hug a Baron. Okay, best not. The British are touchy about Yanks hugging it out in the House of Lords.

——— RAISIN OBJECTIONS ———

Lest you think struggles for property rights are merely a footnote in history, the United States Supreme Court ruled in 2015 that an Agriculture Department program for propping up raisin prices was an illegal seizure of property.

Horne v. Department of Agriculture decided that the rule violated the US Constitution's 5th Amendment and the Takings Clause which states: "private property [shall not] be taken for public use, without just compensation." Framers of the Constitution added such language based on their interpretations of English Common Law and the Magna Carta.

The concepts of **property rights** were essential to building a market economy where goods trade without risk of arbitrary seizure. Without markets, there is no legal or peaceful way to acquire economic resources. When that is the case, human nature being what it is, we've often turned to more violent means like going Viking, invasions, or out-right subjugation and colonization. Thus, the Magna Carta, despite its overt lack of democratic principles, created the beginning of a better, more peaceful world. And it all began with a proverbial spanking for Little Johnny.

How You'll Be Tested...

If you are reading about investing, you know something about ownership and the right to trade it away. But occasionally you may find yourself tempted to over-invest in countries where asset prices are skyrocketing without considering who is making the rules. Many investors become enamored with investment in Emerging Market (EM) countries or the so-called BRICs (Brazil, India, China & Russia). A new wave has taken a liking to Frontier Markets, which are even less developed with respect to property and the rule of law.

All of which is fine, if you understand the risks. Keep in mind that without the ability to control one's property and set a fair price for potentially trading it away, a true market can't exist. Investments in most of those aforementioned countries carries extra danger due to historically weak property rights. So, ask yourself how much of your investment portfolio you want exposed where arbitrary seizure is a possibility, even a remote one. When it comes to owning your portfolio, you shouldn't have to cross your fingers and hope for the best.

EXTRA CREDIT

GO TO THE ARCHIVES: Avoid the dust and centuries old musty smells typical of historians conducting primary source research. Conduct your own inquiries on the Great Charter at the United Kingdom's online archives. Start here: http://www.nationalarchives.gov.uk/education/medieval/magna-carta/.

STEAL THE SHOW: Watch *Robin Hood, Prince of Thieves* (1991). The movie takes place during King Richard's absence while on the Crusades. Even then, Little Johnny caused trouble rebelling against the King's administrators, in this case with help from the likes of the Sheriff of Nottingham, played admirably by Alan Rickman. No, a thief isn't exactly the poster child for property rights, even if he is doing the whole steal from the rich to give to the poor thing. And no, Kevin Costner isn't English. But if you stick it out to the end, Sean Connery makes an uncredited appearance as Richard the Lionheart. And having James Bond as your king is pretty awesome even if he isn't English either (he's Scottish).

GO COUNTRY: If Bryan Adam's soundtrack makes you lactose intolerant due to its high cheese content, you can always opt for the animated version from Disney. *Robin Hood* (1973) has a suitably accented hero, but the music is all American bluegrass and early country.

BUST A RHYME: Yep, the encounter at Runnymede is available in a rap version from a collection called Horrible History. Though I'm not sure anyone wants to claim ownership rights for lines like "How about this, let's barter… we'll stay loyal if you agree to Magna Carta." Why rap about the English times gone by? Because history nerds have spare time and YouTube accounts too.

The proof is at: https://www.youtube.com/watch?v= F_5My8XH-n0.

GET SOME BALANCE: Create a personal balance sheet including your assets and liabilities. Dig deep and inventory all of your personal belongings. It's a good practice for anyone engaging in basic financial planning and insurance agents recommend it anyway. Also, focusing on your assets allows you to appreciate all the stuff you own thanks to a bunch of whining English Barons.

HANG TEN: Think property rights are only nice for Barons? Hit the web and land on this video, part of which uses surfer's rules of the road to explain the momentary ownership of the waves. See, property rights aren't just for the rich. They also help perpetual beach bums finding the endless summer while living in their mom's basement. Hang ten at: https://www.youtube.com/watch?v=jnjPFZV8Wqo.

Building Blocks
Santa Maria Al Fiore & Competition

1418 AD

The completion of the church and baptistery at Santa Maria Al Fiore pitted two famous Florentine masters against each other and resulted in an iconic innovation of the Renaissance. The fact that they hated each other, shows that even the holiest landmarks aren't built by love alone.

The master builder's sturdy hands flailed in exasperation. "You tell them I am sick, and I won't come to work today," he bellowed, his dark eyes flaring above an angular nose. A goldsmith's apprentice as a boy, he had always loved architecture and mastered drawing, painting, sculpture, stone setting, and mechanics. He was a Renaissance man well before the term had any meaning. But Filippo Brunelleschi was a hot-tempered Italian, which is to say he was Italian.

"But you told them that yesterday, and you are not sick at all," protested his apprentice. He worried about his master's temper and where it would leave him if the city fathers chose someone else to continue construction. Brunelleschi had already quit his native Florence for rival Rome once. He'd left with his good friend Donatello when he had lost the commission to build the decorative doors for the baptistery that faced the uncompleted dome. He'd been bested by a man named Lorenzo Ghiberti.

"Just you tell them! And let's see if that idiot they call a genius can finish my work." That particular idiot was the same Lorenzo Ghiberti, his rival for over a decade. "Let's see if he can build the dome of Santa Maria Al Fiore himself!"

The church of Santa Maria Al Fiore, better known as Il Duomo di Firenze, was begun in 1296 by original architect Arnolfo Di Cambio and the design was altered numerous times during construction. Then again, things are bound to change over the course of one hundred and forty years. By 1418, the city fathers of Florence had a massive holy cathedral that also turned out to be massively holey. Nature's elements and creatures entered the church through the void where a vast dome was supposed to crown the masterpiece.

It might have been far simpler to call it a day but nicknaming a church "the hole" instead of "the dome" seemed to be taking the easy way out. And for a religion devoted to the world's most famous carpenter, it just wouldn't do. How they solved the problem of building a one-hundred-and-fifty-foot dome some one-hundred-and-eighty feet off the ground would symbolize the dawning of a new age in Italy that would spread to the rest of Europe. The Renaissance was beginning after one of those extended holidays for which Europeans are notorious and science, art, engineering, and critical thought were back in vogue.

Brunelleschi attacked the problem from a new angle, designing not one, but two domes resting inside of one another for support and proposed to build them without the use of scaffolding. One slight contractual issue: he would not divulge his exact plans fearing his competition would steal the idea. Intrigued but skeptical, the overseers of the project awarded him the contract with the stipulation that he had to work side by side with someone to monitor the designs. His name was Lorenzo Ghiberti. It was like Michael Moore filming a documentary under the supervision of the Republican National Committee. There were bound to be issues. Indeed, it was especially galling for Brunelleschi, as working on the dome meant looking out over the Baptistery where Ghiberti was sculpting relief scenes into the eastern doors. Every day he was reminded of a competition he had lost. Most days he endured it and went to work. But not every day.[56]

The regular antagonism with his more famous compatriot brought out the best and worst in the fiery Brunelleschi. He immediately showed flashes of genius, designing a system of lifts to place massive stone blocks overhead with laser like accuracy. Modern engineers still marvel at the precise placement and the machines used, as better equipment wouldn't come about until the Industrial Revolution. But he also showed peevishness and manipulation by feign-

---

56   The doors would make Ghiberti famous and lead to another endeavor to produce the sculpted doors for the north side of the Baptistery, which became iconic. Michelangelo referred to the second set of doors as fit to be the Gates of Paradise. The name stuck. The location of the Baptistery doors was then changed to reflect their relative importance, with the Gates of Paradise moved to the north entrance in place of Ghiberti's earlier work.

ing sickness and forcing Ghiberti to admit that he couldn't continue the work because it was beyond his capabilities.

At his death, Brunelleschi was laid to rest in the cathedral he finished, an honor previously reserved for high religious figures. Artists would continue to add to the splendor of Santa Maria Al Fiore with statues and bell towers, but all in the shadow of the great dome. It was the beginning of a whole new world of form, symmetry, beauty, and utility.

Competition, you see, brings out the best and worst in all of us. But it is hard to argue with the long-term results of contests and occasional conflict, especially if you can take in The Duomo or any other masterpiece of the Renaissance. Indeed, a primary reason the Renaissance first took hold in Italy was because of the intense **competition** for resources distributed by the church, headquartered in Rome. This competition ensured that the church paid less and got more for each project, which in turn increased the demand for commissioned works.

Driving down prices may have put some craftsmen with less skill out of business and constant rivalry certainly bruised some egos. But the Baptistery doors might not be so fabulous or renowned had Brunelleschi and Ghiberti not found themselves pitted against each other struggling for fame and fortune. And the dome might have gone unfinished, or worse, crumbled under the weight of inferior engineering if there weren't significant rewards for taking on the task. Rivalry, as Brunelleschi demonstrates, required

Patrick Huey

innovation to get ahead. Getting better, advancing, learning new skills: those were the key drivers of the Italian Renaissance. It wasn't always pretty or nice, but the results were often beautiful.

— DOME, SÌ. ARCHES, NO. —

Around the site of Florence's most famous dome, many fast food options vie for tourist's money so that no one ever need sit between The Duomo and David for something so down-to-earth as a meal.

In 2016, McDonalds sought to open a restaurant in the piazza to get in on the action. Italians used the arch to build aqueducts and amphitheaters, and to conquer most of the Mediterranean. But Florentines apparently aren't big fans of arches when they are golden.

Under intense local pressure, the Mayor backed out of a deal to put McDonald's in the square and a lawsuit was filed against the city. To this day, competition still rages in Florence and causes tempers to flare.

How You'll Be Tested...

Today the church of Santa Maria Al Fiore sits like a shining pink and green beacon in the center of Florence. On a sunny day, you can still sit in one of the nearby cafes and enjoy the local Tuscan wine while the light reflects off the Duomo, the Baptistery, and the bell tower. Or you can endure the endless lines and touring groups jostling each other for the perfect selfie in front of the alter. Yes, competition can still bring out the worst in us, as tourists and investors. As the latter, you may one day want to back your preferred genius with a sizable portion of your portfolio. And who wouldn't want the next Musk, Branson, or Zuckerberg propelling them toward financial paradise?

Calm down, don't be peevish and don't get manipulated. Competition is fierce out there and wherever there is a contest, there will be winners and losers. And it is possible, or even likely, that you'll bet on the wrong genius. But that doesn't mean we aren't progressing as a whole, with achievements that soar above the ordinary and last, perhaps, for centuries to come. Take a cue from the Florentines. Most of your portfolio should be betting on multiple geniuses, not just one.

EXTRA CREDIT

TAKE THE TOUR: If you can't jet off to Florence, or you just want to avoid the crush of tourists, sit back with a glass of Chianti and watch the virtual tour here: http://www.360globe.net/italy/florence/florence-cathedral-santa-maria-del-fiore.html.

Then, for more on the most famous doors in the world, take a closer look at: http://www.museumsinflorence.com/musei/Baptistery_of_florence.html.

SHAKE & BAKE: See *Talladega Nights, The Ballad of Ricky Bobby* (2004). What can you learn about competition from the likes of Will Farrell and the hypercompetitive world of stock car racing? Primarily this: "If you ain't first, you're last!"

CREATE A MONTAGE: Any good competition needs a 1980s style montage, so take your phone out and start filming. Add music featuring synthesizer and electronic drums and voila, you are ready for fierce competition. Find a series of handy tips at: http://nofilmschool.com/2014/09/larry-jordan-teaches-us-how-create-video-montage-set-music.

GET INSPIRED: Need a muse? Start with the most famous training montage of all time from *Rocky* (1976). Rocky goes jogging, hits frozen meat, and climbs the art museum steps at: https://www.youtube.com/watch?v=DP3MFBzMH2o.

Then you can follow it with one from every sequel:

Rocky II	https://www.youtube.com/watch?v=ABg0c_E7OOI	Rocky gets faster by chasing a chicken.
Rocky III	https://www.youtube.com/watch?v=6YsfHfHKKh0	Rocky and Apollo Creed frolic on the beach.
Rocky IV	https://www.youtube.com/watch?v=1SUzcDUERLo	Rocky grows a beard and splits wood in Russia.
Rocky V	https://www.youtube.com/watch?v=Jf7CPMh3ZK8	Rocky trains his protégé.
Rocky Balboa	https://www.youtube.com/watch?v=PAvhcLkUIi0	A noticeably older Rocky goes jogging to the museum again.
Creed	https://www.youtube.com/watch?v=-NH1A6CLIrY	Apollo's son revives the genre forty years after the original montage.

Still Not Fired Up? How about a montage of montages? See it at: https://www.youtube.com/watch?v=pOcsBiCaEJ8.

If that doesn't do the trick, maybe this competition thing isn't for you.

Ratted Out

The Great Plague & Equilibrium Pricing

1347 AD

The Great Plague, and several not so great ones, gave survivors plenty of reasons to curse fate and everything else. But when a new balance was reached between resources and needs, it turned out even pestilence had its positives. At a price, of course.

"Oh, *Porca miseria!* Do we have to go in there?" moaned the dockworker, a big Sicilian with rough hands and innumerable scars.

"Si. You go first," whispered his companion. The breeze had died off and they looked out on sloppily furled sails as a boat bobbed lazily at anchor where the Ionian and Tyrrhenian Seas met in front of them.

"Me, *stronzino?* You are the supervisor, no?" Nothing moved. The day was still except for the gentle lapping of the water on the stone quay underneath them.

"*Che palle!* Si, I am the supervisor, so I am telling you

to go open up that boat." They stared, but neither started toward the ship. Time stretched.

"*Che cavolo!* Go on you two," cried out the fishmonger. "We have fish to sell."

"*Fa Napule!* And my wine won't drink itself!" shouted the tavern owner.[57]

Everyone had something to say, but still, no one stirred. The hawkers and merchants were crowding in behind them now. It was a mild October day in the port of Messina and the smells of salt water and decaying fish wafted across numerous decks of ships that had cruised to the end of the Chinese trade routes on the Black Sea. The anxious Sicilian tradesmen waited ashore for the inevitable rush of sailors returning with goods and money in their pockets. And they waited.

Normally, a horde of newly rich, slightly intoxicated adventurers desperate to part with their money would storm the port, spending like, well, drunken sailors. Today, nothing happened: no hollering, no drinking, no gambling, and no carousing. Boats creaked on their mooring lines. The sun beat down and then started to descend. Those plying the world's oldest profession went home alone. In the history of men going to and returning from sea, it may have been a first. And it was truly terrifying.

When curiosity and greed finally overtook caution, the ship was boarded and examined and most of the sailors

---

57 Italian is one of the best languages known to man for cursing. Here is a brief translation of the modest swearing I've included here: *Porca miseria*, pig misery; *Stronzino*, little jerk; *Che palle*, what a pain; *Che cavolo*, what cabbage; *Fa Napule*, go back to Naples (an insult to all Italians not from Naples).

were found dead. Those that survived wished they were departed as well. Feverish and covered with mysterious boils, they didn't have long to wait. The plague or "black death" was again loose in Europe. Quickly it ravaged the city and panicked victims carried it with them into the countryside. In a month, Corsica and Sardinia were infected. Within the year, it would cover Paris and London and reach as far north as Norway, killing upwards of twenty million people, or one third of the continent's population.[58]

The bubonic plague, named for the buboes or tumor sized swellings appearing on its victims, was a bacterial infection originally found in black rats. Once contracted by humans, the mortality rate was eighty percent after the infection took hold. Of course, the limitations of medieval medicine meant that no one would understand how or why the disease was transmitted. It was said that a victim could first show symptoms in the morning and be dead by night, further adding to the terror of the disease. Indeed, the crude medical understanding of the day exacerbated the issue with practices like lancing boils and bloodletting, which helped spread the very disease they were meant to cure. Superstitious methods of disease control included bathing in rosewater or carrying herbs or flowers to ward

---

58　The first major plague pandemic occurred in 541 AD and is known as the Justinian Plague for the sixth century Byzantine Emperor. The Black Death, or Great Plague, began in China in 1334 and spread along the great trade routes leading west. By the 1350s the plague had petered out as a less dense population and culling of the rat population hampered its transference. In future centuries, it would pop up in cities like London or Venice. A modern breakout occurred in the 1860s, and there are still occasional flare ups, but antibiotics and pest control efforts kept death tolls from being quite as devastating.

off infectious miasmas. But nothing worked. No amount of prayer, herbs, or bleeding seemed to stop the dying, and no one could understand why.[59]

Those who survived the plagues would never comprehend what happened, yet they found themselves moving forward in a very different world. As the labor pool in Europe was devastated, it created an imbalance between the quantity of workers and the need for them. It was up to the market to figure it out. When the workforce shrunk, the average laborer smelled a rat (so to speak) and realized he could demand more for his drudgery. Prices rose, and laborers found themselves making more money. With demand and prices for goods dropping at the same time due to fewer consumers, some of those laborers could buy more and better goods, eventually creating something new: a skilled middle class.[60]

When supply and demand are in balance, resources are

---

59   The fleas that lived among those vermin found fewer and fewer hosts as the rodent population died off. After a few days of going hungry, the fleas would turn on humans, many of whom may have been in close contact with each other in restricted spaces like sailing ships or densely populated cities. Once a human was infected, it took three to five days to incubate, at which time they would fall ill.

60   At the time of the plagues, city states came and went, while rulers exercised relatively weak control over their subjects. This left markets startlingly free of interference for centuries until the creation of the modern bureaucratic state, a perfect, if somewhat macabre, laboratory to view economic forces at work. Another example advantage for the burgeoning middle class was a decline in the price of goods. Since dead men tell no tales, nor do they buy wine or fish, the market had to figure out how to deal with an oversupply of goods. Prices fell and life became more affordable, if not less terrifying.

allocated in the most efficient way. When they aren't, the system seeks equilibrium through pricing. That **Equilibrium Price** reflects the available supply balanced against the prevailing demand for any product, be it grain, oriental spices, or hours of toil. Fleas were but one invisible, yet transformational force unleashed throughout Europe at the dawn of the Renaissance, market forces were another. Thankfully, supply and demand are still doing their thing, seeking equilibrium, while the fleas and their plagues are mostly history.

——— THE PRICE IS RIGHT ———

Benjamin Shiller, Assistant Professor of Economics at Brandeis University, wants you to lose your cookies (if you don't want personalized pricing, that is). Online retailers may push what we thought were the limits of equilibrium pricing, creating individual demand charts, and potentially, individual pricing for each customer. Think of it as a dynamic, constantly shifting demand curve using your browsing history and demographic data.

In theory, your definition of a deal may differ significantly from someone else's. But pricing information and feedback have traditionally been too slow for consumers or retailers to use. And one price was chosen as an expedient to get the most people to buy. The Internet changed all that. Consumers now have instant feedback on prices from numerous retailers. To counter, sellers with high speed computer algorithms can create your own personal demand chart if they have enough data on your purchase history. Thus, the right price can change...

...by the day or even the hour depending on how and when you usually buy. Some consumers may end up "paying double the price others do for the exact same product." The only way around it might be to obscure prior purchases by deleting cookies and masking IP addresses.

Think it's farfetched? As of the writing of this book, Amazon has 46 listings for economists on its job site, and a website dedicated to recruiting them for "leveraging big data to drive business strategy." I'm pretty sure on my way to my MBA I learned that "business strategy" is corporate code for maximizing profits, and Shiller found that tailoring prices can add over 12% to the average bottom line. Equilibrium isn't synonymous with equality.

How You'll Be Tested...

Sometime in your investing career you will scratch your head, not because of fleas, but because you can't figure out why markets are going up. *Washington is a mess, the Fed is out to lunch, the economy is growing but not by much...so why are the stock and bond markets so good?* Sound familiar? Get on board and understand what really determines the direction of the markets and how they find their own equilibrium.

Supply: Changes in supply occur at a glacial pace and don't have nearly the pricing influence of overall demand. New issues of bonds and initial public offerings (IPOs) of stocks will increase supply. Retirement of debt, share buybacks, and delisting of companies will decrease it. Yes, supply shocks can happen, but they are almost as rare as modern outbreaks of the plague.[61]

Demand: Changes in demand happen constantly due to one of four main factors: changes in expected returns, changes in perceived risk, need for liquidity, and overall wealth. The first three tend to create short term swings in demand that can be countered in the long run by an increase in overall wealth. When there is more money to invest, it must go somewhere, usually no matter what else is happening.

Keep supply and demand in mind when everyone else is saying: *Oh rats, nothing is going right!* I swear, equilibrium is usually found without you even noticing.

EXTRA CREDIT

GO DIGGING: Join some more rats along with the world's most famous archaeologist, Indiana Jones, and high school teacher Jacob Clifford to learn more about the equilibrium pricing thanks to ACDCEcon. Combining economic education with famous movie quotes? Are you kidding me? This is so good I wish I was back in high school (or had at least thought of this first). Check out the video at https://www.youtube.com/watch?v=RP0j3Lnlazs, then go ahead and create some demand by subscribing to the YouTube feed or becoming a student at www.acdcecon.com.

SHUFFLE UP AND DEAL: We don't talk about them in this

---

61   One example would be 2001's .com bubble where multiple IPOs emerged every day leading to an eventual oversupply of available stocks, especially when cab drivers and baristas no longer offered free tips on tech stocks and demand dried up.

course due to time constraints, but Viking raiders from the eighth to the eleventh century set up trade routes to plunder much of Europe and trade their spoils. Play the card game Birka, a game of strategy where you play the role of a Norseman bartering pillaged loot. Cards with relative scarcity, i.e. lower supply, will have a higher price and you'll have to know when to hold 'em and fold 'em. Check out the instructions and download a scorecard here: http://www. econoclass.com/birka.html.

PLAY ONLINE: Card games too old school for you? The Supply and Demand Game challenges you to get a new kind of charcoal to catch fire. Lighter fluid will only take you so far. Determine supply and demand curves while trying to get to market at a price that will maximize profits. Try it at: http://www.shmoop.com/supply-demand/game.html.

CHECK OUT A SHOW: Go to StubHub.com and pick a show. Watch prices adjust in real time as the supply and demand curves move silently about the inter-webs.

LOSE SOME SLEEP: Read the novel *Inferno* (2013), by Dan Brown. Everything you expect is here in Harvard Symbologist Robert Langdon's fourth novel. Clunky prose and naïve characters cavorting about historical ruins that somehow leads to late nights of frantic page turning and missed slumber. Oh, and references to the plagues abound, especially as a modern one is released to supposedly help balance the global supply and demand equation.

WATCH A MOVIE, DRAW A GRAPH: Check out Tim Robbins in *The Hudsucker Proxy* (1994). Skip the standard evil corporation schlock and the love story with Jennifer Jason Leigh and get to the good part: economic theory in action. The introduction of the Hula Hoop is a colossal flop, its lack of demand driving the price down from $1.79 to zero. Literally, they are giving them away. Until, that is, all the cool kids start doing it and demand soars settling the price at $3.99 for a cheap plastic hoop. Grab a pencil and graph a rough demand curve based on the information from the movie.

DON'T JUST GRAPH, CHOREOGRAPH: If economics makes you want to get up and dance, you'll be happy to know you aren't alone. The folks at wetheeconomy.com, including filmmaker Morgan Spurlock, cut in to provide you with a look at supply and demand that ain't the same old song and dance at: https://wetheeconomy.com/films/supply-and-dance-man/.

Crowd Control
The Battle of Agincourt & Technology

1415 AD

K ing Henry V of England went to war to claim the French throne and was looking for an advantage against his foes. He found strength, and victory, in yew.

"Soldiers of England," bellowed the King. He paused. *What in bloody blue blazes am I going to say next*? he wondered. *Let's all go out and die like men? We're probably screwed but there is nowhere left to run? Bollocks, I probably need to do better than that.*

He cleared his royal throat and began again, "Heroes of England." Yes, that was a better beginning and soon he found himself on a roll. What he said is unknown, though it is passed down through history that he made the rounds that night to encourage his warriors. William Shakespeare would famously write an excellent oration for him a few centuries later, known as the Band of Brothers or St. Crispin's Day Speech. For the next day was the feast day of the

Saint, and the English force would offer battle near the castle of Agincourt.[62]

As a group, they needed a good talking to, for they were probably about to be slaughtered. An inspirational speech was certainly in order. Onto the stage stepped the Knute Rockne of his age: King Henry V.[63]

The French army had appeared on the road early that October morning, cutting off any escape to the Channel and now the English lay encamped and surrounded. A low fog hung over them and the heavy air was rank with the smell of unwashed bodies, recently tilled soil, and fear. A hard rain began to fall, but not enough to dampen the fires of the host which flickered amidst the fall foliage. There were a lot of fires. Outnumbered and outmaneuvered, the English soldiers, archers, and knights had no option but to fight against perhaps as many as five times their own force. Such a gloomy night called for the motivational oration of all time. But, the only known words that night came from one of Henry's squires. Asked by the King to estimate the enemy numbers: "Sire, there are enough to kill, enough to

---

62 Shakespeare's speech: "We few, we happy few, we band of brothers; For he to-day that sheds his blood with me Shall be my brother; be he ne'er so vile, his day shall gentle his condition: And gentlemen in England now a-bed Shall think themselves accursed they were not here, And hold their manhoods cheap whiles any speaks That fought with us upon Saint Crispin's day." There is little direct evidence as to where the battle actually took place, but most historians believe it was in a narrow, wooded patch of land between Tramecourt and the castle of Agincourt. The castle no longer stands and the town erected there took the name in the seventeenth century.

63 Knute Rockne was a college football coach who developed the forward pass and became known for inspirational gems like: "Show me a good and gracious loser and I'll show you a failure." He was not a kinder, gentler type of football coach.

capture, and enough to run away." A good line, too bad it didn't make it into Shakespeare's play.

France and England had been at odds off and on for decades and they would continue to fight on for years in what is known as the Hundred Years War from 1337 to 1453. Yes, it should be the One Hundred and Sixteen Year War, but they took some breaks, and we historians study the days of old to *avoid* math. Then, in the summer of 1415, England invaded France to enforce Henry V's ancient and somewhat tenuous claim to the French throne. In August, Henry's army besieged Harfleur with twelve thousand men and did not leave the town until October, significantly behind his original schedule. For weeks, they were dogged by a French army hesitant to attack but trying to cut off Henry from the English fortifications at Calais. Finally, the French barred the way north and brought battle in a constricted patch of open farmland between two wooded areas. [64]

On came the best of French Knighthood through the thick mud of recently tilled fields. More and more French troops arrived from the country side, eager to take part in the spoils until the crowding got so bad that knights could barely raise their arms or shields. Sometimes, you see, it just doesn't pay to follow the crowd, bad things can happen when you do. Coach Rockne would have known a stalled offense when he saw it, and there was no opportunity to punt. In fact, there was nowhere to go but forward and now it was the English who barred the way and waited.

---

[64] Only under the strict monarchies of the day could conflicts rage for so long without anyone using the term "quagmire" and taking to the streets in protest. This was a multigenerational conflict between the Plantagenet kings of England and the Valois of France.

Their archers, armed with longbows, had stationary targets exhausted by an armored trudge across a muddy field. Arrows were nocked, cords stretched tight, and a barrage of projectiles was let loose. It was almost unfair.

That English longbow was either a technical marvel or a terror weapon, depending on which side of the line of battle you stood. Developed by the Welsh in their wars *against* the English, it was noted as early as the twelfth century that a properly launched arrow could penetrate chain mail, flesh, and bone. Sometimes taller than the man who used it, the bow could be as much as six feet in length, five inches thick in the middle, and two inches at the tips. For such a large bow, it might take upwards of one hundred pounds of force to draw and release an arrow. A mighty effort indeed, but the results were worth it. At Agincourt thousands of those arrows slammed into the French, cutting through noble armor, muscle, and sinew. The French fell in droves and the English, properly inspired, won the day. Overwhelming force had produced underwhelming results in a stunning defeat for the French and the old ways of warfare. The English had perfected a killing machine.[65]

---

65 The outnumbered army of Henry V suffered fewer than one thousand casualties while the French forces lost perhaps as many as eight times that number. Many of the French dead were from the ranks of the senior nobility.

King Henry and his subjects were limited, as we all are, by our resources. There is only so much time in the day to achieve the competing goals of feeding your people and conquering your neighbors. More peasants growing food means fewer soldiers to plunder the French, and vice versa. This tradeoff creates a relationship known as the Production Possibilities Frontier (PPF), which economists use to graph the relationship between resource usage.

Research shows that technology moves the production possibility frontier outward creating a general *increase* in economic activity. *Technological Innovation, Resource Allocation and Growth* authored by professors from MIT, Stanford, and Northwestern analyzed eighty-five years of patents to determine that technology boosts overall wealth and total productivity. Over time, the aggregate economy expanded as technology progressed. Back in Henry's realm, researchers at the consulting firm Deloitte studied employment data from England and Wales going back to the mid 1800s. Their paper, *Technology & People: The Great Job Creating Machine* found that technology created more jobs than it destroyed and replaced boring, tedious, and dangerous work with jobs caring for others. No doubt both sides could have used a few more doctors and nurses at Agincourt.

Taking the *taxus baccata* or yew tree and turning it into a weapon was an ingenious manipulation of nature for waging war; innovation and **technology** at work. Though many worry that **technology** will lead to lost jobs and massive unemployment, historically that belief turns out to be bollocks. Taking the long view, changes in technology lead to more jobs, not fewer. I know, tell it to the out of work craftsmen making crossbows or the jobless French armorers. Progress is hard, and in this case bloody. But when economies seem to be grinding to a halt, innovation and **technology** keep us marching forward without getting stuck in the mud. It certainly helped the English in their wars against the French. Projectile-spewing yew trees altered the balance of power in Europe, and England replaced France as the continent's premier power.[66]

How You'll Be Tested...

Investors tend to be confused about technology and someday you too may be in need of a pep talk. Even great investors like Warren Buffett have shunned investment in tech, finding its twist and turns illogical—valuations can be inflated, prospective growth trajectories baffling. Alternatively, some of the worst investors the world has ever seen, piled into anything ending in .com and got rich before they too were wiped out in droves around the dawn of the

66   The effects of **technology** often go well beyond the obvious. With common bowmen slaying knights in droves at Agincourt, it could well be said that chivalry, and any perceived superiority of the ruling class, was dying. And if chivalry were dead, that weakened the base of power from which all absolute monarchies sprung. Oddly, commoners with longbows may have won battles for their kings, but at the same time they were sowing the seeds of a future demand for democratic reform. Within generations, England, with a constitutional monarchy and burgeoning bureaucratic class, would be on its way to becoming what historians call the first "modern" nation thanks to the innovative use of an ordinary tree.

twenty-first century. Perhaps I can suggest a middle course?

First, note that those who continue to decry the effects of technology, oddly enough, do so using technology. Opinions abound regarding the rise of the robots who will forever put us all out of work and leave us poor. Such opinions are broadcast far and wide via television, the Internet and social media, none of which existed a hundred years ago when we first started to fear the effects of technology. If you find yourself in a funk about the progress of humanity, just think about how many smart people are out there looking to do something innovative with all those proverbial yew trees. Then consider how much the production possibility frontier is being expanded by those folks. That, my band of brother and sisters, is inspirational stuff and worth investing in. Of course, proceed with caution. Be sure to diversify. Winners and losers come and go constantly, and you don't want to overinvest in yew trees when gun powder is about to be invented. There is no talking your way out of that kind of mistake.

EXTRA CREDIT

GET SMART: Want to brag about what you learned at MIT, even though you've never been to Massachusetts and have less tech know-how than your average kid in grade school? Since 2001 they've released their list of the year's top ten technical innovations; think of David Letterman's top ten only geekier. See how life changed in the past decade and a half by perusing previous years of the MIT Technology Review and look for stuff that became mainstream while we weren't paying attention. The Review has featured many advances we now take for granted like cloud computing, biometrics, and nano-medicine. See the lists here: https://www.technologyreview.com/lists/technologies/2016/.

GO TIME TRAVELING: Explainthatstuff.com invites you to look back on the last billion years or so of technological progress and consider the cascade effect of technology, where one advance leads to the next and so on. View the timeline here: http://www.explainthatstuff.com/timeline.html.

LISTEN WHEN THESE PEOPLE TALK: Flying robots, driverless cars, and headsets that read brainwaves may sound like science fiction, but they are here today. Take a break from *The Walking Dead* for a night and view a series of fourteen TED talks on current tech breakthroughs at https://www.ted.com/playlists/2/tech_breakthrough.

BECOME A TREKKIE: There were some pretty far out ideas introduced when *Star Trek* made its television debut in 1966. Since then electric weapons called a Taser instead of a phaser have become common place, we call portable communicators cell phones, and video conferencing has become passé. The Heroes and Icons Television Network airs the original uncut series and CBS launched a reboot in 2017. With the TV and enduring movie franchise to boot, Trekkie tech continues to live long and prosper. Imagine what the transporter will do for your commute time someday.

SAY GOODBYE: The good old days fly by in Amit Ramesh's video ode to the disappearance of rotary telephones, typewriters, and road atlases. Watch cell phones and computers consolidate and dominate. Then think about what might be next. Available at: https://www.youtube.com/watch?v=NoX6mOg2EZQ.

BUY THE BOOK: Merely reading it isn't enough; you need to own a copy of *Economics in One Lesson*, by Henry Hazlitt (1946). How about this for a strong opening: "Economics is haunted by more fallacies than any other study known to man." Yep, my kind of guy. For now, focus on *Chapter 7: The Curse of Machinery*. We'll return again to the rest of the book, but his discourse on technology and how it creates jobs rather than destroying them is one to have handy when watching the nightly news.

King Me

The War of the Roses & Cost Benefit Analysis

1485 AD

During the English War of the Roses, Richard III was rash and impulsive. Henry Tudor was cold and calculating. Richard ruled for two years and died without an heir. Tudor established a dynasty. Coincidence?

"Do you smell that?" asked the King. He inhaled deeply, slapped his chest and let out a satisfied sigh.

"Begging your Highnesses pardon, but if you cut off my nose and buried it in my sweet love's pillow I'd not escape this stink." The younger man grimaced and put his face closer to the sweating horse next to him for relief. There was no breeze here and the air hung heavily about the hillside and over the marshy bog below.

"It smells like victory!" Richard, Duke of York, brother to a king, Lord Protector of the Realm and lately King of England himself was in high spirits. His squire was not.

"It doesn't smell like victory. It smells like the inside of this horse's…ah, there they are Sire." The rebel army was gathering below in the sucking muck of the reedy swamp. Here at the Battle of Bosworth Field, the War of the Roses was hitting full bloom. But surrounded by thousands of warriors in mail and armor sweating in the August sun, perhaps the last things on Richard's mind, or his squire's nose, was the rose.[67]

"Launch the attack. Signal Stanley that he is out of position," Richard purred with easy authority.

"Your Grace, Stanley won't respond. I'm not sure what he is doing."

"No matter, there is Henry!" he bellowed. "I'll be damned if some Welsh puppy who claims royal blood only through his mother will take this crown. Charge!" Richard was a lot of things, but faint of heart was not one of them.[68]

He came in a thunderous assault as long bows twanged, and cannons rumbled. The air was thick with arrows thudding home into armor, leather, and exposed flesh. The ground became slick with blood. A medieval historian who compared

---

67 Henry Bolingbroke, of the house of Lancaster, launched the War of the Roses in 1399 when he usurped his lawful Yorkist king on the way to becoming Henry IV. This split the royal Plantagenet family into warring factions, Lancastrian and York. The disagreement remained relatively minor until the First Battle of St. Albans in 1455 where the Lancastrian Henry VI was captured by Richard of York. Henry VI was the son of the fiery Henry V from our last lesson, but lacked any of the inspirational powers of his father. Richard never made himself king, but he did arrange for his son Edward to inherit the throne. On Edward's death, his son briefly became king, but parliament ruled that his offspring were illegitimate. This made Edward's brother, also named Richard, King Richard III.
68 Nor was he fond of half measures. To seize the crown in 1483 he had either killed his own nephews or hidden their death because his subjects would *assume* he had murdered them.

Richard to the Antichrist nevertheless admitted that, "though small in body and feeble of limb, he bore himself like a gallant knight and acted with distinction as his own champion until his last breath." They were the last nice things anyone would say about poor Richard for centuries. [69]

At the bottom of the hill looking up at Richard's forces, Henry Tudor wondered if it might be treachery he smelled rather than victory or roses.

"You *are* sure about this?" he asked his counselor, the Earl of Oxford.

"Patience, your Grace, let them come meet their lawful king at the end of a lance." Oxford began to move forward to meet the charge forming above and Henry drifted to the rear. Luckily, Henry was plenty patient and recognized his shortcomings as a military leader. Sailing from France and then marching through Wales he'd been told that the crown was his, only to find himself in the face of an overwhelming force. Footsore and outnumbered, neither attacking nor marching away seemed particularly attractive. And so, they had waited. Sometimes not deciding is a decision itself. Now, he looked on pensively as the King's forces rolled downhill like an avalanche. Henry continued to drift backward, staying out of the fray while Richard, who had indeed spotted him in the melee, rode hard and sought a quick end to this rebellion.

As the two men neared hailing distance, the sound of the battlefield changed. Like a gate slamming shut, Stanley's men had rammed into the flank of Richard's forces, changing sides and altering the course of the battle. Richard's charge was

---

69 Richard was quoted as saying he was determined to "die as a king or win." Well, he sort of got his wish.

halted and soon he was surrounded. A halberd swung into his head and a sword punctured his neck. He fell and died, his lifeless body stripped naked, trussed like a hog and paraded about Leicester later that day as a spoil of war. The ignominy didn't stop there but the War of the Roses did. King Henry VII was crowned, and the reign of the Tudors had begun.[70]

While not a warlord, Henry was an expert decision maker as opposed to the impetuous Richard, weighing information and advice and then carefully implementing his strategy. It was a successful approach Henry would employ time and again as he took and solidified his somewhat circuitous claim to the throne. By choosing a path that avoided further war, promoting trade, and establishing an administration to deal with taxes, Henry nearly tripled the royal income in his lifetime. By the time he died, his succession was secured, and his wisdom and his skill at making good decisions were respected throughout Europe. Of course, his successor proved that such discretion is learned and not inherited, nearly ruining it all with a relentless quest for his own male heir which wrecked much of what his father built. But that is another story.[71]

---

70 The Tudors were master propagandists and took to recasting Richard to accentuate their own positives. Art historians have found that portraits of Richard were altered to take a slight and un-athletic man and create or accentuate physical deformities. Writers, including a certain bard from Stratford-upon-Avon who wrote while Henry's granddaughter sat the throne, classified him as a devil, a hunchback and a madman.

71 Henry VIII proved to be more like Richard than his father when it came to Cost-benefit Analysis. Henry radically changed the English monarchy by breaking with the Pope, married six times trying for an heir, and constantly teetered on the edge of financial ruin.

The art of decision making was a key to the success of men like Henry, but it is also quite useful to common subjects like us in the twenty-first century. Economists call this process of weighing actions and determining whether the advantages outweigh the drawbacks **Cost-Benefit Analysis (CBA)**. This four-step process includes: brainstorming costs and benefits, assigning values and financial estimates to costs, assigning similar values to benefits, and finally comparing the two to arrive at a decision.

— TO RULE & OVERRULE —

It isn't just English government that needs Cost Benefit Analysis, today their former American Colonies need a dose too. Cass Sunstein, founder and director of the Program on Behavioral Economics and Public Policy at Harvard Law School wrote the paper: *Cost Benefit Analysis and Arbitrariness Review*. In it, he notes that when federal agencies don't conduct or document a cost benefit analysis, they run the risk of judicial reviewers overturning their decisions. Shockingly, good government requires good decision making. "Cost benefit analysis is the best available method for testing whether regulations increase social welfare." Finally, an economic theory so simple even lawyers understand it.

Here are what Henry's CBA notes might have looked like after he won the Battle of Bosworth:

Action	Cost	Benefit	Decision
Marry Richard's niece, Elizabeth of York	Say goodbye to the carefree bachelor days when larger dowries might come along later Endure centuries of raised eyebrows for marrying your (3rd) cousin Cost: $	Elizabeth was a renowned beauty Unite York & Lancaster clans Start work on producing an heir Benefit: $$	Decisively end the decades long War of the Roses and score the most eligible bachelorette in England. Bonus: fall in love and have a happy marriage and seven children.
Court peace with France	A certain amount of English pride Risk of showing weakness Cost: $	Favorable trade deal Peace and prosperity. Taxes saved not outfitting military expeditions Benefit: $$$$	Raise the white flag and enjoy all that cheese and wine coming across the Channel.
Marry off daughter to James IV of Scotland	Create lifetime of "daddy issues" and awkward family reunions Cost: $	Peaceful northern border. More taxes not going to defense Benefit: $$$	Cue "Here Comes the Bride" on the bagpipes.

Henry balanced things like his daughter's happiness, apparently not worth much to him, against the cost savings of a peaceful ninety-six-mile border, worth a great deal. While he wouldn't win any father of the year awards, in sixteenth century terms, he clearly used cost-benefit analysis to further his goals and those of his kingdom.

How You'll Be Tested...

Some investors focus a lot on benefits, like performance, ignoring the costs. Others are adept at fee avoidance and don't gauge the advantages and disadvantages of their strategy. Before you go charging headlong into an investment plan, consider a full cost-benefit analysis. Better, more informed decision making can help you grow your own treasury and pass something on to your own heirs.

Costs: Everything must have a dollar value assigned when doing a CBA, even if it is approximate. Consider the costs for all phases of your investment time horizon. Add them up and look for anything hidden, like opportunity cost.

Benefits: CBA is not merely cost analysis. You must also tally up the value you get from an investment strategy. Thus, the "best" option may be the most inexpensive, or cheapest, but not always.

Weighing up the total economic impacts of various decisions is a cold, calculated way to live and most of us aren't as decisive, or ruthless as Henry. But that doesn't mean we shouldn't use the tools when appropriate. Tallying the potential costs and benefits of your financial decisions is a good way to discover hidden expenses, ulterior motivations, and emotionally based decisions. Call it what you will—CBA, shopping around, or good planning—a rose is a rose, and by any other name it would smell like victory.

EXTRA CREDIT

GET THE APPS: Find out more about Richard with the help of two apps. First, try Facebook. The Society of Richard III is an international fan club still trying to set the record straight about their misunderstood monarch. Check out their group page for a running recap of the English Monarchy with discussions about Tudor influence on the historical record. Or download the Smithsonian Channel app and look for Season One, Episode Four: *Richard III Revealed*. The video details the successful search for the King's remains, found in 2012 under a parking lot in Leicester.

GET TUDORED: If you want to see how it all came close to tumbling down for Henry's successor, check out the Showtime series *The Tudors* (2007–2010). In four seasons, you get all of Henry VIII's six marriages and thirty years of controversy and political intrigue. In the end, Henry gets his heir, Edward VI, but is haunted by his wives both living and dead. Add it all up and answer the question that likely died on his lips: was this really worth it?

WATCH A DIFFERENT WAR: Tune in for *The War of the Roses* (1989) directed by Danny DeVito and starring Kathleen Turner and Michael Douglas. Turner, as Mrs. Rose, conducts a cost-benefit analysis of her life before and after her husband is out of the picture and opts for the latter. Mayhem ensues as CBA is ditched for pure old-fashioned spite.

ENJOY THE WINTER: "Winter is coming" is the refrain of George RR Martin's as yet unfinished series of novels, *A Game of Thrones*. The author uses many historical events as muse while writing the fantasy series, but the War of the Roses was his primary source. Lancasters become Lannisters and Yorks become Starks as a brutal intergenerational battle is waged for ultimate power. TedEd.com has the full comparison at: http://ed.ted.com/lessons/the-wars-that-inspired-game-of-thrones-alex-gendler. You may have heard that there is a television version of Martin's work, but it isn't recommended for this course as historical nuance and examples of decision making are harder to uncover when camouflaged by full frontal nudity.

The Italian Job
Michelangelo & Opportunity Cost

1497 AD

For an accomplished sculptor, putting down the chisel and picking up the paint brush was an offer Michelangelo couldn't refuse, and his subsequent painting of the Sistine Chapel is considered one of the great masterpieces of all time. But even the great works come with a cost.

Standing in the cavernous silence of Basilica Sancti Petri, he couldn't help but feel small. Yes, the central nave and two surrounding aisles on each side were huge, capable of holding three or four thousand worshipers. And the marbled columns reaching toward the gabled roof towered one hundred feet above, reinforcing the immensity of the building. But, more than the magnitude of the structure, it was the ghosts of Christendom that made him feel minute. This was, after all, the original site of St. Peter's grave, and the thought made him hold his breath. Well, that and the musty smell of ancient parchment, and the early Christian crypts.

Finally venturing outside, his footsteps echoed off the walls and the alter. He emerged briefly, sunlight streaming into the courtyard. As he entered the circular Chapel of St. Petronilla his breath caught again.

"There she is." He stepped back and beheld what he considered the most perfect Carrara marble he had ever seen, a soft ivory color with medium gray veins. He'd loved that slab of rock since he'd first beheld it. Now it was carved and he loved it even more, crafted into the seated figure of the Virgin Mother. It was a dream come true to have his sculpture here for people from all over the world to come and view.

"*Bene,*" the young artist whispered reverently. "*Molto bene.*"[72]

He had spent hours on her, carving the folded fabric that fell back from her young, sad face then draped around her in a flowing gown. Each fold and crease represented hours of work, and he remembered his eyes swollen and mouth full of choking marble dust, but it had been worth it. So very worth it. On her lap lay her son after the crucifixion. It was a stylized version of Madonna and Child vastly different from anything yet done. Then twenty-three-years-old, the artist thought it perfect and was grateful when the Roman Cardinal who had commissioned it agreed, setting a place for it here near old St. Peter's Cathedral.

"My word...this is exquisite." The artist's reverie was broken by a group of religious pilgrims from Lombardy

---

72   "Good" and "very good" in modern Italian. Today's language was adopted during unification in the 1870s and is a descendent of Tuscan Latin with a distinctly Florentine upper-class grammar. It was made popular by the works of poets like Dante Alighieri.

who had stopped to gawk. In his contemplation, he hadn't heard them approach.

"Hmmm.... indeed," mused the second. A smile broke out on the sculptor's face. *Should I tell them*, he wondered? *No, pride is a deadly sin.* But he reveled in their accolades, nonetheless.

"It must have been the work of one of the old masters," mused another of the pilgrims. The artist cocked an eyebrow, the smile faded. *Master, certainly*, he thought. *But not old. Not yet.*

"It must be our Gobbo from Milan." They nodded in agreement and shuffled off toward the courtyard beyond.[73]

The artist subdued a choking noise, stifling it into a cough. The young artisan assumed a face like stone, but inside he churned. *Gobbo? That hack?* Envy, was also a mortal sin. *Heavenly father, I'd like to beat some sense in to these fools.* Wrath, was yet another offence to heaven. *Damn me, the sins are piling up today like the folds on my statue.* He shrugged. He had the tools and the talent, and he could fix this. When the pilgrims were gone, and the chapel darkened with the fading of the sun, he barred the doors. With a chisel, he set to work again, sweat streaming and marble dust flying. Across the Virgin's gown, there now emerged an inscription, MICHAELANGELUS BONAROTUS FLORENTINUS FACIEBAT (Michelangelo Buonarroti, Florentine, made it).[74]

---

73   The sculptor Cristoforo Solari, was also known as il Gobbo, or "the hunchbacked."

74   Michelangelo never again "signed" one of his works, regretting his impulsiveness until he died at the age of 88. The *Pietà* was originally in the old St. Peter's Basilica, begun by the Emperor Constantine that stood in

As the son of a local government administrator, young Buonarroti had showed some promise in the early days of Renaissance Florence gaining the eye of the ruling Medici family. He was a special favorite of the art patron, head of the family, and shadow ruler of the Florentine republic, Lorenzo de' Medici. One wonders what Michelangelo's father, a mid-level government worker, thought of his son hobnobbing with the upper stratosphere of political power. He may not have had much time to consider it, since the Medici family was expelled from Florence in 1494. Taking his show on the road, his son's fame grew as he toured Italian cities and was commissioned for several high-profile works. Eventually, like modern artists such as Sting or Prince, he would become recognized by just one name: Michelangelo.[75]

Michelangelo eventually ended up in Rome at the behest

Rome from the fourth to the sixteenth centuries. Plans for its update were many but progressed little during the 1500s until January 1, 1547 when Pope Paul III named a new superintendent to oversee the completion of St. Peter's. His name was Michelangelo Buonarroti, by then well into his 70s. His *Pietà* eventually found a home in the new Basilica as well, though not until the eighteenth century when it was moved to the first chapel on the right after the entrance.

75 The Medici were often said to be the shadow rulers of the Florentine Republic. A family of merchant bankers, they consolidated power in the first half of the fifteenth century under Lorenzo's grandfather Cosimo. Their bank was the largest in Europe and their political power produced three Medici Popes, two Queens of France, and several Dukes of Florence. Lorenzo, through his own wealth and influence, was an enthusiastic supporter of artists like Michelangelo who lived with the Medici family for several years. Though he never commissioned works himself, Lorenzo aided many artists in finding benefactors, making him one of the most conspicuous supporters of the Renaissance. His son Piero would squander all this good will through political intrigue at a time when the Pope wasn't a relative. The family would be banished from Florence for nearly two decades.

Patrick Huey

of Pope Julius II to paint the famous ceiling frescoes in the Sistine Chapel. He was offered the commission in 1508 but tried to refuse it for various reasons. First, he felt he was more of a sculptor than a painter, as evidenced by his statues such as the aforementioned *Pietà* or his famous sculpture of the biblical hero *David*. Second, he felt swept up in the political whirlwind due to his association with the Medici. He feared the papacy or some other group was trying to embarrass and discredit him by setting him up for failure. But, there are certain Italian organizations, you just don't say "no" to.

PICTURE THIS

A picture may be worth a thousand words but snapping away while touring the Sistine Chapel or viewing Michelangelo's *David* is not without its consequences. Sure, they can add to your enjoyment and provide endless fodder for your Facebook account. But what are you giving up in achieving social media stardom?

In *Photographic Memory: The Effects of Volitional Photo-Taking on Memory for Visual and Auditory Aspects of an Experience*, researchers reveal that taking pictures solidifies visual memories of an event while degrading the non-visual. Shutterbugs may remember more of what was there to see, but their opportunity cost is remembering less about the sounds around them. Could future Italian tourists remember more about the sites but less about the taste of the Bistecca Fiorentina or the smell of the Chianti? The opportunity cost might be too high, and that tradeoff may not so be so *bene*.

So, Michelangelo put aside his major marble works and concentrated on the vault ceilings until 1512. He worked on specially made scaffolding to paint stories from Genesis, including the most famous fingertips in the world, the divine spark given to man in *The Creation of Adam*. He painted in vivid colors to make the scenes stand out from the floor below. The magnificence of the work induces a hushed reverence on those below, or it would if not for the jostling of large crowds speaking loud slow English to Papal security guards ruining the effect.

Twenty-five years after finishing the ceiling, Michelangelo would return to paint *The Last Judgment* over the altar, taking four years to finish the massive sixteen-hundred-square-foot fresco. Critics disliked the use of nude figures, stripped bare for their final judgment. Two decades later the Council of Trent would condemn such nudity in religious arts and the offending genitalia were painted over with draperies. But in the last judgment of the critics, Michelangelo's raw, naked talents were undisputable. And he was equally brilliant no matter the tools put in his hands.[76]

The artist's decision to put down the chisel and take up the brush is an example of the concept of **Opportunity Cost**. If Michelangelo had said no to the Sistine Chapel and focused on what he thought he knew best, it would have cost us one of the world's treasured works of art.

76   The fresco's figures were not restored to their original until 1980.

Likewise, painting the chapel may have deprived us of great sculptures that might have eclipsed his *Pietà* or done what centuries of public nudity haven't, put *David* to shame.

While we will never grasp what great virtuosity was on the road not taken, what we do know is the single great truth of economics: you have to give up something to get something. Economics is, after all, the study of finite resources and infinite desires. To make good decisions about those resources it is important to know the value of the next highest alternative, the **opportunity cost** given up. Understanding the tradeoff between two choices, and thriving after that choice, might have been Michelangelo's greatest masterpiece of all.

How You'll Be Tested...

Many investors say that "sell discipline," the decision to ditch a fund, stock, or bond, is confusing. Often, they sell when envious of some other financial instruments performance and wrathful that their own hasn't kept pace. You too might find yourself, especially after a period of underperformance, attempting to add to your portfolio by subtraction. Do your wallet a favor and analyze your opportunity cost before you sign your name on any trade orders.

If you sell: you lose out on the potential returns of that investment *going forward*. Yes, it may have been a stinker for a few months, but if its prospects are equal to its peers *in the future*, then there is no reason to dump it. That would merely add the cost of the trades without any change in your overall potential returns. Incurring costs without any upside? That just might be the eighth deadly sin.

If you hold: you are foregoing the opportunity to reinvest and earn a better return somewhere else if it is available, while also avoiding any real costs (i.e. trading). Sometimes holding on will limit both your opportunity cost and your real cost, which is ideal and why long-term investors tend to be the most successful.

So, if you have a very specific and compelling alternative, feel good about moving on from your current holding. But if not, it is okay to stay put, assuming you are well diversified. Yes, these decisions are more art than science and can make you feel small. But for an investor, that is an acceptable tradeoff for a portfolio that gets bigger.

EXTRA CREDIT

FEEL SOME PITY: *Pietà* means pity and is a general artistic term for the scene of the Virgin Mary supporting the body of Jesus after the crucifixion. The form first began in Germany and there are pietas by other artists and even several by Michelangelo. But there is only one *The Pietà*. Find out more here from the series titled Spencer's Painting of the Week: https://www.youtube.com/watch?v=JdXmygDQCNc and see the statue in its home at St. Peter's courtesy of a virtual tour: http://www.vatican.va/various/basiliche/san_pietro/vr_tour/Media/VR/St_Peter_Pieta/.

MAKE GUNS OR BUTTER: The classic example of tradeoffs used since the early twentieth century is the mythical country deciding on how many guns or how much butter to produce. Arm to the teeth? Or use your teeth to eat something slathered in soft, creamy butter? This clip might help you make an informed decision: https://www.youtube.com/watch?v=E3tkrkgLo5Q.

GO RETRO: MyAbandonware.com has the global game of guns and butter domination available for free download. The game is from 1990 and ran on an operating system called DOS. So, things have changed a bit in the last thirty-odd years. The technology has changed (see previous lesson) but your choices are still between cannons and dairy products. Download at: http://www.myabandonware.com/game/the-global-dilemma-guns-or-butter-wk.

GO THROUGH THE GALLERY: Check out the website http://www.wga.hu/frames-e.html?/bio/m/michelan/biograph.html for all things Michelangelo including a biography and links to all his works in one place. There is nothing like it for il Gobbo of Milan, so take that, pilgrim.

GO PUBLIC: Public Broadcasting delves into the lives of the most famous family in Tuscany in *Medici, Godfathers of the Renaissance*. Fortunes rise and fall, sometimes just as violently as in those other Godfather movies. Episode two features the relationship between Michelangelo and his benefactors, but check out the premier as well to revisit the building of the Dome in Florence, which the Medici also bankrolled. Originally aired in 2004, check the PBS website or your favorite streaming service for reruns.

LOSE YOUR MARBLES: Apparently marble quarries don't last forever. After centuries of harvesting marble from the tip of western Tuscany, demand for toilets and fixtures in China and Dubai may be outpacing supply. Read *Demolishing Michelangelo's Mountain* in BBC Magazine, it's online at: http://www.bbc.com/news/magazine-36865396.

Upward Facing Dogma
Copernicus & Inflation

1514 AD

Whether it was the coinage of the kingdom or the path of the planets, the Canon of Frauenberg was burning to be at the center of things. Though recognized as a genius, some of his ideas would take longer than others to catch on. He just had to be careful he didn't literally burn in the meantime.

The two ecclesiastical scholars looked at each other across the table warily. Outside, the street carts noisily rumbled past on their way to a sunny, bright market day. Inside the Cathedral in Frauenberg, it was silent, cool, and dark. The men sipped ale and ate hard cheese, enjoying a companionable silence punctuated by occasional drabs of conversation.

The Canon had made his case and sat placidly while his counterpart sipped and nibbled. Finally, the Polish Bishop wiped foam from his mouth with a flourish of his homespun sleeve. "Why not devalue the currency? It makes perfect sense to me!" He tapped the table with a good-natured fist to accentuate the point to his subordinate.

"Respectfully, Bishop, because it is too much money. If this ale cost a shilling today, how much would it cost if there is more money to buy it?"

"The same, why should it change?"

"Because money is a measurement of value. And this ale will be more valuable when more money tries to buy it, meaning the price will go up. You create more marks, skoters, and shillings to buy the same amount of goods and it can only serve to raise the price of everything! My studies demonstrate that an excessive amount of currency should be avoided."

The Bishop smiled and polished off his glass. "Well, I'm glad I got to that one before the price went up." He reached to rectify the emptiness of his glass.

The Canon shrugged and was about to wade back into the argument, but his elder merely held up a hand. "I'll take it under advisement Nic, but I don't think anyone is going to agree with you. Debasement means more coin for running the government, it shouldn't have any effect on prices! I like you and you have a tremendous mind. But I think you are wrong."

"Well, if you think I'm wrong about that wait until you hear my other idea. I think we've been mistaken about the sun revolving around the earth. I believe it is the other way around," announced the Prussian Canon.[77]

A silence ensued. Old boards groaned and somewhere

---

77   A Canon was one hierarchical step below a Bishop in the administrative structure of the church.

a shutter hinge squeaked. The men eyed each other across what seemed to be a widening distance. Then, the Bishop slapped the wooden table as if he intended to split it in half. He bellowed and snorted, then nearly giggled with joy. Tears streamed from his eyes. "Nic, that's funny. Really funny." His face sobered, the mirth draining like a tankard of good beer. "But don't let anyone else hear you joke about that stuff. I don't want to see you burned as a heretic."[78]

Nicolaus Copernicus, Canon of Frauenberg, was undaunted in both of his pursuits. His idea that the sun was the center of the solar system broke with the classical theories of Greek philosophers like Aristotle and Ptolemy. Yet in all the time since classical antiquity, no one could accurately say why some bodies seemed to move across our sky and then move backwards, or retrograde, before continuing their primary path.[79]

Copernicus's controversial concept made sense to those who could draw circles but contradicted clerical dogma in the circles of the church. He trod a delicate path, sharing his ideas with close friends and fellow astronomers in his

---

78   In reality, Copernicus seemed to be quite careful with whom he shared his ideas about the earth and sun. Though he likely developed the theory sometime after 1500 and put it in writing around 1514, it only circulated within a tight circle of astronomers. His great work, *On the Revolutions*, did make it to print, though barely in time for the leader of the Scientific Revolution to behold it on his deathbed in 1543. The delay may have been driven by fear of retribution from the Church, or by the continuing demands of his day job. While other believers such as Giordano Bruno were burned at the stake as heretics, none was targeted specifically for merely believing in the Copernican system.

79   Copernicus sought "...a more reasonable arrangement of circles, from which every apparent regularity would be derived while everything in itself would move uniformly, as is required by the rule of perfect motion."

lifetime to avoid awkward conversations.[80]

Meanwhile, responsible for the accounting, records, and administration of local currencies in an area of shifting national allegiances, he found that there was more than a single accepted legal tender. At the time, there were three of them circulating at different rates of exchange, and Copernicus took to the pen to sort it all out, writing an essay on coinage, the folly of devaluing currencies and poor monetary policy.[81]

Monetary policy is, simply put, the control of a realm's money supply through the issuance of currency or credit. It should not be confused with fiscal policy, which is the amount a government spends on goods and services through a budget, or lack thereof. Copernicus sought to study how the introduction of new money affects prices throughout the rest of the economy. "Money loses its value most of all through successive abundance" he wrote, which is an early way of recognizing that quantity will vary inversely with

---

80   Copernicus became famous throughout Europe for his works and his mathematical equations, but it would take years before anyone would widely accept that they weren't at the center of the universe. Some, in places like movie studios and the hallowed halls of Congress, still don't believe it to this day.

81   Nicolaus Copernicus had likely always felt like something of an outsider. Originally a Prussian from the city of Cracow, his family had moved to Torun on the Vistula River, which the Prussian Union ceded to the kingdom of Poland. Thus, he was a Prussian who became a Pole, a sort of foreigner even in his own home. As an adult, the theme continued as Copernicus rose in the church hierarchy while, to the chagrin of some, spending significant amounts of time on his scientific pursuits.

value, obeying the laws supply and demand. This quantity theory of money, of which Copernicus was an early adopter, theorized that increased demand for money would lead to **Inflation** as more coinage was now available and the quantity of goods hadn't changed. More money meaning higher prices? Some wondered if it wasn't Copernicus's wits that were in retrograde.

ONE FOR THE MONEY

Copernicus wrote *Monetae cudendae ratio* or *On the Coinage of Money* for Sigismund the Old, King of Poland in 1526. Even then, "old" folks wanted to know why their money wasn't worth what it used to be.

Copernicus found currency debasement to be right up there with dissension, amorality, and barren soil as ways to wreck a country or principality. And he theorized having less pure coinage damaged the worth of the better-quality coins.

Finally, he noted that increases in the money supply, through new coinage or debasement of the currency, would mean a lower value of money. In turn, this would mean consumers had to carry more currency to buy the same amount of goods, meaning more demand for money. Ale, beer, and wine all increase in price as the general level of prices rise. Today this is known as **inflation** to economists and a buzz kill to the rest of us.

And that hasn't changed much, even after many thousands of revolutions around the sun. While most agree that Nic was prescient about the solar system, not everyone is ready to believe him, or those who expanded on his work, that changes in monetary policy alone create **inflation**. Sometimes it takes a few decades of awkward conversations to change dogma, sometimes it takes a bit longer. [82]

How You'll Be Tested...

This is a lengthy test for most investors and you may not know what a tremendous mind you have, until your cost of living doubles. That won't be funny, and it will take about thirty years at present rates. But when it happens you will know just how much attention, if any, you paid to inflation when retirement and investment planning. For retirement, the ongoing level of inflation will tell you how much of a return you need in order increase your purchasing power or standard of living. Not enough growth increases the time you must work to replace your current income and makes sure that you won't live any better. Also, if you aren't careful you will wear away purchasing power, reducing the real value of a portfolio and leading to a shortfall in retirement years.

The rate of inflation is one of the biggest variables in your investment plans too. But the ultimate impact will depend heavily on what you own. Stocks are usually good

---

82   I can hear you out there already: *what about the lack of inflation after the financial crisis when the Federal Reserve printed money like they were making real life Monopoly games.* Indeed, many use the period after 2008 as an example of huge increases in the monetary supply having little effect on inflation. But when there is no *demand* for increased supplies of money, banks merely park it as excess reserves and the velocity with which money changes hands is not modified. Thus, inflation remains tame even when it looks like it shouldn't. You may want to accumulate an "excessive amount of currency" yourself in case inflation does see the light of day.

hedges against inflation with earnings and revenue increasing at roughly the same rate as inflation and equities rising along with general consumer goods. Fixed income or bond investors tend to be hardest hit by inflation as they are locked in to potentially long-term rates of interest that may not be higher than inflation throughout their life. The mixture of assets you choose will depend on a lot of things, but it should revolve primarily around planning for inflation.

EXTRA CREDIT

MAKE AN OBSERVATION: Apparently, demonstrating the correctness of heliocentric theory is as easy as taking measurements of the variable binary star RZ CAS, which is visible with a decent pair of binoculars. An amateur astronomer has done all the calculations at http://www.student.oulu.fi/~ktikkane/AST/helioc.html. Check his work or take a few hundred years of scientists' word for it.

DO MORE GAZING: Don't know your Ursa from your Big Dipper? Try Google Sky or The Night Sky™ app available on iTunes or Android. Avoid the lengthy late-night observations and keep your day job.

TAKE A LESSON FROM UNCLE MILT: A bunch of economists get together in the 1970s to talk about inflation and it looks and sounds like something out of Mad Men. Fashion miscues and bad jokes about wives spending habits abound (there were, apparently, fewer female economists than ad executives), but Milton Friedman's theory on the money supply mirrors that of Copernicus: "Inflation is always and everywhere a monetary phenomenon." Enjoy the madness here: https://www.youtube.com/watch?v=6LfUyML5QVY.

BECOME A DESPICABLE MINION: No, not a Federal Reserve Governor, Mr. Clifford is back with a look at monetary policy via the movie *Despicable Me* at https://www.youtube.com/watch?v=RaeIBeJT5hY.

PUT THE FED IN FOCUS: Get an introduction to modern monetary policy from the folks at the Federal Reserve. Learn about monetary policy and how Fed officials attempt to use or abuse it to achieve various economic outcomes. Read up and take the quizzes here: https://www.federalreserveeducation.org/about-the-fed/structure-and-functions/monetary-policy/.

GO TO IT: Got all that? Then give your money supply management skills a try and unleash your inner Yellen, Bernanke, or Greenspan: https://sffed-education.org/chairthefed/default.html. You'll note that events such tightening labor markets and tax refund checks have rather large effects on inflation. Again, not everyone believes Nic's (or Milton Friedman's) theory that inflation is a monetary phenomenon.

ENJOY A KIT KAT: Check out *Cabaret,* Liza Minnelli's 1972 musical turn as a young American performer at the Kit Kat club in pre-World War II Berlin. The film received rave reviews, won more Oscars than any film not to win best picture (thanks to The Godfather) and probably saved the career of director Bob Fosse. What does a film version of a Broadway musical have to do with monetary policy? The Weimar Republic, which was in its death throes during the setting of the film's plot, had the most famous bout of hyper-inflation in modern history. A decision to devalue the currency in the 1920s to pay off debts from World War I was catastrophic, leading to political and social disruption and the rise of the Nazis. Lest you think there are no real-world repercussions to the performance of monetary policy.

Brave New World
Thomas Morton & Trade

1624 AD

From the literary circles of London to the colonial frontier, Thomas Morton got around. His comings and goings demonstrate how crossing borders can help efficiently move resources, though never without controversy.

"I think I am quite soused," said the nobleman to the ceiling. Neither of his two table companions was terribly surprised, nor did they take much notice. The inn was loud, the din of patrons who'd been overserved on ale and cheap wine rising and falling with the tides of disparate conversations. They had heard a few taking to song or proclaiming their opinion of this or that with the certainty reserved for drunks and politicians. Smoke curled in the rafters from a roaring fire and there were pleasant smells of meat pies wafting in from the small kitchen.

Will, the young man with a high forehead and a trimmed pointed beard, acted as if he hadn't been interrupted: "And then my character says 'the first thing we do is kill all the lawyers'.

What do you think?"

It took Morton, a non-inheriting son of a noble family, a moment to focus, his wits dulled as they were by hours of excessive consumption. "Damn it Will, you know I am a lawyer! You do me wrong."[83]

"Yes, of course I know it. Why do you think I wrote thus?"

Morton arched an eyebrow at the playwright and drummed his fingers clumsily on the table. Then he let out something between a sigh and a chuckle. It was, he knew, a pretty good line. The tension of the table melted away, replaced with an easy familiarity.

"What's got you all bothered tonight Morton?" asked the second man, whose unkempt facial hair and reddish-brown curls were in stark contrast to Will's meticulous whiskers and bald pate. "Shouldn't you be out somewhere sitting astride a horse leaping hedges, with horns blaring, dogs howling, and in chase of a sporty but ultimately doomed fox?"

Morton yawned. "Boring," he said with his head hung low, his companions straining to hear his voice. "There you have the heart of it Ben, nothing is exactly wrong. There is nothing to do and I am bored. Bored of fox hunts, bored of literary conversation with the likes of you two, and bored of England."

"That is good news for the foxes," Ben jibed.

"And for us," countered Will.

---

83 Primogeniture, the feudal succession rights of the first born, meant younger sons were more or less on their own. Regardless, Morton received an Elizabethan education, went on to practice law and enjoyed an early life of leisure as befitted his class. A lover of literary culture in the London of the late 1590s, it is also easy to imagine him in late night conversation over too much claret with the likes of Ben Johnson and young William Shakespeare. Johnson, at least, was a friend. Whether he knew Shakespeare is pure conjecture, but really fun to imagine.

"I should very much like an adventure. And I think I will find it in the New World," sighed Morton.

"Wonderful!" cried Ben. "We shall trade you to the colonists…for what? What will we get in return?"

"I have it," announced Will after some thought. "We shall get a reprieve on claret prices once all of this demand dries up." He turned over Morton's empty glass for effect. Not for the last time, Morton wondered if he really ought to try and verbally spar with such men.

Morton eventually found his adventure, arriving in the New World in 1624 to match wits with the colonists already established around Plymouth. He was entranced by the natural beauty and wide-open spaces of the New World and grew to love the land and most of the people, including the Indian tribes whose ingenuity and toughness he respected. But Morton, an unapologetic Anglican Royalist, and the separatists at Plymouth Rock were bound to clash. Morton set up a profitable trade with native tribes, making the original settlement of Pilgrims nervous and angry. They felt it was their exclusive charter to treat with the locals and they were not happy to have the competition. So, clash they did.

During a spring celebration, Morton, the locals, and his employees celebrated by dancing around the Maypole, a Germanic tradition that included drinking ale and engaging in the "harmless mirth made by young men."[84]

To Plymouth, it was a pagan ritual and just the sort of thing they didn't want in their new utopia. Or, at least, it was a

---

84 Nathaniel Hawthorne's uses the plot in his story *The May-Pole of Merry Mount* to revisit his recurring theme of Puritans suppressing individuality à la Hester Prynne of *The Scarlet Letter*.

great excuse to head on up there and put a halt to the offensive dancing and trading. An armed troop of Pilgrims attacked the trading post at Merry Mount and arrested Morton, calling him the "Lord of Misrule." He was jailed for allegedly selling guns to the natives, and Morton the lawyer, trader, and adventurer became the first person ever deported from the colonies. Turned out and put aboard a ship headed back to England, you might say he was their first export. [85]

Back in London he set about clearing his name, which was no great feat given his background in the law and the flimsy charges against him. When thirsty he likely went back to his old haunts and found some of his old comrades.

"I'll be damned, but you were right." Morton likely would have said with a grin. "It would seem that one of the first things they did was get rid of the lawyers."

Little good it would do them, as the courts in England found the evidence against him feeble at best and dismissed the charges. Vindicated he returned to America and was again arrested and deported in 1630, whereupon he took up the pen to describe his treatment by the Pilgrims in his three-volume dissertation *New English Canaan*. In 1643, he returned for the last time and, after arrest for writing the aforementioned book, was again imprisoned. Eventually, he was allowed to settle in Maine where he fades from the historical record.

---

85   The expedition to capture him was led by military advisor Myles Standish who also led preemptive attacks on several local Native American tribes. His brutality was just the kind of thing the more liberally minded Morton would come to detest in his dealings with the Pilgrims of Plymouth Colony.

Morton's adventures are a reminder of how easy, frequent, and sometimes alarming it is for things and people to cross borders, an example of **Trade** and exchange on a global level. And this was centuries before the term "globalization" crept into the English language. The English traded something they had plenty of...young, bored, noble males. They received, in turn, a reprieve from explosive population growth. The Colonists gave up some land to attract another settler, presumably a man of letters who could be relied on to help expand the culture of the colonies. It was a win-win situation until personal feelings got in the way. Isn't it always?

It can all become rather complicated and divisive, and there are advantages and disadvantages to **trade.**

Advantage	Disadvantage
Specialization: Each country produces what it is good at and in turn we get all the best stuff.	Exhaustion of resources: Maximizing my production may prematurely use up the kind of stuff that isn't easy to replace.
Access to more products: Good ideas have huge market potential, meaning new stuff continually seeks to surprise and amaze.	Impediment to home industries: I can't make a living in a new business if prices are so low and quality is good. Give me a break.
Potential goodwill: Give me more good stuff at a lower price and we will be friends.	Economic dependence: I really like your goods and if I'm not careful you can use that against me.
Lower prices: Maximizing supply should lower overall prices, so we get more, newer, and cheaper stuff.	Potential bad will: Please stop flooding our markets with your cheap goods, I'm addicted, and I hate myself for it.

In the long run, most of us realize that the benefits of **trade** far outweigh the negatives. Though international commerce can be quite an adventure, it is an integral part of modern economies and the companies that navigate them. We all need friends in this world. They usually make us better, even if we don't always feel equal to their literary wit or productive capacity.[86]

How You'll Be Tested...

As you learned in History 101, investors have many biases, and you may reach for the claret when you realize you've fallen for another of them. Investors like to keep their friends close and exhibit regional biases and country biases when developing their portfolios. Regionally, they overweigh sectors that are large employers in the area because of familiarity. And, though the US is just above fifty percent of the global market capitalization, the average American's investment portfolio is as patriotic as hot dogs, apple pie, and reality television. They often justify their lack of international exposure via trade. It is estimated that slightly less than half of the sales earned by S&P 500 companies come from outside of the United States, the result of foreign exchange. So, many investors think they are just fine.[87]

---

86 Adam Smith would later note that **trade** was beneficial for both parties: "If a foreign country can supply us with a commodity cheaper than we ourselves can make it, better buy it of them with some part of the produce of our own industry, employed in a way in which we have some advantage."
87 Research by JPMorgan demonstrates if you live on the west coast, your investments have a higher proportion dedicated to technology because you have Silicon Valley in your back yard and either speak computer code or know someone who does. If you live in the south, closer to the oil patch, you are more likely to be overweight in energy because your brother-in-law works in the oil fields. Near the heartland, you'll favor industrials because grandpa built automobiles in Detroit. And if you are within a few area codes

It's oaky, no one will send you away for that, but this approach ignores a weakening trend in just how much those companies earn overseas, the percentage of which has consistently declined since 2006. It also overlooks huge segments of foreign markets, like small companies and the growing middle class in far off lands that uses local products. Time to take charge and invest directly. Doing so can reduce some risk from US markets, diversifying into foreign assets whose correlation to ours is moderately low. You miss that boat if you just buy American. Yes, this can be an adventure. Some foreign markets are volatile, especially when the effects of currency are factored in and correlations tend to be higher during sell offs. But whether you are young, noble and bored, or old, common, and a little afraid, an adventure away from home is just what you need.

EXTRA CREDIT

GO BACK A LONG TIME: Before Adam Smith and Thomas Morton there was Luke Skywalker in a galaxy far, far away. Yes, Mr. Clifford made his YouTube debut using Star Wars to demonstrate several concepts including scarcity, voluntary exchange, and the woeful state of the XP-38 Landspeeder market. Like the Star Wars movies themselves, the first really is the best. The force will be with you at https://www.youtube.com/watch?v=Np-dZSdzymk.

TRADE AWAY: Play the Trading Around the World game courtesy of the International Monetary Fund. Start with

of New York or Boston, you will have a higher exposure to financials because you know at least one person who used to peddle stocks by phone à la Charlie Sheen in the movie *Wall Street*.

money to buy goods and try to maximize your wealth buy buying and selling on an intercontinental scale. Beware of trade barriers, currency restrictions, and the inevitable disappointment of not getting what you want all the time. Consider that a life lesson on top of a history lesson. Corner the market at: https://www.imf.org/external/np/exr/center/students/trade/index.htm.

BE FAIR: "Fair trade" is a relatively recent designation that, has less to do with trade than it seems at first blush. Instead, the certification focuses on the ethical manners of production. Good or bad? Probably neither, but form your own opinions by reviewing what it means to be fair, at least according to the non-profit organization that approves the labels at: http://fairtradeusa.org/what-is-fair-trade/faq.

CELEBRATE SUCCESS: Did you know your tax dollars support something called the The International Trade Administration? Neither did I, but rest assured your tax dollars are hard at work promoting international exchange. According to its mission, the ITA works to foster economic growth through global trade. A division of the Department of Commerce, you can read more about their success stories here: http://trade.gov/success/.

Going Around in Ellipses

Johann Palitzsch, Edmond Halley[88] & The Business Cycle

1758 AD

F or centuries, fear and loathing reigned when a certain comet blazed its way through the Earth's sky. Then someone showed that it happens with regularity. Well, what comes around goes around, though if it takes long enough, we tend to forget that we've been there before.

"*Frohe Weihnachten* Johan!" The horse and sleigh went charging past, kicking up plumes of snow along the road between the two farmhouses. Children were laughing and the smells of burning wood, living evergreen trees, and frying meat mixed wonderfully in the early morning air. It was Christmas Day 1758.

"Ja, ja, Merry Christmas," came the distracted reply from

---

88   His first name is often spelled Edmund, though his will has it spelled Edmond. I choose to honor his last wishes. Also, the last name rhymes with valley.

the figure hunched over an eight-foot reflecting telescope. No amount of pleasant smells or holiday cheer was going to distract him this morning. The riders shrugged and smiled, used to the somewhat eccentric ways of their neighbor farmer and amateur astronomer.

Johan's breath came in foggy gasps against the cold air, and snow crunched under foot as he shifted positions to move the eye piece across a blessedly clear sky. And then his breath caught. The silence of the morning stretched on and on. He shivered against the cold, absently tugging a scarf around his exposed neck as he lost track of time. When he finally exhaled, his eye was firmly focused on a clump of terrestrial leftovers from the formation of the solar system. Out there on the final frontier of space, cosmic detritus was hurtling around the sun in irregular orbits, coming and going for millennia without any perceived regularity. Until that Christmas Day.

He stood up and wiped his eyes, barely suppressing a grin. "It is back," he whispered to the heavens. "This changes everything!"

Johann Georg Palitzsch, gentleman farmer and future science advisor to the royal German court had just viewed the comet foretold by Edmond Halley before his death. Comets are remnants of the cosmic dust bin; large dirty snowballs of ice chunks careening about space trailing rubble behind them in a luminous tail. From earth, they can be imperceptible to the naked eye or, when conditions are right, fill the sky like a falling star with a bad attitude. They have appeared in the written historical record since

Chinese astronomers first noted an appearance in 239 BC.[89]

But with their seemingly random comings, humans tended to see them as omens, both good and bad. The appearance in 1066 was thought to be a bad portent, and indeed it was for King Harold who was killed at the Battle of Hastings. And it is sometimes suggested that Genghis Kahn turned eastward into Europe following the comet's appearance in 1222. Regardless, Palitzsch's Christmas Day observation proved that Halley had been accurate about the periodic nature of comets and that his colleague, Isaac Newton, had correctly worked out the basic principles of gravity. Comets didn't fly haphazardly about the cosmos and appear at random intervals to signify anything, they traveled elliptical orbits due to the pull of gravity. Johann Palitzsch was ready to spike the eggnog and have a Merry Christmas indeed.[90]

Edmond Halley grew up a century before his German counterpart, the squeaky-clean son of a wealthy soap maker in Derbyshire England. Though the family lost much of its fortune in the great fire of 1666, they were still prosperous enough to afford good schooling for their promising child. While at St. Paul's School, he demonstrated a knack for physics, mathematics, and astronomy. A local globe maker noted that: "*if a star were displaced in the globe he would*

---

89 Other sources such as the Babylonians continued to mark their passing on tablets back when they were clay and touch screen meant something entirely different than it does today.

90 Newton's theory was supposedly sparked by the infamous falling apple striking him in the head. The story is apocryphal though apples falling in an orchard where he was taking his tea did lead him to wonder about the nature of gravity.

presently find it out." How literally true that would prove![91]

When his comet returned to earth after seventy-five trips around the sun, Halley had been dead for fifteen years. But there was no doubt now that the orb seen by the Chinese and mentioned by other sources such as the Babylonians, Normans, and the Italian painter Giotto was the very same hunk of stellar debris he and Johann Palitzsch gazed upon.[92]

So, what were once thought to be portents of good luck or imminent doom became normal and expected occurrences as we learned that we don't need to irrationally fear explainable natural phenomenon. Unfortunately, we fail to remember similar lessons in the "dismal science" of

91   Halley eventually fell into the orbit of the English Royal Astronomer John Flamsteed, who supported his studies and research. Halley's main preoccupation, along with contemporaries such as Isaac Newton, was explaining the motion of planets. Halley and Newton admired each other's work and took care of each other through patronage and political appointments, which managed to alienate Flamsteed as well as his widow. Upon Flamsteed's death and Halley's elevation to Royal Astronomer in 1720, Mrs. Flamsteed cleaned out the Royal Observatory leaving it bare, claiming the instruments were personal and not public property so Halley couldn't benefit from them. The government agreed and Halley had to request funding to re-equip it at a cost of five hundred pounds. The scientist thus also demonstrated that hell truly did not know any fury quite like a woman, or her deceased husband, scorned. Despite missing a few tools from the proverbial tool box, Halley persevered in his study of the heavens.

92   Giotto's fresco paintings in the Arena Chapel in Padua include the Adoration of the Magi featuring the Star of Bethlehem in the form of a conspicuous comet and tail. Painted around 1304, the comet had appeared just three years earlier and apparently made quite an impression on the painter. Having come in to view in 12 BC and 66 AD the comet would not have appeared around the time of Jesus's birth.

economics. Instead, through the magic of modern media, we turn every production statistic, employment figure, and Federal Reserve meeting into a signal of impending global calamity. Might we be calmed by the thought that, economies, like comets are cyclical?

DON'T CALL IT A COMEBACK

In the dull days of 2006, researchers noted in *Business Cycle and Stock Market Volatility: A Particle Filter Approach* what they thought was a "new normal" when it came to the business cycle and stock market volatility.

The authors discovered "a significant decrease of broad macroeconomic risk, as represented by an exogenous decline in business cycle volatility" and found that "the switch to lower variability has occurred in both business cycle and stock market variables along similar patterns."

The next year, the US stock market peaked before losing over half of its value and the ensuing recession was deeper than anything since the Great Depression. Turns out the business cycle hadn't gone anywhere, and volatility was just a few bad mortgages away.

There are four defined periods of the **Business Cycle:** expansion, boom or peak, contraction, and recession. Factors such as variations in spending and technological innovation keep economic growth cruising along or begin dragging it out of orbit, though it is nearly impossible to predict exactly when or why. Unfortunately, business cycles don't appear with the certainty of comets. Since 1900, we have endured twenty-two comings and goings of the business cycle, ten since 1950, and two just since the year 2000, each lasting a different amount of time and ending for different reasons. Yet news outlets and commentators will be astounded when the cycle runs its course once again, including a dreaded recession. But with time, shouldn't expected downturns become less of a spectacle since we know they are a normal phenomenon? Well, that hasn't happened yet, and we can trace major slumps further back than Halley's lifetime. Details of economic downturns and can be traced as far back as the Dutch Tulip Bulb Mania of 1636.

Four Phases of the Business Cycle			
Contraction	Recession	Expansion	Peak/Boom
Growth decelerates	Economic activity falls	Activity rebounds	Growth accelerates
Credit tightens	Corporate earnings drop	Credit grows	Credit growth strengthens
Earnings under pressure	Inventories grow, sales fall	Profits grow rapidly	Inventories and sales growing
Inventories grow but sales growth falters	Credit dries up	Inventories are low, and sales are improving	Profit growth peaks
Monetary policy is contractionary	Monetary policy eases	Monetary policy stimulates	Monetary policy is neutral

How You'll Be Tested...

Investors frequently fret over the business cycle and eventually you might find yourself scrutinizing retail sales data or dissecting employment figures looking for something out there to show you the way. But this test is one of the easier assignments yet presented, just stop doing that. Don't get distracted. It comes. It goes. It isn't a portent of doom, but a natural part of a growing economy. Plan for it, don't panic because of it.

Sitting still and observing from a distance isn't easy. And taking such a logical (and admittedly laissez faire) approach to the future of the economy probably won't happen for most investors, whose emotions tend to rule them. But if you can force your own stars to align that way, it just might change everything.

EXTRA CREDIT

GET A DATE: Check out a timeline of U.S. business cycle fluctuations from the 1850s to present provided by the National Bureau of Economic Research: http://www.nber.org/cycles.html. Of course, the methodology of timing a recession is always controversial. President Harry Truman offered the non-mathematical method: "It's a recession when your neighbor loses his job; it's a depression when you lose yours." A candidate for President in 1980, Ronald Regan expanded the definition to include "recovery is when Jimmy Carter loses his." Stick with the hard data.

GIVE YOURSELF A B: *Lifeforce* (1985) screams B movie. Come to think of it, there are a lot of screams as a race of vampires from space arrive in the tail of Halley's Comet. Or you can try *Night of the Comet* (1984) to see what two Valley Girls do after one wipes out most of life on earth. Of course, if you are looking for disaster movies about objects from space you can try more recent fare like 1998's dueling disaster flicks, *Deep Impact* or *Armageddon*. Given these choices, you may want to curl up with a good book. Read on!

BECOME MANIC, THEN PANIC: Another book where merely reading it isn't enough, you must own Charles Kindelberger and Robert Aliber's study of *Manias, Panics and Crashes* (2005). Trace the history of economic growth, irrational exuberance and credit expansion leading to inevitable contraction and sometimes outright anxiety and alarm. This book neatly summarizes the business cycle and all the fun and horror it can produce when accompanied by untimely monetary policy.

RAISE A TOAST: Overcome the gravitational pull keeping your beer on the table and raise a glass at Sir Edmond Halley's Restaurant and Freehouse in Charlotte, North Carolina. There you can belt out a drinking song to Sir Ed first penned by the Members of the Royal Astronomical Society in 1910:

> *Of all the comets in the sky,*
> *There's none like Comet Halley.*
> *We see it with the naked eye*
> *And periodically*
> *The first to see it was not he,*
> *But still we call it Halley.*
> *The notion that it would return*
> *Was his originally.*

Can't make it to Charlotte? Belt it out at your own favorite watering hole where it will make no sense whatsoever. Bonus points for posting the evidence on YouTube.

DROP IT LIKE ITS HOT: Using a paper cup, poke a hole in the bottom and fill it with water. When you release your finger, the water streams out of the hole. Now, with a refilled glass, simultaneously release your finger and drop the cup. Water no longer sprays out the hole as the cup and water fall at the same speed toward the floor. Nice work Newton, gravity at work. And no produce was harmed during this experiment.

Fowl Play

W.B. Tegetmeier, Charles Darwin & Specialization

1859 AD

W hen two scientists swapped stories about what they excelled at, one gave the other the bird. Or, more precisely, the birds, which helped explain how to use distinction to avoid extinction. It turns out you can't be equally good at everything, and both history and science back that up.

———————

The throng of scientific minds milled closely together talking over the din of silverware put to dishes of small hors d'oeuvres. Coffee and wine made the rounds and the air was sweet with the smell of small cakes and confections.

"My name is Charles. I study barnacles," he said over the background noise of conversation. His drink sloshed in his glass, his white knuckles contrasting with the red wine. Perhaps I should go back to sea and get away from human socializing and Scientific Society meetings?

The older man gave a polite nod. "Ah, do you indeed?" The ensuing silence grew awkward, then uncomfortable. Finally, the elder raised white eyebrows as if recognizing a friend across the room. "Will you excuse me?" And he was gone.

"Oh, don't concern yourself with him," said a man nearby who had clearly overheard. "He only has a head for studying beetles. Thinks anything else is a waste of time. If it weren't for the wine, I shouldn't think he'd bother to attend these Society meetings at all." There was a smile there and Charles relaxed his grip. The eavesdropper's avuncular face was framed on top by a bald head and below by an expansive beard.

"Tell me," said the newcomer leaning in, "out of all the creatures in our ever-expanding world, what brought you to study barnacles?" It was a genial question, collegial and straightforward. Charles found himself smiling.

"I spent five years aboard a ship of scientific discovery. With that much time on the water, what else could one do but become acquainted with barnacles? Besides, the variation of the species is really quite amazing." He stopped himself short of a longwinded exposition on the wonders of *Thecostraca Cirripedia*. Charles had sailed in 1831, spending years at sea on the Beagle and continuing his observations on land. But now he feared boring this new acquaintance, so he asked: "What do you study?"

"Ah," the fellow sighed. "I have settled down like a lonely man in his dotage to feed the pigeons, and occasionally to kill them in the name of science." He laughed easily. "My name is Tegetmeir, William Tegetmeier. Hard to say, but easy to remember. And my friends call me W.B." They each extended a hand.[93]

"I'm Charles Darwin. Tell me more about your pigeons." Upon such introductions, the world turns. For Darwin didn't just study barnacles while sailing about the globe. While on land in Brazil, Patagonia, and the Galapagos Islands he collected numerous specimens, including those of small birds. Like barnacles, the birds demonstrated immense diversity though they seemed to be related. He theorized that his finches particularly had most likely come from a single ancestor yet evolved differently into identifiably distinct species. To prove it, he needed to find other such adaptations at work. On return to England after the voyage of the Beagle, Darwin had limited means but a voracious appetite for knowledge and bird skeletons. He wrote often to his new friend for help, and W.B. obliged him, sharing his library of remains, living birds, and decades of knowledge.

Pigeons, his new friend Tegetmeier had learned, were selectively bred for various traits including beak size and length of legs. If humans could force such adaptations, known as artificial selection, what would prevent nature

---

93   Born in 1816 to an English surgeon who emigrated from America, William (W.B.) Tegetmeier apprenticed for his father before attending University College in London to train as a physician. Like many young men who are forced to follow their father's calling, he thought it was for the birds. Though "for the birds" in Tegetmeir's mind wasn't a put down or a dismissal, it was a plan for his life's work. He studied and wrote extensively on domestic fowl, becoming secretary of the London Philoperisteron Society by the time he was forty. His published works included *A Manual on Domestic Economy* and *Pigeons: Their Structure, Varieties, Habits, and Management.* For the birds, indeed.

from carrying out the same process? This would be selection by the environment instead of man, or natural selection. For Charles Darwin it was the last remaining research project before publishing his theory of evolution at the end of 1859. Though he is more often associated with the Galapagos finch, it was the lowly pigeon whose selective breeding helped him solidify his thesis for *On the Origin of Species*.[94]

Through the finches, pigeons, and barnacles, Darwin saw not every animal was good at the same things and that nature was better and more beautiful for all the constant variations. It wasn't a big leap to see that human endeavors were organizing similarly. After all, The Industrial Revolution (1760–1840) had demonstrated the efficiency and effectiveness of splitting up work responsibilities. There was no single "best job" that everyone could do productively, just as there was no single series of traits that was best for a species. Efficiency increased as workers maximized unique talents at specific and varying jobs.[95]

---

94   Darwin's theory was that nature forced species into changes like those in selective breeding or artificial selection in a process known as "adaptive radiation." There was no single best type of animal for a particular place, or else they would all evolve to the same end. Slight variations in their surroundings forced them to evolve differently. The eventual differences showed that an original species found individual niches they could exploit, becoming the best new organism for a certain task or environmental factor. From one species, several variations radiated outward depending on the different climates, predators, or food sources nearby. The variations were heritable, and the most useful ones were preserved in future generations. Evolutionary victory went to those who efficiently specialized and adapted to changing circumstances.

95   Economist Adam Smith wrote extensively on the effects of division of labor and specialization in *The Wealth of Nations*. He used pins as an example. Separately workers could make about one pin per day and with ten workers there would be ten pins produced. But if each of the eighteen sepa-

From a few talents such as hunting and making fire, we have evolved to have many, whose combinations can make economic magic when creating things like cars or smart phones. Humans evolved to do different jobs and their combined talents increased production through what is known as **Specialization** or division of labor. Not everyone saw this as progress. Carl Marx warned: "The more the division of labor and the application of machinery extend, the more does competition

---

rate steps to make the pin were separated and assigned to different, specialized workers, productions soared to forty-eight thousand pins per day.

extend among the workers, the more do their wages shrink together." But history has been less than kind to Marx's predictions, as societal wealth has increased drastically thanks to **specialization**. Generally, we are a better, more productive species when we divide the work and get really good at specific things. To think otherwise seems to fly directly in the face of history.[96]

How You'll Be Tested...

Many investors think, or have been taught to think, that working with anyone on their investments is too expensive, provides little or no value, and is generally for the birds. Perhaps, you too will consider flying solo or avoid advice because you are firmly convinced you can do it all. Hey pigeon, time to evolve! Ask yourself the question: *What am I special at?* Look, I don't mean to bring back feelings of latent inadequacy due to your overachieving siblings or the coach who wouldn't play you in the big game. What I mean is this: *is crafting your own financial and investment plan your specialty?* Are you good at it now and dedicated to honing your craft for the rest of your life? Are you committed to being up to date and educated? If your answer is a resounding yes, good for you! Call me, I may be hiring. But if your answer is somewhat less confident, then call someone like me. Because, *you* should be hiring.

We'll talk more about the nature of advice in History 401, especially on what to look for when networking so you find the right specialist, and I don't want to spoil the fun now. But suffice it to say, that if you aren't concentrating on what you are

96   After all, pin making ain't exactly a growth industry these days. Economic victory goes to those who efficiently specialize and adapt to changing circumstances.

best at, you aren't maximizing your total satisfaction or personal utility. To do that, you have to spend more time on your own profession to maximize your current income and savings for retirement. Recall a bit of Darwinian theory, specialize and get so good at your own job that you don't need it anymore. And when you do retire, concentrate on that to maximize your happiness, without taking on a second career as an investment guru. Yes, the fittest survive. But the specialists thrive.

EXTRA CREDIT

MEET WB: The lesser known of the two scientists, William Bernhard Tegetmeier gets short shrift in most history books, but not this one. Find out more about the bird man here by reading his obituary at: https://britishbirds.co.uk/article/obituary-william-bernhard-tegetmeier/. Then see the man himself in portraiture: http://friendsofdarwin.com/articles/tegetmeier/tegetmeier-painting/. And in caricature as one of his beloved birds: http://friendsofdarwin.com/articles/tegetmeier/tegetmeier-as-pigeon/.

DIVIDE AND CONQUER: Professor Don Boudreaux of George Mason University expounds upon specialization and how, in turn, it leads to new technologies and trade. Trade provides a market big enough to make specialization worthwhile while technology advances to meet production requirements. A nice summary of previous lessons as we near the end of History 201 at: https://www.youtube.com/watch?v=r43dv8k8M1k.

FIND A TRAIT: You need one to be first rate, at least according to Marilyn Monroe and her co-star Frankie Vaughn. Their 1960 musical tribute to specialization includes the following shout out to Charles Darwin:

> *"The Pharaohs did it with Sphinx.*
> *And Darwin did it with links.*
> *Some robbers did it with Brinks.*
> *Carnegie used a Hall.*
> *Specialists all."*

Sing along at: https://www.youtube.com/
watch?v=jd14ztiGMHc.

STAY IN THE POOL: Yes, Darwin made adaptive radiation and evolution famous. But there is another Darwinian legacy: the dark humor and cautionary tales of the Darwin Awards. Author Wendy Northcutt highlights those who have voluntarily removed themselves from the gene pool. The Berkley grad with a degree in molecular biology seems to be on to something about the self-selection of humans, at least those who make it into her books. Read and heed the collection including *The Darwin Awards Volumes I–V* and *The Darwin Awards: Countdown to Extinction*. Or evolve to the Internet and see more at http://www.darwinawards.com/ and hear it straight from the award committee here https://www.youtube.com/watch?v=PixJ_y_ilmI.

BREAK BREAD: Think humans are the only ones making questionable decisions with disturbing consequences? Darwin and pigeons return in this news story from Russia where the birds were unable to pass up the allure of free grain: https://www.rt.com/viral/362458-pigeons-mill-russia-video/. Unfortunately, that grain was being sifted into a mill to be processed into bread and the birds were unceremoniously sucked into the machine. Ironically, on a park bench somewhere, that bread was probably fed back to the pigeons. It's the circle of life!

A House of Cards
World War I & Unintended Consequences

1914 AD

There are people in this word known to neglect considering the consequences of their actions. They are called
teenagers, and at the beginning of the twentieth century,
millions of lives hinged on the judgement of one of them.
It didn't go well.

"Damn," he muttered walking briskly with his head down,
the weight of his pistol heavy in his pocket.

His mission was a failure and what he needed was a
smoke and perhaps a stiff drink to calm his nerves. The
comfort of a crowd and a cocktail would give him precious
time to think. And a shady, anonymous cafe might be just
the place to come up with a plan for the future, if he had
one. As he hurried along he saw an open seat at a table and
ducked off of Franz Joseph Street into the shade. He ordered
nervously at Moritz Schiller's Cafe and drank quickly, thick

smoke curling into his nostrils and clutching his cigarette in a trembling hand.[97]

"A good plan," he murmured into his drink. "A good plan."

To begin, the day's operation had gone perfectly. The Duke had come to Sarajevo and ridden the route they expected in an open car. They'd stalked him like game and closed in for the kill. But the driver, he had ruined it all. Gavrilo Princip sat and replayed it all in his mind, seeing the grenade arc toward the car, a black mark on the blue sky tumbling toward its target. The crowd screaming and the car's engine roaring to life. The driver had reacted quickly, making a split-second decision to accelerate at the oncoming object and not stop.

"Damn him," he whispered. Most men would have stopped.

Instead, Princip had watched the grenade bounce off the windshield and explode under the trailing vehicle. There was panic and perhaps death among some of the Duke's Austrian entourage, but the man still lived. *But will I*, Princip wondered? Failure was never good in such operations and The Black Hand, leaders of the fight for Serb independence, might not be very forgiving. Perhaps it was better to take the poison now and be done with it. He had failed to kill the Arch Duke of the Austro-Hungarian Empire. His mission was over and his time on earth likely very short.

---

97   In years to come, legend would arise that Gavrilo Princip was eating a sandwich when he opened Pandora's proverbial box. This seems apocryphal given the lack of sandwich fare in the early twentieth century in and around Bosnia. To be fair, there is no evidence that he had a drink at Schiller's deli either, given that the assassination took place sometime after 10:30 AM.

He withdrew the vial of cyanide from an interior pocket and set it on the table next to his drink.[98]

Looking up from the table with heavy eyes, the young Serb noticed commotion from the way he had come. His heart skipped, goose flesh rippled up his arm and he clutched his poison. Police? No, he realized, calming slightly, just a nondescript touring car hesitantly making its way up the street toward him. A motorist lost in the tangle of Sarajevo streets had turned into the milling crowd that congregated on Franz Joseph. The car had a familiar look to it, black, with an open roof and a man and woman in the back. Princip saw a flash of medals and a uniform. Recognition began to dawn. At the wheel was the driver, hero of the day, now lost on the city streets and trying to make a slow three-point turn to head back the way he came. Princip downed the drink and doused his cigarette. He drew his Browning FN 1910 semi-automatic pistol and started walking.

Cold despite the heat of a June morning, he strode purposefully toward the open car, the weight of the now exposed weapon in his hand barely noticeable. He was twenty feet away and someone was screaming. He marched

---

98   The Black Hand (Crna Ruka) also known as Union or Death, used terrorist methods to attempt to unite free Serb territories from Habsburg or Ottoman rule and unite them. Inside Serbia the group eventually grew so powerful as to threaten the army and government, leading to their persecution and purge from within. Princip's failure, had it lasted would have saved millions of lives as the spiraling events leading to World War I would not have happened. No ultimatum would come from Austria who would not be backed by Germany. No threats from Russia of retaliation, and no declaration of war between France and Germany in August of 1914. Of course, there is more to the story. Ferdinand, alive and well, insisted to be driven to the hospital to visit the wounded. On the way to the hospital, the Arch Duke's car took a wrong turn and got separated from the motorcade.

forward, ten feet away, and could make out the features of the man, the target, with his curled mustache. There was also reaction from the car, surprise on the faces. They seemed to know what was coming but were unable to move. At five feet, he opened fire. The pistol barked and spit smoke. More screams came from all around the busy thoroughfare. He'd hit the woman. She slumped and now he had a clear line of fire for his second .38 caliber bullet. He fired. Blood splattered the interior of the car. The Duke clutched his throat, the motor on the touring car was cut. In his impatience to get the car moving, the driver had inadvertently stalled just as Princip approached. With the car silenced, he could hear the Duke struggling to breathe in choking rasps.

He reached for the cyanide capsule and brought it to his lips, choking down the vile liquid. Now he could die a hero, not a failed freedom fighter. He grimaced at the revolting taste that wracked his body and waited for the darkness to come. But nothing happened.[99]

He thought perhaps he should turn the gun on himself, but it was too late. The crowd had rallied, were on him now, dragging him down to the street, hitting and kicking him as he fell. He smelled the acrid smell of gunpowder, tasted blood and acid, then felt the pressing weight of angry men on top of him. It was over. He had done it. He was, he thought, a hero.

---

99 His co-conspirator, Nedeljko Čabrinović who had thrown the grenade at the Duke's car, had likewise taken the poison only to find that it was old and past its lethal date. Čabrinović then tried to jump in the river and drown himself but it was only four inches deep where he waded in. He was captured by police, wet and sick but very much alive. If not for ensuing events, it might have been comical.

Within hours the Duke and his wife were dead. The Austro Hungarians demanded satisfaction from the Serbs and when they didn't get it, picked a fight backed by their big brother Germany. But the Serbs were old allies of the Russians and so the dominoes began to fall as alliances lined up to defend each other. Six weeks after Princip's successful mission, European heavyweights Germany and France declared war on each other and The Continent and the world plunged into bloody chaos that lasted for generations. Princip, who was nineteen at the time of the assassination, developed tuberculosis while in prison. Depending on your point of view, he either perished a terrorist or a freedom fighter, take your pick. Either way he died with only the vaguest notion of what he had wrought.

Unintended Consequences are a keystone of sociological and economic theory. Human beings, for a variety of reasons, often engage in actions we find rewarding now without regard to what may come later. And there is no better historical example of the concept than the story of Gavrilo Princip, a teenager who brought about mass poison gas attacks and the laments of The Lost Generation. His single act led to World War I, its sequel and eventually the Cold War and its many offshoots. In numerous ways, he shaped the modern world we live in from the Middle East to Main Street USA. Reverberations from the assassination continued to plague Europe long after. The settlement negotiated at Versailles in 1919 to finally end hostilities did that and, of course, much more. A punishment that was supposed to leave Germany incapable of further aggressive war instead led to economic disaster, the rise of the uber-militant Nazi party and a large, armed, and angry populace in the center of Europe who began the greatest conflict the world had ever seen. Other than *that*, it pretty much worked as planned.

—— BREAKING THE LAW ——

First mentions of unintended consequences go back at least to Adam Smith, though Robert Merton's 1936 paper *The Unintended Consequences of Purposive Social Action* popularized the term.

Today, there is often talk of the "Law of Unintended Consequences" though Merton never put any of his work up for a vote in Congress. Like that optimist Murphy, (if anything can go wrong, it will) "the law" has become idiomatic, meant to convey the idea that human's rarely control the world as much as we think. No, but controlling ourselves is an admirable start.

Achieving your primary goals is nice, but as Princip shows, you can achieve a short-term goal and still set in motion unintended and potentially life-altering, far-reaching effects. Even if, like Princip or the Duke's hapless driver, you feel like a hero for a little while.[100]

---

100 The French economic journalist Frédéric Bastiat famously noted that there is only one difference between a good economist and a bad one: "the bad economist confines himself to the visible effect; the good economist takes into account both the effect that can be seen and those effects that must be foreseen."

Without understanding our potential for letting loose inadvertent outcomes we run this risk of getting lost in the tangle of a complex world. Identifying the potential catalysts that lead us to **unintended consequences** might just help keep the aftermaths from being catastrophic. American sociologist Robert K. Merton systematically analyzed the problem and advanced five causes for inadvertent outcomes, so arm yourself accordingly.[101]

---

101 Merton acknowledged what he called a "relevance paradox," where decision makers ignore or neglect information that would allow them to better analyze potential unintended consequences. Sounds like confirmation bias to me. Notice that you couldn't make a good decision, even knowing about unintended consequences, without first understanding how your brain tries to trick you?

Merton's Five Causes of Unintended Consequences

Cause	Description	Example (Black Hand)	Example (Investor)
Ignorance	Incomplete analysis. After all, it is impossible to anticipate everything.	"We're just going after the Duke to prove a point. What is wrong with that?"	"These tech companies are amazing. What could possibly go wrong?"
Error	In analyzing the problem, we follow previous habits that worked in the past despite potentially new fact patterns.	"We killed our own Royal Family and made an attempt on the Governor and that wasn't the end of the world."	"I killed it last time I bought stocks from the list in that newsletter."
Immediate Interest	I need something now and I'll cross the bridge of consequences when I come to it.	"We have to make our voice heard! No one is listening."	"I can't keep watching my account go down. I'm done."
Basic Values	Prohibit or require certain actions even if the long-term results are unfavorable.	"We are fighting for something bigger than ourselves, we have to do something."	"My father lived through the Depression. He taught me not to take risks."
Self-Defeating Prophecy	Fear of a consequence driving people to find solutions before the problem occurs. Nonoccurrence of the problem isn't anticipated.	"If we don't do this, we will all end up as slaves to the Austro-Hungarian Empire."	"I'm not going to get burned again like I did in 2008."

How You'll Be Tested...

In your life as an investor, the ghost of Robert Merton may haunt you too, as you find yourself acting out of ignorance or immediate interest to feel less pain or find more gain in your portfolio. Yes, some combination of Merton's causal factors might lead to a short term, feel-good-effect in swapping mutual funds, chasing hot stocks, or seeking safety in cash, pick your poison. But you must remember your overall mission when things get a bit exciting. Doing the right thing is often a matter of perspective, taking the long view, demonstrating wisdom beyond your years.

During the lessons in History 201, you should have retained enough basic economic theory to bore anyone at a dinner party. More importantly, you should have begun to develop a decision-making process that promotes analysis deeper than the gut feelings of the here and now. You should know how to tally up hidden costs (such as inflation and opportunity cost) and to create a cost benefit analysis that includes a variety of potential outcomes, many of which are often overlooked in heat of the moment decision making. And if you aren't feeling up to the task, you've learned to ask for help.

Investors are constantly faced with decisions that, due to the nature of compounding, effect their investment outcomes forever. We'll return to compounding and other investment terminology specifically in History 301. In the meantime, if you want to be able to live with the decisions you make, you need to have considered a variety of potential outcomes. After all, forever is a mighty long time to watch dominoes fall if they weren't the ones you intended to play.

EXTRA CREDIT

PICK A PASSWORD: Go ahead and change your e mail password, the class will wait. Now, how many different combinations of letters, numbers, and special characters can you remember? Most tech users when urged to make their passwords more complex for security reasons resort to version 1.0 and write them down or store them in a text file. This, of course, has the unintended consequence of making them less safe.

PICK YOUR POISON: You would think that after helping to end World War I, Americans would want to have a drink and either celebrate the end or mourn the casualties. Not so much. Instead, the United States began a massive social experiment with Prohibition in 1920. Historical film maker Ken Burns recaps how going dry meant unemployment, business failures, bootlegging, and a rise in attendance at church…for the still legal sacramental wine: http://www. pbs.org/kenburns/prohibition/unintended-consequences/.

GO HARDCORE: Discover storyteller Dan Carlin's Hardcore History podcast. A veteran journalist with two extremely popular podcasts, Carlin gives history the kind of passionate analysis it deserves. Check out part one in his history of the Great War, *Blueprint for Armageddon* at: http://www. dancarlin.com/product/hardcore-history-50-blueprint-for-armageddon-i/.

GET FREAKY: Take a listen to the Freakonomics podcast about The Cobra Effect. In Colonial India, it was decided by the powers that be that fewer cobras would mean a safer environment. So, a bounty was placed, and the government paid for cobra carcasses. And some people will do anything for a buck, including raising their own cobras in captivity in order to kill them and collect. When the program was cancelled, the snakes were released. Thus, the population of cobras likely increased due to the program. Hear more about snakes on the Indian plain at: http://freakonomics.com/podcast/the-cobra-effect-a-new-freakonomics-radio-podcast/.

GO GOOGLING: Unintended consequences aren't just about lone gun men and economic theory. An Internet search for the term should return somewhere over 6 million hits. Browse the results and the news to review the unintended consequences of things like airline safety measures, school discipline, China's one child policy, seat belt laws, airing your politics on Facebook, and new rules to protect NFL quarterbacks.

THEN MAP IT: Google itself comes under scrutiny for changing the way we live in seemingly strange and unpredictable ways. Did Google Maps start a war in 2010? Read More from the New York Times: http://opinionator.blogs.nytimes.com/2012/02/28/the-first-google-maps-war/?_php=true&_type=blogs&_r=1.

GET CHAOTIC: "Chaos happens, let's make better use of it." Historian Edward Tenner takes us back forty thousand years into the past to show how our ability to innovate also creates a lot of positive outcomes. We learn a lot, it turns out, from our disasters. His TED talk is a good reminder that not all unintended consequences are negative. He notes that we're all in this together and your decisions can have consequences for others, presumably to include me. So, study up and read on: http://www.ted.com/talks/edward_tenner_unintended_consequences?language=en.

HISTORY 301

The Building of America & Basic Investment Theory

"Facts are stubborn things; and whatever may be our wishes, our inclinations, or the dictates of our passions, they cannot alter the state of facts and evidence."

-JOHN ADAMS

"It is better to be alone than in bad company."

-GEORGE WASHINGTON

"...think calmly and well upon this whole subject. Nothing valuable can be lost by taking time"

-ABRAHAM LINCOLN

"If you could kick the person in the pants responsible for most of your trouble, you wouldn't sit for a month."

-THEODORE ROOSEVELT

LESSON ONE: New World Disorder
Christopher Columbus & Time in the Market
1492 AD

LESSON TWO: A Pilgrim's Lack of Progress
The Mayflower & Corrections
1620 AD

LESSON THREE: A Gage of the Randomness
Thomas Gage & Random Walk Theory
1768 AD

LESSON FOUR: All About the Benjamins
Ben Franklin & Diversification
1790 AD

LESSON FIVE: Going Postal
Wilson Hunt & Risk v. Reward
1811 AD

LESSON SIX: On the Money
Salmon P. Chase & Compounding
1862 AD

LESSON SEVEN: Shaving Face
Ambrose Burnside & Action Tendency
1863 AD

LESSON EIGHT: Extrapolation Celebration
Marmota Monax & Financial Forecasting
1887 AD

LESSON NINE: Rough Ride Rewrite

Theodore Roosevelt & Asset Allocation

1898 AD

LESSON TEN: Salt of the Earth

Patillo Higgins & Cyclical Investments

1901 AD

New World Disorder

Christopher Columbus & Time in the Market

1492 AD

Christopher Columbus left Spain to find a new trade route to Asia in the summer of 1492. The result was the opening of a new continent to good things like opportunities for trade and bad things like small pox. While the story is complex, we can learn a simple lesson from Chris and his crew about hanging in there when the voyage is a yawner.

"Face it. We are lost." The accusation was as clear as the blue sky unfolding like and endless blanket in front of them.

"We are not lost! Just a little bit farther and I'm sure we will find it." He was tired of having to justify himself. He had this under control. How many times did he have to say it?

"Seriously, I think we should turn back. Maybe we can fill up back there and get better directions."

He kept his eyes forward. White knuckles on the wheel.

"Better directions? You really think I don't know where I am going?" He practically shouted it out of frustration.

"I didn't say you don't know where you are going. I said that we are lost trying to get there!"

There was a tense silence, neither party willing to bend. Then, Admiral Christopher Columbus sighed audibly. He forced himself to calm down, gave up the ship's helm and smiled patiently at the assembled crewmen and their designated spokesman. They were gathered on deck, lean and emaciated bodies packed close, angry faces looking to him for a solution. An argument here was not to his advantage.

"Please," Columbus pleaded, "just give me a little more time. A few days more and I'm confident we will make land." A few months sail out of Spain, the three ships of Columbus's party were drifting on light winds and weighed down by heavy thoughts. Aware of the crew gradually turning against him with each passing mile, the Admiral kept two log books during the journey, one to show the officers and men, and one he kept to himself. Columbus thought it best if they didn't know how far away from home they truly were. But as the days dragged on, tensions grew regardless of the distance traveled. Outright mutiny seemed a real possibility.[102]

The crewman sighed and looked back at his compatriots. "Two days," he bellowed to them, "and then we go back no matter what." The men gave a half-hearted cheer and scrambled back to their watch stations aboard the flagship,

---

102 Aside from a brief stop in the Canary Islands to fix the rudder on the Pinta, not much had happened on their voyage across the expanse of the Atlantic. The Pinta's rudder was thought to be damaged by her own crew in an act of defiance. Even at that early date in September 1492, it was clear that not everyone was "on board" with Chris's plans for riches and glory.

careful to avoid Columbus's eye.

Exhausted, the Admiral retired to his cabin. He slept fitfully, constantly waiting to hear them coming for him, that they had changed their minds and were set to mutiny after all. He tried without success to distract himself with thoughts of the riches awaiting them should they indeed find what they were seeking. It was almost a relief when he heard the cabin door creak open well after midnight. Would they set him adrift he wondered? Or feed him to the sharks?

"Admiral," came the whispered voice of his steward. "Begging your pardon sir, but the lookouts report seabirds and floating grass. Land is near." Columbus raced on deck where the once mutinous crew had broken into song.

"Quiet on deck! I need lookouts not songbirds. Land? Where?"

"Two points to starboard, Admiral."

Columbus scanned the horizon and focused on what seemed to be a darker part of the sky. Then a star flickered where his eyes rested. He closed them, tried to reset his brain. But it was there when he opened them, a light in the distance that seemed to flicker like a candle rising and falling on the horizon. "Strike the sails. Drop the anchor. We've reached Japan!"[103]

---

103 The Nina, Pinta, and Santa Maria left Spanish waters on August 3rd seeking a westward passage to the East Indies. Between September 6th when they left the Canaries and October 12th when land was spotted, calm winds made for slow going. Several false sightings of land didn't help the mood, nor did the chart they referenced that turned out to depict entirely fictional islands and landmasses. The men complained to Columbus who convinced them to hang in there during a meeting on October 10th. Actual land was sighted on the 12th by Columbus who noted a light seeming to dance on the horizon. Rodrigo de Triana was the lookout who originally thought he had spotted

Of course, you should know that Columbus had not discovered Japan and that there was a substantial land mass blocking him from ever doing so with his current flotilla of ships. If, perhaps, that *is* news to you, I'm not sure how you got this far in the book, or in life. Nevertheless, Columbus had struck out from the European continent and found land to the west. He returned to Spain a celebrity, convinced he had reached Asia, his report to the Royal Court of King Ferdinand and Queen Isabella, glowing, if somewhat exaggerated. For a brief while, he was on top of the world.[104]

But after that first voyage, things started to go very wrong. Given control of the newly discovered lands, Columbus forced many of his new charges to look for gold, producing little but hatred for him and his compatriots. Returning in 1493 he found the settlement of Villa de la Navidad in Hispaniola, built from salvaged timbers of the wrecked Santa Maria, had been attacked and wiped out. His third voyage saw a near revolt by settlers who complained about his mismanagement on the island and little gold to show for it. Back in Spain, Columbus was arrested and stripped of his titles including the Governorship of the discovered lands. This was enough to void most of the monetary promises he'd been given, including his lifetime pension. He received some measure of redemption after convincing King Ferdinand to finance one last voyage, his fourth and final.[105]

---

land, but Columbus claimed his sighting of the unidentified light source as the crucial event, thereby claiming a lifetime pension from the Spanish crown.

104 The persistent belief that Columbus sailed to prove the earth was round, not flat, is a myth. The spherical nature of the globe was well known long before his voyages.

105 Notorious among the Caribbean natives by this time, the Spaniards

The old joke goes like this: *A pedestrian walking in New York City sees a musician getting out of a cab. Encouraged, he asks, "Excuse me, how do you get to Carnegie Hall?" Without pause, the artist replies wearily, "Practice, practice, practice."*

A 2015 study says the joke may be getting it wrong. Researchers point out that the punchline should really be "persistence, persistence, persistence." But people, even creative types, "may undervalue and underutilize persistence in everyday creative problem solving." You don't always need a new direction; the critical determinant of performance is the ability to endure setbacks and keep the music playing.

The new joke goes like this: *A pedestrian sees a New York Rangers hockey player getting out of a cab and breathlessly asks, "How do you get to Madison Square Garden?" Without pause, the player says, "Stick with it, eh?"*

The last voyage allowed him to recoup some of his fortune, but not his titles or the support of the crown. At his death, he still insisted he had reached the Orient. Of course, he hadn't, but he had expanded the known world and opened new trade and settlement to Europeans. Unfortunately, he'd also opened the Americas to disease and forced labor. His voyages made him famous and led to his arrest; made him rich and ruined him; expanded the known world and ended a civilization.

---

were denied provisions in Cuba. Columbus punished them by taking away the moon, or at least telling him he would before the lunar eclipse on February 29, 1504. The alarmed islanders quickly changed their minds, though there weren't enough celestial events to win over the rest of the New World.

The story of Christopher Columbus remains complicated. Less complicated is the lesson that persistence can lead to great discoveries. Explorers call it patience or perseverance, investors call it **Time in the Market**—letting your plan work and accepting the occasional lull in the action. It beats trying to time every ebb and flow of the marketplace.

How You'll Be Tested...

You'll be adrift, floating for days, weeks, months and seemingly going nowhere. You'll be bored and frustrated, feeling like you've made a mistake when you charted your course. You may even be moving backwards. And you'll be tempted to move money in or out of an investment purely for the thrill of doing *something*. Avast ye landlubber! Don't just do something, do the right thing. Get your thrills elsewhere and maintain some discipline.

Focusing on **time in the market** is maddening when nothing much happens for months in your explorations or your retirement portfolio. But let there be no doubt, you must stay on the boat to enjoy the ultimate destination and the fruits of your journey. It is a port of call you can't afford to miss.

EXTRA CREDIT

GO HOLLYWOOD: Ridley Scott is justifiably more famous for movies like *Alien* & *Blade Runner*. But he tackled the discovery story in *1492: Conquest of Paradise* (1992). The movie never quite manages to sail out of the doldrums, so you'll need a bit of persistence to make it all the way though.

GET ANIMATED: Or, get all the drama in a fraction of the time. Fans of the Simpsons and Family Guy can get their Columbus fix in cartoon form at: www.youtube.com/watch?v=aF_unlvjccA&feature=youtu.be.

GO SIDEWAYS: I'm talking about the markets, but if you want to grab a glass of pinot noir and watch the movie *Sideways* (2004) before hitting the books, I won't judge. Then enjoy Vitaliy N. Katsenelson's *The Little Book of Sideways Markets: How to Make Money in Markets that Go Nowhere*. His thesis? Stick with your strategy, collect your dividends and do not, under any circumstances, drink that merlot.

STOCK UP: Some books you read, some you own and some you revere. *Stocks for the Long Run* is one of the latter. Billed as *The Definitive Guide to Financial Market Returns & Long-Term Investment Strategies,* Jeremy Siegel's classic tome demonstrates the benefits of time in the market the way no historian ever would: with numbers.

TURN OVER A NEW LEIF: Columbus was not the first European to set foot on the American continent. The Icelandic explorer Leif Erikson is thought to have reached Newfoundland some five hundred years prior, though Leif the Lucky may have followed a trail pioneered by other Norsemen even earlier than the eleventh century. Celebrate his memory on Leif Erikson Day next October 9th. Yep, Leif deserves that kind of respect.

MAKE TIME TO REVIEW: Aside from **time in the market**, this lesson also reviews previous material including:

Anchoring bias: It has nothing to do with where Columbus parked the Nina, Pinta, and Santa Maria. Columbus underestimated the size of the globe, believing it was 63% of the actual circumference and to the end of his days he couldn't accept anything much different.

Confirmation Bias: Columbus wanted to believe the islands he found were off the coast of Japan or China. But the natives in the New World looked and sounded nothing like the traders he had met from Asia, which might have given him pause. He saw everything that seemed to confirm his theories and ignored whatever didn't. In retrospect, Columbus came closest to the Asian continent as a teenager on a trading voyage into the Aegean Sea when he landed at the island of Khios in modern day Greece.

Unintended consequences: Columbus didn't intend to sicken and enslave a native population when he left Spain, he was just looking for a shortcut. But, as so often happens, shortcuts lead to outcomes not foreseen before the journey.

Patrick Huey

A Pilgrim's Lack of Progress
The Mayflower & Corrections

1620 AD

ny journey worth taking will have its challenges and the Pilgrims who established colonies in America withstood an awful lot to get here. But they endured, even when "awful lot" became a perfect description of their fellow passengers. Not everyone on the Mayflower was a saint.

"Can they not hurry this along? I'm damnably tired of waiting and this bloody old tub is going to sink before we get ashore!" John Billington had left England for adventure and to make a bit of money. Instead, he'd been occasionally bored, often scared, and hungry nearly all of the two-month ordeal in crossing to the New World. Rations were as short as his temper and passengers, men and women alike, were growing frail and sickly. Some had breath that smelled like bilge water and had begun to lose teeth.[106]

---

106 Their ship was actually known to have a fairly sweet bilge, the product of years plying the seas between France and England with a hold full of wine, and the inevitable spillage. But a two-month journey through North Atlantic

"Aye, me too. Wait for them to sail from Holland, wait for them to meet us in Southampton, wait for them to fix their ship, wait below until the storms pass. Damn all this waiting three times to hell." Stephen Hopkins was equally agitated, and though his friend Billington was known as the most profane man onboard, he was willing to match him oath for oath. Especially now, crammed into a dank passageway with less than five feet of clearance "tween decks" leading toward the main cabin of the old ship. She was a three-mast merchantman about one hundred feet long, crowded with over one hundred and thirty men, women, and children. It was hell on earth, though the two tradesmen were surrounded by men who called themselves Saints. And it had the decidedly non-floral smell of sweat and vomit, though she was named the May*flower*.

Aboard the ship were four parties, those called The Pilgrims from the Leiden Congregation, their servants, the ship's crew, and The London Merchant's Adventurers. Those of the Congregation were religious separatists, dissatisfied with King James and his leadership of the Anglican Church. Having left England, they found themselves living second class Dutch lives, working six days a week at menial jobs in Holland. Deacon John Carver had managed to secure rights to land in the Americas. To fund the voyage, he had accepted the merchants as fellow travelers. The Congre-

---

winter gales would have soured much including the water in the hold. Provisions might have been shorter had not so many passengers become so violently seasick that they'd ceased eating altogether. And even shorter had they not lost one of the passengers who died of the sickness just days before land was sighted. Foul breath and loose teeth were indications that scurvy had set in.

gationalists called themselves Saints and referred to the merchants as Strangers. It wasn't the most cohesive group to begin with and the ordeal of the crossing hadn't helped. Now, after averaging just over two miles per hour in getting to New England, the passengers waited in line to hear what would happen next.[107]

"The hell with it. I've had it." Billington wedged himself around and started to move away from the men huddled near the hatch.

Hopkins put a hand on his shoulder. "Where are you going John?"

Billington turned with a strange look on his face. "I'm so tired of waiting around that I am going to strangle someone. Weston ain't here, damn his soul. So, maybe I should kill Jones? He's the one that anchored five hundred miles from where we were supposed to." He snapped his finger and grinned. "Or I'll kill Carver. Yes, that's it. John Carver is the damn fool that started this mess." With that he shook off his friend's arm and disappeared down the dark passageway.[108]

---

107 Having already anchored once in present day Cape Cod the ship had attempted to sail further south but was battered by wind and tide. News that she had turned around and again anchored in New England caused all kinds of mayhem below decks including "mutinous speeches" by men such as Hopkins and Billington who would develop and nurture reputations as rabble rousers.

108 Thomas Weston was the recruiter of the Merchant Adventurers in London. Though he financed part of the expedition, he remained in England and quit the enterprise in 1622. Jones was one quarter owner of the Mayflower and the ship's master. He had planned to leave England in August but was delayed by the Speedwell, a ship bringing the Leiden contingent from Holland that became unusable for a trans-Atlantic voyage. Taking on new passengers delayed him until September and overloaded a tired ship that sailed poorly before the wind. Jones did his best to beat westward, anchoring near today's Provincetown in a hook-shaped inlet that sheltered them from

"Kill him? Have you gone daft?" But he was gone. Hopkins stared after him dumbly for a moment and he heard his feet stomping on the deck above. Part of him thought about giving chase, but he was loathe to lose his place. For a few minutes, he kept his head down, shuffling forward at odd increments toward the light in the cabin. Billington reappeared, red faced and fell in line again behind him without a word.

"Well?" whispered Hopkins. Sneaking a peek toward the great cabin to see if they would be overheard.

"Well what?"

"Did you kill him? Holy God man, is it the hangman's noose for you?"

"No brother, I didn't. The line waiting to kill him was even longer than this one." Billington waited a beat and then let loose a great chortling fit of laughter. He slapped a knee, wiped his eyes and doubled over at the waist, shaking with mirth. "Honestly, you really thought I was going to do it? I just had to visit the head, that's all. This slop they serve does the worst things to my insides."

"Strangers, if you are quite done? Step into the cabin," said a man beckoning them. It was John Carver, alive and, for the time being, quite well. Billington dug an elbow into his friend's side and stifled a giggle.

They proceed inside the cabin where early morning light streamed in from the two windows over the stern that looked out on the giant sand dunes towering before them on the

---

battering winter seas. Their original charter for lands in Virginia became a moot point when they realized that getting into the waters around Cape Cod was a lot easier than getting out.

cape. Carver, seated at a squat table, proceeded to ramble on for a few moments about a legal compact they were all signing since their original charter was null and void in Massachusetts. They shrugged, neither one particularly moved, stepped forward and placed an X to mark their consent to the Mayflower Compact. No matter what, going ashore had to be better than what they had already endured.[109]

 Wrong. During the ensuing winter, forty-five of the one hundred and two original immigrants died of scurvy, exposure, disease, and hunger. Hopkins and Billington survived. Hopkins became a tavern keeper who occasionally ran afoul of the Saints in later years, though it was often overlooked due to his adroit handling of relations with local tribes, including those who attended the first Thanksgiving. Billington became the first person hanged for murder in Plymouth Colony in 1630 after he argued with a neighbor and then shot him when he encountered him hunting in the same field. Governor Carver would die in the spring after their arrival and be replaced by William Bradford, who viewed the misplaced landing, the ensuing winter or any other setback as nothing more than "a **Correction** bestowed by God." In any worthwhile endeavor, we should expect obstacles, complications, and adjustments to our plans. Often, the way to reach an ultimate destination is, like the Strangers and the Saints, to endure.

---

109 The original version of the text was lost, but its language and list of original signers was dutifully transcribed by William Bradford, future Governor of Plymouth Colony. Forty-one of the sixty-five males aboard signed the compact. Thirteen minor sons were excepted as their father's signatures were sufficient. Nine servants and two sailors never signed. Even then voter turnout was a problem.

MISSING INACTION

Whether you are bored or terrified, jumping ship on your investments is a bad idea. Missing just the ten best return days over the twenty-year period from 1997–2016 reduced the return of the S&P 500 from 7.7% to 4.0%. If you missed the best thirty days your return was as negative as the attitude of a few of the Mayflower's passengers.

Think you are pretty nimble? Over that twenty-year period, six of the best ten days occurred *within two weeks* of the ten worst days. Okay, got the market timed to the week? How about to the day? On August 24, 2015, the Dow Jones Industrial Average lost 588 points. Two days later it rose 609 points. That's a tight time-frame to turn your investments around unless you know something I don't. In which case I should be reading *your* book. Face it, market timing is still for lubbers.

How You'll Be Tested:

It is not coincidence that severe tests of fortitude in investment markets are called **corrections**, echoing Bradford's description of the Pilgrim's trials. As an investor, perhaps it won't be the periods of calm that get you, it will be the turbulent periods where you are tossed about by the whims of the markets and want to deviate from the plan that brought you to such peril. If so, go ahead and put your X next to the following:[110]

---

110 Any drop of more than ten percent in value over a relatively short

Patrick Huey

A Compact List of Investment Lessons from the Mayflower

- *If it is important, put it in writing.* The Pilgrims needed clarity since they were in the wrong place and lacked legal standing. Put a plan in writing that gives you similar clarity of purpose. It will help you focus on the long term when **corrections** are bestowed upon you.
- *Don't wreck a good plan because it isn't perfect.* A well-constructed and written plan is not something to pitch overboard at the first sign of difficulty. Be sure to include occasional bad markets in your projections. Then update your plans and assumptions after the worst is over.
- *Be flexible.* Virginia, New England, what's the difference? Quite a bit, but a good plan also requires the occasional revision. Planning and investing are a constant process of revising and evaluating your options.
- *Don't let the judgment of others affect your own.* In England, they called it a fool's errand. Maybe, but the voyagers aboard the Mayflower are known to history and most of those who didn't get on the boat, aren't. When **corrections** come, the naysayers on television and other mass media are not your friends. You'll give thanks later if you just unplug and ignore.
- *Be hardy.* The Pilgrims responded to setbacks, even major ones, with what the English would later refer to as a "stiff upper lip." When the seas get roughest, mind your temper and recognize that swapping your current situation for another

---

period of time is referred to as a correction, while a more protracted dip of over 20 percent would be called a bear market.

isn't necessarily an improvement. A good investor during a **correction** is the one with the patience of a saint.

EXTRA CREDIT

GET THE FACTS: A long voyage can be broken into smaller parts to make it more bearable. *Deconstructing History: Mayflower* does that too, bringing you all the stats about America's most famous ship in a bit over three minutes. All the details you need to annoy your family with trivia at the next Thanksgiving dinner are here: http://www.history.com/topics/mayflower/videos.

TRIP OUT: Get your permission slip signed by a parent and then queue up on the miniature yellow bus that smells like stale Gummy Bears and has no seat belts? Only to be dropped into a bad historical reenactment hosted by over the hill theatre wash outs? No thanks. Save time, money and self-respect with a virtual voyage on YouTube: www.youtube.com/watch?v=p5qi3Meqy24.

SPEND TIME WITH FAMILY: About thirty-five million people can now trace their family tree all the way back to The Mayflower. You'd think with those kind of numbers, someone might get around to developing a site to reveal if you make the cut. Nope, this too will require some patience and fortitude. Start your research project at: www./familyhistorydaily.com/genealogy-help-and-how-to/are-you-one-of-35-million-mayflower-descendants-heres-how-to-find-out/.

GIVE THANKS: Celebrate Thanksgiving, the celebration of friendship between the survivors at Plymouth Colony and the local native tribes, as we do each year. Eat too much and fall asleep during a football game. Then set to reading Nathaniel Philbrick's book *Mayflower: A Story of Courage, Community, and War (2007)*. Spoiler alert, I already told you most of the story.

SURVIVE & THRIVE: Kiplinger's has their own ideas about how to weather a correction at http://www.kiplinger.com/article/investing/T052-C008-S002-how-to-survive-a-stock-market-correction.html. Unfortunately, all of their ideas include doing something, feeding into investors bias toward action, which is often self-defeating. However, there are two recommendations here worth keeping in mind: turning off the TV and having a strategy. Extra points for those of you for whom turning off the TV *is* the strategy.

LET THE DOGS OUT: People acting irrationally to come out on top at all costs? Pilgrims versus Strangers? Investors versus the world? Neither. It's the annual Mayflower Kennel Club Dog Show as depicted in the mockumentary *Best in Show (2000)*. And if you thought the original passengers had geography issues, meet the play-by-play announcer for the show, Buck Laughlin: "Mayflower, combined with Philadelphia—a no-brainer, right? Cause this is where the Mayflower landed. Not so. It turns out Columbus actually set foot somewhere down in the West Indies. Little known fact." During the next correction, feel free to tune in for a few laughs whenever needed.

A Gage of Randomness

The Braddock Expedition & Random Walk Theory

1755 AD

T he problem with history is that it all seems so obvious in retrospect. Modern Americans tend to think of our experiment with independence as preordained, obvious, destined to happen. But the path to Revolution was as haphazard of a march as any other in history, hinging on two men and an unused sick day.

"Ahem. Ah, listen, I'm not sure I can make it today." He'd awoken and felt okay, but his stomach was a bit sour and he was pretty sure it was going to get worse. No sense in pushing it, and if he had to exaggerate a bit to get his point across, so be it.

Silence. The boss wasn't buying it.

"No, I'm telling you, I'm not well." He coughed once or twice, but since he was complaining of dysentery wasn't sure why. This wasn't going well at all.

"I see."

"I'm sure someone else can handle it. I mean I'm not the only one, right?" He was one of three people doing the same job, and he had just joined, so was it really that important he get up and go with them?

"Mmmm…"

"Besides, there is more. I have other medical issues as well." He went on to detail them at some length.

"Alright Georgie. Do as you will. We can't expect a lad from the backwoods to pull his weight in the real army, can we? We'll move on without you." General Braddock, commander of the expeditionary force sent to drive the French out of the Ohio River Valley and open the west to British expansion, stood to leave.

Damn his mental trickery; his warfare of the brain, thought the younger man. It hit him where he hurt, wishing to shed his Colonial label and fight with the real soldiers. Sighing deeply, his new aide said: "Wait General. I'll saddle up." He was a British subject, after all, and a good performance might put him in line to lead the militia in Virginia someday.[111]

"Wonderful Georgie, it will be better if someone who has been down this road rides with us." Washington had led his own smaller foray into the woods west of the Alleghany Mountains the previous summer. "And I'll get you some cushioning for your saddle."[112]

---

111 Later in life he would apply for a commission in the regular British Army, which was denied. To say that the British later would regret that decision is one of the great understatements of history.

112 If he was hesitant to embark toward Ft. Duquesne, it was with good reason. He had literally been down that road before, meeting with disaster

"Cushioning?"

"Yes, old boy, for your hemorrhoids. You said you could barely sit in a saddle."

"Yes sir. Yes, I suppose I did say that. Uh, thank you sir." Young George Washington of Virginia would do his duty, riding into battle perched on pillows.[113]

Meanwhile, ahead of Braddock and Washington, Lieutenant Colonel Thomas Gage, fussed continuously over his men as they marched toward Fort Duquesne.[114]

"Major, dress that column!" Gage barked commands like others breathed air. He had a naturally clipped manner of speaking that lent itself to giving precise orders. The second son of Viscount Gage, he had taken to the army to make a name for himself and been on campaigns in Scotland and Holland before coming to America.[115]

---

at Ft. Necessity the previous summer when he was attacked and defeated by French and Native American forces.

113 This was no random walk for three thousand British Infantry and their Colonial comrades, they were readying an attack on the French Fort Duquesne where the Monongahela flowed into the Ohio River. Young Washington complained of both hemorrhoids and dysentery before the campaign but there is no evidence that he was embellishing. Indeed, he was said to be feverish throughout the march and barely able to get out of bed on July 9th. But isn't it fun to think of the same man who "could not tell a lie" exaggerating an illness? Nor would it be out of character at this point in his life, or any other twenty-something. His reports from the Fort Necessity campaign are a study in artfully dodging the truth, if not the enemy.

114 The fort, where the Monongahela joined at a right angle to the Alleghany and flowed southwest as the Ohio River, is the site of modern day Pittsburgh, Pennsylvania.

115 A Viscount is a member of the British peerage beneath an Earl but superior to a Baron. Gage had a mixed record on campaign having lost a bitter battle as a Captain in Flanders and won at the Battle of Culloden in Scotland. Though no definitive biography of Gage exists save a 1948 effort that glosses over many of his faults, it is known that he was an able admin-

"Yes sir," replied the harried junior officer. More-or-less automatically, he went through the motions of properly spacing the marching infantrymen. The infractions, minute ones at best, were easily corrected. But that didn't keep Gage from noticing, commenting, or correcting. On they plodded through a deep, sun-dappled forest that muffled sound and gave a welcome reprieve from the summer sun. Known as an able, even outstanding administrator, Gage paid attention to spacing, step, polish, supplies, manpower, and sick lists. But he was not paying attention to what was ahead when his column spilled out into an open glade, the sun momentarily blinding them to the armed men emerging on the other side. The French, equally surprised, looked across the open space, waiting.

"Deploy line, Major, double time." The French began shaking out into a loose formation as well, but some men seemed to be drifting away from the back of the lines. "Shirkers," Gage sneered.

"What's that sir?"

"Nothing Major. Give the order to load and fire." *Too bad*, he thought, *what I wouldn't give for a proper siege*. Gage should have been relieved to be out in the open and perhaps avoid laying siege to the fort. Sieges were long tests of supply lines and organization. A battle was won or lost in a bloody roll of the dice, but a siege was administered to, managed to the last detail. Personally, he would have loved a siege. Instead, a wild, disordered firefight soon overtook the

---

istrator but a less than effective tactician. Failing to secure or even scout the high ground on the march to Duquesne is a failure many historians continue to, rightly I think, take him to task for.

clearing. Bullets began to angle down on them. The "shirkers" had enveloped the clearing by climbing the heights.

"Sir, they're firing from the high ground." Gage also had neglected to pay much attention to the high mounds that gave the Monongahela its name, "falling banks" or "high banks that wash out and collapse" in the Native language. But it wasn't the banks that were collapsing, it was his formation. Troops began streaming backward from the front, some bloodied others merely shocked by the devastation being rained on them from above.

"Sound the retreat Major. Double time. Smartly now." They'd need to evacuate along the road which Washington and Braddock were advancing on and hopefully regroup with the main body.

For the orderly, precise Gage, the disorder that greeted him when he found the headquarters staff made him breathless. He had to put his hands in his pockets to keep from wringing them like an anxious school child.

"George, is that you?" He had recognized one of the General's aides, a decent enough fellow whom he had taken a liking to. "You look ill."

"You have no idea," Washington sighed. "Gage, what is happening?" Washington was calm, and he spoke plainly. Gage didn't even notice the lack of rank preceding the question.[116]

---

116 Trial under fire led to a friendship between Gage and Washington, but not one that endured. Though they exchanged occasional letters over the years, by the time of the Boston Massacre, Washington had no problems publicly criticizing his former colleague. Gage was by then the military commander of British troops in North America, including those occupying Boston.

"We're retreating. Why aren't you? Where's General Braddock? They've got the high ground and we need to keep falling back. To regroup in good order."

Washington glanced around him. Good order seemed to also be a rather tall order. "General Braddock is dying. Maybe dead, I don't know. He was shot while calling on the men not to hide behind trees like cowards. We've loaded him into a wagon but he's barely conscious. I think the orders are now yours to give Lieutenant Colonel Gage."[117]

"Very well, let's get the men and wagons formed up... smartly."

It was but a single battle in a long fight, known as the Seven Years War, or in America, the French and Indian War. Based on the descriptions of that day, would you guess that the British would win that war? Despite a pummeling near Pittsburgh and a mauling by the Monongahela, they did. Would you guess that, denied permanent command of Braddock's force for failing to secure the high ground and standing accused of poor combat coordination and tactics, Thomas Gage would still be promoted? That he would be lauded for his administrative abilities and ascend to the rank of Major General over all British Forces in America?

---

117 Braddock is often faulted for favoring old tactics over the shoot and cover techniques espoused in the French and Indian War mostly due to his notorious comment equating shooting from concealment to cowardice. But he was no great practitioner of his own tactics either, charging forward into an unknown engagement on a confined road and failing to order the scouting or securing of the high ground by his subordinates. He paid with his life, dying four days into the retreat.

All that happened too.[118]

And would you have guessed that the General's aide called Georgie, a tobacco farmer with modest political ambitions, would become the most renowned soldier of the age? That he would fight side by side *with* the French to give the Colonies their independence? And that he would become the first President of the United States? Who knew?[119]

No one knew, because it would be folly to predict anything based on the actions of a single day. Looking backward we can see patterns where none would have existed at the time. Washington, we surmise, was a man on the rise, with considerable ability for a young officer demonstrated on that day by his bravery under fire. And Gage, clearly, had administrative skills more suitable to governing than fighting, good news in times of peace, but disastrous when it came to war and revolution. Yes, we can make much of the significance of that day in our minds. But it was only one day, and it really means nothing at all.

Economists call this a **Random Walk.** The term, coined by mathematicians in the early 1900s, describes processes defined by a succession of random steps. Looking backward our minds create patterns to explain how things turned out. But it was haphazard all along. Only in retrospect does it

---

118 Gage's career should have been in jeopardy, but family connections probably helped and continued to be of assistance, along with the attrition of British commanders, in his repeated promotions. By 1764 with the war at an end, Major General Gage was viewed as just the person to take over administration of the North American Colonies.

119 There were more French soldiers at the surrender of British forces at Yorktown than Colonials. I know the French aren't always popular allies, but some credit is due.

seem possible that these two begin and end the American Revolution. Gage was clearly the wrong man at the wrong time in history to save British influence in North America. And Washington was clearly better off for having gotten out of bed and joining the fray that fateful day. Wonderful coincidence...unless you are British.

FLIPPED OUT

Burton Malkiel, an economics professor at Princeton, published his famous treatise: *A Random Walk Down Wall Street* in the 1970s to formalize the concept of unpredictability in stock returns. To show how stock prices move randomly, and how we can misinterpret that to have meaning, he flipped a coin. Each coin flip, heads or tails meant that a hypothetical stock either gained or lost money in a given day. He charted the results and showed them to a stock analyst who immediately recommended he buy the stock, based on the completely random series of returns. Like Thomas Gage, the analyst is mostly forgotten by history.

How You'll be Tested:

In many ways, the military careers of Washington and Gage aren't unlike stock markets: unpredictable and random, but demonstrating an upward trend over time. Yet many investors, and you may find yourself in this camp, see patterns developing from the day to day movements. And there are a host of what are known as technical traders, trying to glean buy and sell signals while looking for patterns in historical movements of stocks, bonds, or indexes. By now, knowing the biases of the human brain, you should realize that if you are looking for a pattern, you will probably find one.

Such patterns, available only in hindsight and subject to our cranial foibles aren't of much use at all. If you think you can determine what will happen today based on what happened yesterday, and are thinking of acting in your portfolio, it is time to take a walk. Or perhaps to call in sick.

EXTRA CREDIT

WALK ON: You could spend a lot of long random walks listening to audio books about George Washington. One recent biographer estimated that there are over nine hundred works about this American icon. Give *His Excellency (2005)* by Joseph Ellis a listen. From impetuous, debt ridden youngster to father of his country, you get it all in just 352 pages. That means, if you are listening on the move, you can go from Georgie to Mr. President in just over fourteen hours.

GAGE YOUR INTEREST: On the other hand, there is almost nothing currently in print about General Thomas Gage. Well, to the victors go the biographers, I suppose. John Richard Alden wrote *General Gage in America, Being Principally a History of His Role in the American Revolution (1948)* but it is out of print. So, readers must be satisfied with Bonnie Hinman's *General Thomas Gage: British General,* a history book for young adults that summarizes his life in a mere eighty pages of large font. More suitable for short jaunts than long walks.

DON'T GET FOOLED AGAIN: Need more for your reading list? Then include *Fooled by Randomness: The Hidden Role of Chance in Life and in the Markets (2005),* Nassim Taleb's landmark work urging us to never mistake luck for skill and to always expect the unexpected.

GO NATIVE: Finally, add *The Last of the Mohicans* (1826) to the list. James Fenimore Cooper's classic novel takes place during the French and Indian War, where Native Americans allied with both sides in a fight to maintain their traditional way of life. By the time the novel was written almost seventy years later, it was becoming clear that they hadn't succeeded.

GET SOME DIRECTION: Washington loved camp music, believing that "agreeable and ornamental" tunes were a necessity that officers should provide their men. But it wasn't all waltzes and show tunes. Eighteenth century armies used the music of a fife and drum corps during the commotion of battle to control the movement of troops. Musician Don Francisco demonstrates how to keep long walks a bit less random at: http://www.mountvernon.org/george-washington/the-revolutionary-war/music/.

GET IN THE SPIRIT: If you can't get enough of the fife and drum or just want to jazz up your next July 4th barbecue, queue up The Spirit Of '76: Music for Fifes and Drums. Get it on YouTube: www.youtube.com/watch?v=dWf0BZ1yyTM.

DECLARE YOUR INDEPENDENCE: Watch the *The Patriot (2000)*. Mel Gibson plays Benjamin Martin, who is reviled by the French for his alleged atrocities during the French and Indian War, a secret he had hoped to carry to the grave with him. Yet, he must ally himself with the French to achieve independence. Sound familiar? Enjoy what is basically Braveheart set in South Carolina and without the kilts. Even the enemy is the same. Will those British never learn?

DOODLE LIKE A YANKEE: Drawing, or doodling, is more than just a random time waster. Studies show it can aid concentration and productivity as well as providing an outlet for your everyday creative impulses. So, grab a pencil and sketch and scribble when you can. Check out a few examples on Pinterest: www.pinterest.com/explore/random-doodle.

All About the Benjamins

Ben Franklin & Diversification

1706–1790 AD

For Ben Franklin, offering homespun advice came easily. The author of Poor Richard's Almanac invented idioms as easily as he mastered science, played politics, and charmed the ladies. But the expression which he exemplified best was one he couldn't claim as his own: "don't put all your eggs in one basket."[120]

"Grandfather, are we there yet?" The coach and four rumbled over cobblestones, jostling the whining seven-year-old about his seat. His sixteen-year-old companion sighed and elbowed the boy, though he too was wondering the same thing.

"Hush child," said the elderly man on the bench across from him, barely glancing up from his book.

"But grandfather… I need to go," the boy whined.

---

120 The origin of the phrase isn't known, but is believed to have its roots in Miguel Cervantes' *Don Quixote,* written in the 1600s.

The man sighed and put down his book. "You should have gone before we left Palaiseau." His French was rough, but passable and he smiled to himself with a trace of vanity. He could, he thought, learn whatever he put his mind to.

"Yeah," chimed the older boy "you should have gone before we left Pally's Zoo." His French was non-existent. He stuck out his tongue and for added emphasis he gave the younger boy a swat on the back of his head.

"Boys," said the elderly man in a plain brown suit and coonskin hat, "I will have this cart pulled over and no one will go to Paris if you two don't settle down." Benjamin Franklin showed his best stern face.

The boys glowered but remained mercifully silent as the coach rumbled on. Their grandfather returned to his reading, though how he could manage it with his poor vision and the dim light of France in the winter, neither boy could tell. After what seemed like everlasting eternity to the boys, the coach rumbled and skidded to a stop.[121]

"Monsieur," called the coachman, "Nous arrivons."

"Merci," Franklin exclaimed, suddenly full of energy. "Merci indeed." Franklin, five feet ten inches tall and squarely built, emerged from the coach into a maelstrom of humanity on Paris's Ponte Neuf. To his right was the seemingly unending pale stone colonnades and gray-green rooftops of the Louvre Palace. The River Seine flowed in front of him;

121 The older boy, William Temple Franklin was the illegitimate son of Ben Franklin's own illegitimate son, yet still called the old man grandfather. Benny Franklin Bache was the (legitimate) son of Franklin's daughter Sally. William would be Franklin's personal secretary and learn French quite well, returning there to live out his days and be buried in Père Lachaise Cemetery. Grandfather would fix part of his vision problem, inventing bifocal spectacles around 1784.

a dark, frothy smudge with a few hearty boatmen lolling in the current, seemingly rowing only in order to keep warm. Over his left shoulder loomed the gothic shadow of the Cathedral of Notre Dame and to his left, in the distance, the great golden dome of the Hôtel des Invalides reached into the sullen winter sky. After weeks of travel and intrigue, Benjamin Franklin and his unusual entourage were in Paris.[122]

Franklin's oval face at once took on the pensive look he became known for in portraiture. He didn't travel abroad often, few really did, but he had seen cities as large as London, and his immediate impression of Paris was not grand. To be sure, his native Philadelphia was a quaint backwater in comparison. But while the city around him was large and bustling it was not *beautiful*. Beyond the gold and stone facades were ramshackle buildings and tenements and a pervasive smell of human beings and horseflesh working and living in near proximity.[123]

"Monsieur Franklin?" He turned and bowed deeply to a lovely woman in her mid-thirties surrounded by a phalanx of servants.

"My name is Anne-Catherine, and my servants are here

---

122 Franklin was dispatched by the Continental Congress in October of 1776 and departed Philadelphia on October 26th. He and the boys dodged British patrols aboard the sloop Reprisal for over thirty days, landing at the mouth of the Loire River in early December and reaching Paris on the 21st.
123 Paris in the latter part of the eighteenth century lacked the modern charm of what became the City of Lights (La Ville Lumière). The plan of the modern city, with its wide avenues and large green spaces, wasn't instituted until the 1850s, when many slums and tenements were demolished. Monuments such as the Arc de Triomphe and Tour Eiffel wouldn't appear until 1806 and 1889, respectively.

to help you secure lodging. Welcome to Paris."

Franklin instantly transformed from a pensive old man to a frantically attentive suitor, bowing, scraping, and kissing her proffered hand. "Ah, did you now my dear? I am happy to have you…I mean have your company." The boys, extricating themselves stiffly from the carriage, rolled their eyes.

"And all of France is happy to host someone of your stature. I personally have followed your career and scientific discoveries and simply must insist you join my salon as soon as possible." Franklin lit up like the key at the end of his kite.[124]

Linking arms with the lady he would come to admire if not adore, he beamed at his charges as they fell in step behind them. "I believe we'll be alright here in Paris boys."[125]

It wasn't always easy for Franklin to mix with high class Parisians. He'd been born seventy years prior in a Boston home that reeked of beef fat. His father, Josiah made candles and soap from rendered fat or tallow, a decent trade but barely enough to sustain his seventeen children and stepchildren. Clearly, young Benjamin had to do something

---

124 Franklin's experiment with a kite in an electrical storm was well known, as was his attentiveness to the fairer sex. Thomas Jefferson was amused: "I have marked him particularly in the company of women where he loses all power over himself and becomes almost frenzied." The more Puritan minded John Adams was less so: "Franklin at the age of seventy-odd has neither lost his love of beauty nor his taste for it."

125 Anne-Catherine de Ligniville, Madame Helvétius (July 23, 1722–August 12, 1800) was a widowed aristocrat whose gatherings, known as salons, attracted the wealthy and powerful of Paris and beyond. Franklin would come to call her Notre Dame, profess his love, and ask for her hand in marriage. She would decline, but they remained friends and saw each other often.

special to stand out among his brood. With little formal education, he fell in love early with books and reading, became a writer, and opened his own printing business. He founded the first public library, experimented with electricity and ocean currents, retired at forty-two, and dabbled in politics. He was doubtless the most interesting man in the world of the eighteenth century. Indeed, it was Franklin's varied career that opened the doors to the salons of Europe where he gained prominence in the political arena. His celebrity would be the key to the French Royal Court and American Independence.[126]

Franklin did not speak French all that well, despite his confidence in his abilities, and it might have been difficult to do much good barging in to see the King. So, Franklin used social engagements around Paris to flirt with women of power like Madame Helvétius, gaining introductions to men he would find useful, such as the Comptes de Vergennes, Minister of Foreign Affairs. In parlors of elegant mansions along the Tuileries Gardens, the upper-class citizens of Paris wore the finest fashions and held elaborate parties. Franklin ambled onto the stage with a furry hat, no powdered wig, and a few simple suits. To French eyes, he was a fascinating cross between genius and backwoods simpleton.[127]

---

126 During the creation of America, Franklin is the only person to have signed the Declaration of Independence, Treaty of Alliance with France, Treaty of Paris, and the United States Constitution, the four major documents that helped establish this country.

127 The French grew to adore him and threw their own wigs into the ring against Britain. In 1790, when Franklin passed away at the age of eighty-four, his death sparked the largest funeral ever seen in Philadelphia with some twenty thousand attendees. Not to be outdone, the French National Assem-

Writer, scientist, printer, humorist, rake, statesman, inventor, political theorist; Benjamin Franklin was a man whose diverse talents were as immense as the country he helped establish. Franklin's notable range demonstrated an important concept both in colonial life and for those who have endured the subsequent centuries. **Diversification** mitigated his risk of becoming obsolete in one area and negatively affecting his earnings, net-worth, or prestige.

Franklin's wide-ranging interests made him an eighteenth-century star, one whose financial security was without doubt. Lacking politics, he could easily make a living as a scientist. Devoid of science, he could go back to printing or writing. **Diversification** means having a wide spectrum of varying skills to reduce overall volatility and risk. Over time it just may earn *and* save you many dollar bills featuring Ben's likeness. If you put your mind to it.[128]

---

bly proclaimed three national days of mourning.
128 Franklin appears on the one-hundred-dollar bill.

How You'll Be Tested...

For investors, diversification can be difficult because it violates a primary rule of great financiers like Warren Buffet, who tells us to "invest in what we know." But what if "what you know" is tallow candle making, dial up internet, or some other antiquated industry? You probably wouldn't get one kid through college investing there, much less seventeen of them. And forget about retiring at forty-two. You likely need a lot more than just "what you know."

Diversification is also difficult because it goes against natural tendencies to hoard "winners" and become emotionally attached to companies we like. Someday you'll be tempted to either 1) let a hot stock or fund ride because it has been on a tear or 2) buy and continue to buy in irrational quantities either the stock of the company you work for, or the one your grandfather swore you should never sell. Either way, you will be concentrating your 'Benjamins' and hoping it doesn't come back to bite you. When you do, imagine Franklin glaring down at you from over his bifocals. Hope is usually a poor speculative strategy while **diversification** is a key to enlightened investing.

EXTRA CREDIT

GET BIG ON BEN: Learn more by reading *Benjamin Franklin: An American Life (2004)*, by Walter Isaacson. Or, if you want the highlights, check out the author as part of the Gilder Lehman Institute of American History lecture series: www. vimeo.com/19297476. And if that is still too much work for you, you can read and watch a biographical sketch at: www. biography.com/people/benjamin-franklin-9301234. I'd recommend studying up though to take the Ben Franklin quiz at: http://quizzes.howstuffworks.com/quiz/benjamin-franklin-quiz.

GO DEEPER ON DIVERSIFICATION: If you put all your money on one number when spinning a roulette wheel, you can win a lot if you get lucky. But spreading out your bets gives you a better chance of a more modest take and a lower chance of breaking the bank. A perfect example of diversification at work, or rather at play. Read up on the magic of more at: https://money.howstuffworks.com/personal-finance/financial-planning/diversification.htm.

GO MAVERICK: Enjoy an alternate perspective from billionaire and owner of the Dallas Mavericks, Mark Cuban. Cuban says diversification is "for idiots." He of course made all his money from the sale, at the height of the internet mania, of broadcast.com which didn't quite have the staying power of the Franklin stove or the lightening rod. So, in a single lesson, I'm basically telling you to go ignore advice from Warren Buffet and an Internet billionaire with an NBA championship ring. What can I say? Buffets are where you eat, and Cubans are for smoking. Light up at: www.youtube.com/watch?v=u5Pp1HEKSPM.

HAVE FUN WITH FICTION: Check out Disney's *National Treasure (2004)*. Benjamin Franklin Gates, played by Nicolas Cage, is a historian adventurer, and hey, aren't we all? He's out to find a lost Templar treasure hidden by the Founding Fathers, at least those, including Benjamin Franklin, who belonged to the secretive sect of Freemasons. Yes, it is a poor man's Dan Brown novel. Disney, poor? Jeez, how many American icons can you insult in one lesson?

TRY, TRY, TRY TO DIVERSIFY: Or don't, it is your choice using this simulation where you can put together one or more portfolios and then see how they do over time on Market Watch's Virtual Stock Exchange. Launch your own experiments at: www.marketwatch.com/game/.

GET UP AND ADAMS: See the mini-series, *John Adams*, on HBO Now or HBO Go. Episode Four introduces the puritanical Adams to Franklin in France at the height of his Parisian powers of persuasion. Sparks fly: www.hbo.com/john-adams.

Going Postal

Wilson Price Hunt & Risk Premium

1817 AD

Amerian explorers and adventurers of the nineteenth century grasped that there were great fortunes to be made on the frontier. But there is no free lunch, rewards being proportional to risk. Indeed, the privations of the frontier meant there was often no lunch at all unless you were well provisioned.[129]

The damn streets are a mess! thought the shopkeeper, wading through ankle-high mud on Main Street. It had been a hard, rainy winter and as he approached his store, the mighty Mississippi River came into view over one hundred feet below, brooding and storm swollen. Down the bluff it churned and thrashed its way south through a narrow but deep channel toward New Orleans and the Gulf of Mexico.

---

129 Sources vary on when and where the free lunch was terminated. But Ben Franklin didn't say this either. Scripps-Howard Newspapers published an article in 1938 in response to the New Deal titled *Economics in Eight Words*, the punchline was: "There ain't no such thing as free lunch."

But spring was coming and soon the first of the travelers heading west would be provisioning here in St. Louis. In fact, he could already hear American voices with eastern accents mingled with French, Spanish, and Native Americans around the city's two taverns. So, he wasn't surprised to find two men waiting for him as he approached the door to the shop.

"We've come to fit ourselves out," announced the taller of the two. He had to repeat himself. The three blacksmiths in town were hammering out the necessary wares for the horses coming to and from the west, adding their clamor to that of carriage wheels on unpaved roads. The shopkeeper, who had some familiarity with New York, recognized the accent.

"Heading west? Furs?" He asked.

The second man held a handkerchief over his mouth and nose and bobbed his head in affirmation. Not much had changed in the shopkeeper's time in St. Louis, including the treatment of human and animal wastes and a distinct frontier odor permeated the town. It looked, sounded and smelled every bit like a border outpost in 1817.[130]

"You are that Hunt fella, aren't you? The one who set up Astoria before the war?" asked the first man, following him into the dimly lit anteroom.

"That's me. Wilson Price Hunt, shopkeeper turned wayward adventurer and now back again." He shook their hands in turn.

---

130 St. Louis had only replaced the French Flag with that of the United States in 1804 and wouldn't incorporate as a city for another five years. The boom period between 1820 and the breakout of the American Civil War would see the streets paved and fix most of the sanitation problems.

"Why, you are famous!" proclaimed the taller man, clearly the one more prone to chat. "Tell us what it was like to get all the way the Pacific." Hunt's store had been in New York City when a bull of man with a slightly Teutonic accent dropped by in 1809. John Jacob Astor, head of the American Fur Company was looking for a young and able administrator to lead an overland expedition following Lewis and Clark's route westward. There they would set up a fur trading community on the coast. Astor's money and sense of adventure were irresistible, and Hunt had signed on, getting much more than he had bargained for in the process.[131]

Now, Hunt stood still for a moment and he gradually got a dreamy, far-away look in his eyes. "It was hard," he murmured taking a seat near the counter and beckoning the men to do the same. "Really hard." He went on, over the course of an hour to tell his story in the same, slightly haunted tone. Hunt had struck out from St. Louis in the fall of 1810 with a party of fifty-nine including a pregnant woman, and two children despite lacking meaningful experience with an expedition of the intended size. Just fifty-four of them made it all the way to the west coast.

"We canoed up the Missouri River for a few hundred miles, made winter quarters, and then set out on foot and by horse. The progress was slow. The Natives tracked us, sometimes threatening to attack, sometimes wanting to trade and sometimes merely curious. But it was hard to know the difference. By the time we reached the Snake River

---

131   There was also the inconvenient fact that, notwithstanding his surname, he wasn't much of an outdoorsman.

we were hungry and exhausted. You don't sleep much when you are worried about having your throat slit in the night." Hunt ran a finger across his Adam's apple for emphasis. The men's eyes went a bit wider and their faces lost color.

"We lost our first man at the Snake River, though we called it the Mad River then. We had abandoned the horses and were on canoes. Nine days in we hit heavy water that tossed the boats about like child's toys and sprayed cold water all over us. Two of the canoes overturned and we never saw them again, dragged under and probably smashed on the rocks. Everyone was thrown in the water and we were able to get to them except for that one man. We barely recognized his body when it came out of the rapids. Bruised and bloated, neck cracked like a twig." Hunt snapped his finger and both of his listeners visibly flinched.

"We split up then, four groups trying to make it through the mountains and find the mouth of the Columbia River. Well, we made it. Some of us anyway. It took us 340 days in all. Most of them we were hungry, many of them we were cold or freezing. All of them I was scared for my life."[132]

With that, he seemed to come back into the room, to the present. "So, gentlemen. Since you are heading west for a great adventure, what can I get for you?"

---

132 Hunt's adventure wasn't quite over. Established at the outpost of Astoria in Oregon he ranged as far as Alaska trading for seal skins, and Hawaii where he found himself stranded by a ship in need of repairs. On his return to Astoria, he found his partners ready to abandon the post in the face of the British military threat when war broke out in 1812. He returned to New York in 1816 and remained on good terms with Astor. Astor, however, published a book somewhat critical of Hunt's long absences from Astoria where he might have prevented his Scottish partners, who retained British citizenship, from selling out to the Crown for pennies on the dollar.

The man with the kerchief dropped it to his side for the first time, revealing a mouth agape. "You know what? Let us think on it." said the taller man, "Come on!" He said to his partner. "Let's see if the saloon is still open."

As the men retreated, Wilson Price Hunt called after them, "If you decide to stay in St. Louis, I've got some prime real estate for sale." He laughed when the door closed. Voyages like his weren't for everyone.

The experience of crossing the continent may seem like the stuff of adventure tales, but those who did it were often left scarred by the journey. For Hunt, the feeling was more of being lucky to have survived despite his inexperience. His journal of the year-long journey reads more like a newspaper column about the abundance and variety of prairie grasses on the route than a dime store novel. He skims over the swamping of his boats on the Snake River and their encounters with Native tribes. Excitement was apparently *not* his thing, despite his early desires to the contrary.[133]

A frontier hero to some, and romanticized in future years as exemplifying the spirit of wild adventure, Hunt's later life reveals a desire to live a much quieter existence. After settling affairs with Astor in New York, Hunt returned to St. Louis, eventually making his living in real estate when the town boomed. He also went on to become the city postmaster. For a man who had crossed great mountains and rivers it was probably the most boring position imaginable.

---

133 Meriwether Lewis also blazed the trail of men and women left mentally bereft by their experiences in the west. He suffered deep bouts of depression and committed suicide in 1809.

And that was how he appeared to prefer it.

FLUCTUATING FIGURES

While most investors know that they should get something for taking on risk, for instance, buying stocks instead of bonds, they are widely confounded as to how much reward is realistic. In turn, estimates of the ERP or Equity Risk Premium (how much return you should receive from stocks above a risk-free investment, like a US Treasury bond) vary widely and are subject to a fair amount of mythology.

A number of investors believe that an 8% ERP is normal, and others are convinced that it is 5% and static across markets. Neither of these beliefs withstand much research and scrutiny. The 8% figure only held up during the last half of the twentieth century, while 5% prevailed during the first half.

Current backward-looking risk premiums range from 3–5% when comparing bond and stock indexes since 1950. So, it is reasonable to expect something for your efforts, but while there are no free lunches, there are no guarantees either.

Wilson Price Hunt was initially all for taking risks to get wealthy, the rewards seemingly well worth it. Then he endured those very risks and found the rewards insufficient to make him ever do it again. Understanding the **Risk Premium,** how much you would need to earn in return for exposing yourself to peril, is the key for those of us who are merely risking our personal fortunes and not our lives. Over the long term, taking on more risks should mean bigger rewards than taking few or more moderate ones, otherwise, there is no incentive to brave the wild at all.

How You'll Be Tested...

Investors tend to worry about risk when markets are frothy and focus on returns when the bourses are becalmed. They forget that the two are related, that you don't get returns without risk, and the occasional setback is the price you pay for long-term earnings. If you feel yourself becoming less adventurous when the market turns against you, it is time to revisit your plan. What premium are you seeking and what risks are you willing to take?

Luckily there is an easier way to think about **risk premium**. You don't need to assess it for every position in your portfolio. You just need to plan a reasonable rate of return that meets your goals and build an assortment of investments that together will realistically reach that return. Let history be your guide. But also, be sure to look at how that portfolio performed in tough times. What kind of results did it produce in 2008 or 2001? Is the potential loss worth the potential gain? Can't handle the periodic adventures to the downside? Then it is okay to avoid them. Stay home. Be boring. But realize that without some risk, your overall returns are destined to be boring too, and so might the retirement for which you are saving.

EXTRA CREDIT

BUILD AND LOSE AN EMPIRE: No one outside the Pacific Northwest seems to remember much about the Astor party. Peter Stark, writing a book about the last open spaces in America checked into a hotel in John Day, Oregon and began to change that. Who was John Day, he wondered? When he found out that the trapper had come west with an overland expedition, was robbed and stripped naked in the wilderness, only to survive physically but lose his mind, Stark knew he had a book in the making. Check out his work *Astoria: John Jacob Astor and Thomas Jefferson's Lost Pacific Empire: A Story of Wealth, Ambition, and Survival (2014).* And get a taste for the adventure at: www.opb.org/artsandlife/article/author-peter-stark-explores-astoria-the-lost-pacific-empire/.

PLAY AROUND: If you can't read the book, see the play. Chris Coleman wrote and directed an adaptation of Stark's book for the stage in two parts. See a behind the scenes peek with the actress who plays the lone woman on the Astor expedition: www.youtube.com/watch?v=arFQ65hdgls. So far, the play's only run has been at the Portland (Oregon) Center Stage. Worth the trip, even if it is an adventure for you to get there.

GET THE FULL MONTY: Check out the official Let's Make a Deal YouTube feed at: www.youtube.com/user/LetsMakeADeal-CBS. The CBS gameshow is now hosted by Wayne Brady in the role that Monty Hall made famous. Now imagine yourself as a contestant, having done well enough to win $500. But Wayne asks you if you'd like to walk away with that money or choose from one of two doors? Behind one door will be $1,000, but behind the other is nothing. For $500 risked, you can win $500. Contestants who are risk averse will take the money and run. To get more contestants to make things interesting, the show might change the payout behind one of the doors to $1,500. They've doubled the risk premium. Note that gameshows, like the lottery, are not for investment purposes and should be played for entertainment only.

DON'T BE DAUNTED: The original historical recounting of a trip through the wilderness to the Pacific is Stephen E. Ambrose's *Undaunted Courage: Meriwether Lewis, Thomas Jefferson, and the Opening of the American West.* After reading of their trials and the suicide of Lewis, it is a wonder anyone followed in their footsteps. Which tells you just how high the potential profits were for Astor and Hunt.

BE BRIEF: The University of Texas McCombs School of Business presents a series of videos decoding various financial lingo. Their explanation of the risk premium takes about a minute: www.youtube.com/watch?v=u6HTfuCB2nY. If you are watching while on a wilderness journey, roaming and data charges may apply.

On the Money

Salmon P. Chase & Compounding

1861AD

The easiest way to make more money is to already have some at the start. Earn it yourself or ask your parents for it, whatever it takes. And then? Just picture where you might end up if you leave it alone and let it work for you.

Great beads of sweat formed on his prominent dome of a forehead as Washington D.C. baked in the heat of July. Even a late afternoon breeze blowing off the Potomac gave him no respite. He was anxious, feared the worst, and now had to go to Father for help.

"Sir, I need to ask you for something. You won't like it." He felt meek and small and he continued to dab at his forehead with a kerchief.

"Well, it won't be the first time, now will it?" Father said, not unkindly.

"I need money." There, it was out now. He felt relief. He pocketed the handkerchief and wrung his sweaty hands.

"Money?" Father seemed disappointed. "You've gotten quite a bit already."

"Yes, I know. But…" There was so much to say, but none of it new nor particularly compelling, so he just stopped.

"Tell me about it." President Abraham Lincoln, Father Abraham, arched an eyebrow and waited, arms crossed.[134]

Treasury Secretary, Salmon P. Chase frowned, furrowing his ample brow. He thought, *how to explain such things to a backwoods lawyer?* For it wasn't personal funding Chase required. No, Mr. Chase was always more concerned with power than personal gain and wealth.

It was the funding of a country suddenly tearing itself apart that interrupted his sleep and gave him sweating fits. That and the damnable Washington weather and the occasional rumble of guns far away to the south and west. [135]

"Well, sir, you realize we are just a few years clear of the Panic of 1857 and have had no paper money in circulation since the 1770s." Lincoln nodded, and Chase continued. "The United States needs a way to raise funds for more men and supplies, while being virtually shut out of the global bond market."

"Yes," Lincoln sighed, "who would want to buy bonds

---

134 "We are coming, Father Abraham, Three Hundred Thousand More" were the opening lines of James Sloan Gibbons 1862 poem enthusiastically endorsing Lincoln's call for more troops to defeat the Southern insurrection.
135 The former Senator and Governor from Ohio had his own Presidential ambitions derailed by the man who became his boss, a little-known lawyer from Illinois named Abraham Lincoln. Chase had been instrumental in forming the Republican Party and may have expected the nomination at the 1860 convention. When it became clear that he didn't have much support outside of his native Ohio, he backed Lincoln. This earned him a spot in the administration, though that was a blessing and a curse due to their tempestuous relationship.

Patrick Huey

from a country split in two?"

"Quite right, Mr. President. Congress authorized non-interest-bearing notes on whatever credit we still have. But the demand notes can be exchanged in various locations where we hold sufficient coin on hand to redeem them."

"And?" One knew Lincoln, the noted storyteller, was agitated when his sentences consisted of a single word.

"Well, we are finding that many banks won't accept the notes at all. After Fort Sumter fell, redemptions soared and depleted our stores of coin, silver, and gold. It has happened again in the last few days as the Rebels have threatened Harper's Ferry. If we aren't in Richmond soon we'll find ourselves insolvent."[136]

Lincoln was quieter than Chase had ever witnessed. Part of him was relieved to have unloaded the problem on his Chief. And another part was happy to see Lincoln's discomfort. *Father Abraham, indeed.* A knock at the door interrupted the reverie of the two sometime rivals. A secretary appeared and handed the President a note.

Lincoln took the note and grimaced. "It is worse than we thought Chase."

"Worse. Dear God, Mr. President, how could it be any worse?"

"The war won't be over quickly. We'll need more men. And probably more money than even you can dream up. The Rebels have pressed their attack at Bull Run. We are retreating." He looked at Chase and then quickly seemed to move

---

136 Clearly the ability to convert notes on demand was not going to work unless the war was won quickly, which everyone assumed it would be with troops bellowing "On to Richmond!" and massing in Northern Virginia for an impending movement south.

on from the shock.

"We'll endure Chase, we have to," he said. "Why, it reminds me of the story about the boy who wants a horse for his birthday but only gets a pile of horse manure. He doesn't weep or wallow, he grabs a shovel. When everyone asks what he is doing, he says, 'Digging. Because there has to be a horse there somewhere.'"[137]

The Secretary looked at the bumpkin turned politician and knew that he, Salmon P. Chase, had a golden opportunity to get the wheels of finance moving, win this war and supplant his boss as President in 1864. It was time to get to work.

In the aftermath of the defeat at Bull Run, Chase took his own pay in the suspect demand notes. He also encouraged soldiers in the field to use them to send money home. Those notes came in three denominations: $5, $10, and $20 and featured pictures of Lincoln, Alexander Hamilton, and a depiction of Lady Liberty. On the back of each note was a green design field spelling out the dollar amount and the infamous reminder that: "This note is legal tender for all debts public and private..." The notes became known as greenbacks. The nickname stuck and eventually became synonymous with American dollars of all types and denominations.[138]

---

137 Lincoln was well known to use, or perhaps overuse, stories and anecdotes to get his points across. When another Ohioan, Congressman James Ashley, disapproved of one of them, the President told him: "Ashley, I have great confidence in you and great respect for you, and I know how sincere you are. But if I couldn't tell these stories, I would die." This particular story, though, comes from a different presidential source. It was a favorite of Ronald Reagan.

138 When the legal tender notes were first printed, Chase had his picture put on the one most widely circulated, the $1 note. After all, at the time he was still aiming for his boss's job. What better way to run for President in 1864 than to distribute your picture every time people got paid? Despite

Chase also pushed through Congress, in February of 1862, a second series of "legal tender" notes. Legal tender notes did not entitle anyone to convert them into any physical specie or precious metal. They were fiat money, obligating all parties in a domestic transaction to use them as payment. A month later demand notes were also given legal tender status. Since the legal tender notes were not yet in circulation and the demand notes were, the latter became the first paper money to change hands in the United States. Having the hard currency on hand without worrying about backing the notes helped Chase and the government fund and eventually win the American Civil War.[139]

It was important to the war effort that the populace avoided pulling money out of demand notes whenever the whim struck. And it is equally important for individuals to allow their own greenbacks a respite from the world at large. That's because in a market-based economy, the concept of

the free marketing scheme, Lincoln defeated Chase at the 1864 Republican convention and eventually moved him out of the Treasury. Chase's picture was removed from the $1 note and replaced by George Washington.

139 While Chase turned out to be uniquely fit to the task of leading the Treasury, he became a victim of his own success. Having moved the United States onto surer financial footing in his term, he became expendable given his frequent arguments with the President and his cabinet. Chase offered to resign numerous times in the first term, but Lincoln dared not lose the support of the secretary's Radical Abolitionist wing of the party. With the 1864 election won, the hot-tempered Chase overplayed his hand. Lincoln simply accepted the next resignation offer Chase made, moved him out of the executive branch and then nominated him to be Chief Justice of the Supreme Court. Only Father Abraham could make a sacking look like a promotion.

Compounding is the largest creator of wealth we have. An asset that generates earnings on its own earnings accelerates and amplifies its growth, even if you don't add more money to it. Which, of course, you should do anyway; contributing more money and saving whenever possible.

──── IT'S ALL RELATIVE ────

With compounding, the rate of increase is proportional to the amount or quantity of capital, but this concept also works in other fields. It isn't always *just* about the money. The compounding phenomenon of continuous growth is a natural law of organic development and transformation.

In chemistry, it can be said that the hotter a body is relative to its surrounding, the more rapidly it will cool. Also, the velocity of a chemical reaction will increase the more of the chemical is present. Research botanists have found that ordinary plants increase their leaf area faster, all things being equal, when the leaf is larger.

In general, across numerous disciplines "the rate of change in some quantity is proportional to the quantity itself." That is, the rate of change is relative to the size of the object. That would make this the Theory of Relativity except some hack named Albert Einstein already turned that phrase. Speaking of Einstein, the world's most famous physicist allegedly called compounding one of the universe's most powerful forces. But there is scant evidence he ever said such a thing and a lot of stuff gets misattributed to geniuses. Yet the more people believe he said it, the faster the misconception spreads. You could say the problem compounds.

The reinvestment of earnings or interest creates exponential growth as long as you do something seemingly simple: leave things alone. Redemptions hurt the greater cause. And bad news shouldn't coax you into bad decisions like moving money. Chase got that right. Indeed, it is too bad money never mattered as much as power to Salmon Chase. While he never became President, from 1928 to 1946 his picture reappeared on circulating money, this time on the $10,000 bill to celebrate his role in creating the currency. Lincoln and Washington *combined* only ever amounted to six bucks and some change.

How You'll Be Tested...

Investors are notorious for schemes to use money before it is time, like loans on their 401(k) or early distributions for dubious expenses. Even worse, their attempts at market timing usually mean they have money on the sidelines when markets rally and miss out on potential **compounding**. In the future, you may be tempted by such seemingly innocent ideas as to pull a bit of money from a retirement account early, or to partially go to cash when the market is going against you. But once you've missed out on any amount of earnings, that money and its own future earnings are gone. Those funds will be forever missing from your accounts. And, unless you print your own money, they can never be recovered.[140]

Run the numbers. Websites like Bankrate.com or Inves-

---

140 Not a recommended strategy as it breaks more than just the law of compounding.

tor.gov have free calculators to determine what a sum now would be after compounding for a number of years. By now, you aren't a financial bumpkin and can determine if you want to part with the future sum for today's short-term gain. The idea is to make more intelligent choices, so you can out do Salmon Chase and have both the power *and* the money.

EXTRA CREDIT

CREATE A RIVALRY: Learn more about the election of 1860 and the *Team of Rivals* (2005) that Abraham Lincoln assembled, including a scheming Secretary of the Treasury. Doris Kearns Goodwin's book won the annual prize for the best book about Lincoln, but it is his lieutenants who steal most of the show.

TEAM UP: Steven Spielberg used Goodwin's book as a basis for the move *Lincoln (2012)*, which is worth a look too. For his portrayal of Father Abraham, Daniel Day-Lewis became the first winner of three best actor awards. Chase doesn't appear in the film as he was out of the administration by 1865 when the film takes place. But the movie gets a lot right about Lincoln, his personality and how he managed his team. Though the teammates are a bit less historically accurate: www.theatlantic.com/entertainment/archive/2012/11/fact-checking-lincoln-lincolns-mostly-realistic-his-advisers-arent/265073/.

FOLLOW THE MONEY: You might expect a website like www.moneyfactory.gov to take you to a payday lender or the Federal Reserve. Instead, you get introduced to the Bureau of Engraving and Printing where you can turn in mutilated currency, buy sets of $2 bills and explore how our money is designed, engraved, and sent to the printers. You can also read up on the history of cash in the United States, including the fact that "all currency issued since 1861 remains valid and redeemable at face value." Yes, a few bucks from the Civil War can still be redeemed if you have them. But try not to think about all the compounding you missed over one hundred and fifty years.

GO MAD WITH ME: You may think I've lost it and gone completely crazy. After bashing Jim Cramer, television pundits, and mass media in general, I'm sending you to a link from his show on CNBC: www.cnbc.com/2017/09/22/cramer-how-compounding-can-help-you-double-your-money-in-7-years.html. Jim calls compounding "magical." And I could agree with him... if the sidebar in this chapter hadn't clearly shown that it is science!

PUMP UP: You only see results in a fitness program, as previous successes build upon each other. The key is to work out regularly and see gains over a long period of time. That is a decent metaphor for explaining how compounding works courtesy of the Department of Defense and their retirement plan: www.youtube.com/watch?v=6YssFtJ1J58. Then pump up even more with a motivational video courtesy of Saturday Night Live: www.nbc.com/saturday-night-live/video/pumping-up-with-hans-andamp-franz/n9619?snl=1.

Shaving Face
Ambrose Burnside & Action Tendency

1863 AD

Asoldier on either side of the American Civil War spent long periods of time fighting nothing more than boredom. From time to time, that was replaced by the terror of combat which produced the highest proportion of casualties, compared to population, of any American war. Soldiers in blue and gray learned the more exciting path isn't necessarily the safest or most prosperous.

It was a cold January night, clear and biting. The Federal encampment at Falmouth was a barren, brown gash cutting across the Virginia countryside. Blue clad soldiers sat in circles around small fires amidst the ghostly, billowing white shapes of camp tents. They were grateful for the warmth on their dirt smeared faces and their lean hungry bodies. Flames leapt and cast a gloomy glow, while an occasional spark popped loudly enough to make them all flinch. Otherwise they sat stone faced, occasionally clanking a metal spoon into a bowl of brown broth. The only other sounds were the low murmurs of conversation, hundreds of them, across the campground.

"Looks like a rider headed this way." The enemy for many days now had not just been the army on the other side of the Rappahannock River, it had been boredom. Boredom that sapped any energy, leaving them sluggish, slow, and irritable. The only thing worse than boredom was some damn fool interrupting you with a menial army task. So, no one even moved when the messenger appeared and dismounted.

"New orders boys, fresh from the top." The word fresh hung in the air as they lingered over a meal of stale hardtack and some moldy vegetables softened into a soup.

"Wonderful, what damn fool thing have they cooked up at headquarters this time?" The word "cook" also drew sharp glances. Before the New Year the cooking had been just fine. An occasional deer from the woods, or a ham illegally acquired from a nearby farm. Sometimes preserved peaches for desert, whiskey, and Virginia tobacco. But the holidays were over, the luxuries from home long consumed and the local farmers fled to retain some of their possessions and dignity.

"Yeah. New orders for what? Don't they know it is January up there at headquarters? Don't they have a dang calendar?" Throughout the nineteenth century, armies in the field followed a seasonal schedule, maneuvering and fighting during the summer months and digging in to lie low during the winter. Traditional wisdom held that maneuverability was too difficult in the wetter winter months, as roads drained poorly, and animals and wagons easily bogged down in such conditions.

"Well, I suppose, you ignorant farm boy, that General Burnside, graduate of West Point Military Academy figures he knows a bit more than you do."[141]

"Yeah, well even I could see we shouldn't have been attacking Fredericksburg. Any idiot could have seen it." They all went quiet at that, a silence spent remembering the horrors of friends cut down on an open expanse of upward sloping field. The messenger turned on a heel, mounted, and rode off without further discussion.[142]

The orders, it turned out, were to prepare to move again.

---

141 A graduate of West Point in 1847, Burnside was a good student, but lacked much of the discipline necessary to succeed in such a regimented life. He graduated eighteenth in a mostly undistinguished class of thirty-eight. Confederate General A.P. Hill was the only other notable Civil War officer in the class of '47. Contrast that with the likes of Thomas (Stonewall) Jackson, George McClellan, and George Pickett in the class just ahead ('46) all of whom became General Officers on one side of the conflict or the other. Burnside went on to serve primarily on garrison duty in the Mexican War. He resigned in 1853 to manufacture rifles but the company failed. Defeated in a Congressional election he found work as the treasurer of the Illinois Central Railroad, joined the militia, and won on his second try at Congress. Back in the army at the outbreak of war, Burnside led a brigade of infantry at Bull Run and an expeditionary force into North Carolina for which he was promoted. His early date of rank and successive failures by those ahead of him propelled him into leadership of the entire Army of the Potomac in the winter of 1862. Things got a bit hairy after that.

142 Immediately after taking command the previous December, Burnside had directed his men straight into the Confederate forces at Fredericksburg and was bloodily repulsed. The crescendo of the four-day engagement came at a low rise above the river plain called Marye's Heights. The Confederate Artillerist Lt. Col. Edward Porter Alexander told his boss that he had the field of fire approaching the crest of the hill covered so well that a chicken wouldn't survive once they opened their bombardment. Burnside attacked several times to test the theory, resulting in thousands of casualties and an eventual withdrawal back to his winter encampment.

Burnside had something to prove and he couldn't do it sitting still, he needed to be in motion. Showing a disregard for history, precedent, and the weather, he ordered his entire army out of winter encampments and onto the roads leading north and west along the river, to flank Robert E Lee's smaller force.[143]

Fredericksburg had been a head-on attack with all the tactical nuance of a drunken saloon fight. Now Burnside's men tried to maneuver, relying on speed and the element of surprise. January, to that point, had been a dry month. But no sooner were they on the roads when it began to rain. And rain. And rain. Roads became bogs, traffic ground to a halt, and hourly progress was measured in yards. In one day, some units managed to move no more than a mile and a half. Confederates lined the opposite bank of the Rappahannock River and shouted insults, clearly destroying any notions of a surprise movement.

The rain continued. And, unfortunately, so did Burnside, whose ability to determine the worst possible course of action and then follow through on it became army lore. A contemporary complained that he "had no sense of timing and never knew when to stop." Which was hard to argue with as Burnside continued to throw resources at a bad plan until he was forced to turn back. Wet, cold, and with

---

143 A Lee versus Burnside matchup is laughable in retrospect. But Lee was still months away from his apogee as a commander, the bold strike at Chancellorsville that nearly wrecked the Federal Army. And Burnside had proved a decent officer and a good Corps Commander, so there was still some hope he might rise to the occasion of commanding the Army of the Potomac. It wasn't to be, and one suspects Burnside knew it all along. He had twice previously refused offers to direct the army perhaps knowing he would be out of his element.

a distinct air of defeat, the Army of the Potomac stumbled back to gather around the same fire pits, with the same complaints, to the same brothers in arms, minus the needless casualties inflicted on the infamous "Mud March."

"We should have had Hooker," someone groaned, flopping to the ground in exhaustion. Joe Hooker, had charge of a Grand Division at the Battle of Fredericksburg and was known for being an aggressive commander. He was also known for repeatedly conniving to replace his superiors and for the debauchery of his staff headquarters. Burnside was known to loathe him.

"We'll probably have him now."[144]

The night grew quiet but for the fire and the scraping of a razor across one man's face. They all turned to stare at him. He had shaved his chin and neck, leaving tufts of hair that emerged from the front of the ear and connected to each other via a mustache. It was the exact style worn by their commander.

"Hey boys, look at me, I've got me some Burnsides!"

"Call them sideburns instead. It's only right given how that damn fool is always mixing things up." For Ambrose Burnside, taking control and forcing the action were bad decisions. He might have faded from history had it not been for his distinctive facial hair. [145]

---

144 Hooker's tenure was short lived as well. His stunning defeat, and uncharacteristic lack of nerve at Chancellorsville forced Lincoln to continue searching for someone to command in the Eastern theatre.

145 While dramatized here, the story of sideburns becoming the term to honor the General's propensity for muddling things is true.

It is human nature to try and make things better by effort, motion, or change. That is our innate bias toward doing something, or **Action Tendency**. Action can feel good, especially when things are going badly. If we just do *something* it will be better than sitting still and letting things run their course. Burnside's example shows that this is not always the case. Indeed, we can often make a bad situation nearly intolerable with ill-conceived action.

How You'll Be Tested...

An investor is supposed to have a long-term outlook seeking price appreciation and using compounding of returns to her advantage. A trader, meanwhile, has a short-term outlook and seeks short term, incremental profits. He craves action and volatility and is concerned with the day-to-day or even minute-to-minute swings of the markets. As an investor, is it possible you might cross over and fall into the trading trap because you aren't ready for the emotional swings that markets can throw at you? When things go badly, will you satisfy your emotional needs with movement, effort, and action?

You know that you should choose a portfolio that won't scare you into making bad decisions and not deviate from that no matter the day-to-day temptations. But some day in the future, you may not want to hear that, despite the logic. Why? Because fear and greed are more powerful forces than many realize. Fear tempts people to sell low after suffering losses and greed to buy high when everyone else has already joined the march. This type of cycle does nothing for long-term investors but get them stuck as they shuffle back and forth between bad decisions. Sometimes doing nothing is the best strategy, especially for the clear majority of us who lack a perfect sense of timing. Here is an order to follow instead of blindly following your emotions: Soldier, don't just do *something*, stand there.

EXTRA CREDIT

FIGHT IT OUT: Civil War buffs have their own internal division over who wrote the greatest books on the conflict. Bruce Catton won the Pulitzer for *A Stillness at Appomattox* (1953), which is the completion of his *Army of the Potomac* trilogy and one of the first history books I ever owned. Shelby Foote's own trilogy, *The Civil War a Narrative* was an extension of his fiction *Shiloh: A Novel* (1952) and has its own place on my bookshelf. So, who wins? I am Maryland on this, a border state trying hard to be neutral. Don't get that joke? Then read them all.

BE MORE CIVIL: Shelby Foote figures prominently in Ken Burn's PBS documentary *The Civil War* (1990), now available in a restored high definition format: http://www.pbs.org/kenburns/civil-war/. At six hundred and ninety minutes, time still flies thanks to the narration of America's greatest historian David McCullough. If he ever writes about the Civil War, I may secede from the argument above and install David as the clear winner.

SING ALONG WITH SIDEBURNS: From the mind of standup comedian Toby Turner comes *The Sideburn Song* at https://www.youtube.com/watch?v=6TXWzlT02_s. Turner, also known as Tobuscus, lists himself as an Internet personality, which I always thought was synonymous with unemployed. But apparently, this is a paying gig, and while this little ditty tends to wander off track, so did the man for whom sideburns are named.

ROAD TRIP: Find "celebrated sites and structures" of the War Between the States by visiting the Civil War Trust and looking up local heritage spots at: https://www.civilwar.org/visit/heritage-sites. Pack up the car and, hopefully you won't endure long periods of boredom like the combatants often did.

BE BETTER THAN BURNSIDE: Give your skills in the field a test with Ultimate General: Civil War, available at http://www.ultimategeneral.com/. If you find that standing still doesn't win you many points, remember video games are not real. Which is something movie executives should have kept in mind before making a move like *Pixels (2015)*: http://www.imdb.com/title/tt2120120/.

HAVE ONE ON THE ROCKS: Portland Oregon's Eastside Distilling makes a 92 proof Burnside Bourbon that featured the flaring whiskers of the Major General until a rebranding in 2017. Pick up one of the older bottles if you can find it and pour a little out for Old Ambrose, who still gets no respect.

USE YOUR ILLUSION: In previous lessons, we used the example of guns and butter to showcase the efficient frontier. Here are more guns, this time paired with roses at the unofficial Guns N' Roses YouTube channel: https://www.youtube.com/watch?v=O1fHxPY3TJo. There we can all try to answer the unanswerable question: what's so civil about war anyway?

Extrapolation Celebration
Marmota Monax & Financial Forecasting

1887 AD

We're all looking for answers, trying to shed light on the shadows and have a deeper understanding of our world. But consider your sources. When it comes to making predictions, even the most famous of our fellow mammals go on lengthy cold streaks.

The dawn was still far off and the fields covered with a recent dusting of fresh flurries. Boots crunched on the snowpack, cresting the small hill a few miles southeast of town as stars twinkled above giving the revelers enough light to see. They'd come from near and far to find out what no one else could tell them: the future. In a clearing at the top of the knob was the one they had come for, the one whose counsel they sought on a biting cold morning in February. They crowded into a circle, some signing and some quiet with anticipation. Or perhaps a sense of foreboding.

"Call to him and he will come!" Someone shouted.

"Shhh…" someone hissed, "it isn't time yet."

"Yes," came a quiet retort. "It is now. Summon him." The sun was starting to rise, casting a subdued golden shadow around them.

"Bring him!" The crowd began to chant softly. The appointed hour had indeed come and they moved toward a mound of earth, sizeable enough to house the One. They beckoned.

"He comes," someone whispered. The sun rose high in the sky, which was cold but startlingly blue, and a breath of wind touched the open hill where they stood. A small figure appeared and looked around blinking in the bright new day-light.

"He goes." The figure had turned and gone back from where he came.

"That's it?" Many were befuddled and began to mill around with confused looks on their faces.

"Aw, hell. That's just great!" One of the angry followers barked. Those gathered looked askance at him, horror showing on their plain, wind chapped faces. "What, you guys wanted six more weeks of winter?"[146]

The One, on that February day in 1887, was a Marmota monax, the common woodchuck or groundhog, as he was locally known. Pulled from his slumber and asked to predict the weather, he cast a shadow long enough to plunge the eastern seaboard back into wintery chill. On such a clear day, it would have been hard to miss, especially if he stood on his hind legs (making himself appear taller than usual) as the Marmota monax is known to do. But the spectacle caught on

---

146 Contrary to popular opinion, the One need only cast a shadow to pre-dict more winter, not actually see it.

in Punxsutawney, Pennsylvania and soon people came from other counties, then other states to see the one they came to call Punxsutawney Phil. Indeed, this humble groundhog would become bigger, more colorful and gain wider appeal than any squirrel or woodchuck dared to hope. He would become the world's most famous weatherman.[147]

— UNUSUALLY UNRELIABLE —

Alfred Cowles was an American economist who had a fairly simple question: can people who make stock market predictions predict the stock market? In 1932, he delivered the answer in front of a 'raucous' party combining the Econometric Society and the American Statistical Association. His verdict was, well, usually not.

In 1931 forecasters were almost uniformly positive that the markets would rise. Almost no one thought it would fall. For every sixteen bullish forecasts, there were but three that were bearish. The stock market fell 54% in 1931. Not only could forecasters not predict the direction of the market, they couldn't see the second leg of the Great Depression bearing down on them.

Cowles also tracked the performance of William Peter Hamilton, editor of the Wall Street Journal and found that ...

---

147 The largest member of the marmot family and cousin to the squirrel, the groundhog may also appear to be everywhere at once, his habitat being broad and varied. Groundhog habitats range from Georgia northward along the Appalachians and the Atlantic coast into Labrador and then westward nearly to the Alaskan border. This marmot gets around, figuratively as well as literally, taking numerous mates during the spring after a long hibernation.

...he had predicted the right direction of things forty-five times in twenty-six years...and wrong forty-five times. And he was one of the better prognosticators of the early twentieth century. Today with all our technology and lessons learned from nearly a century of investing, we must be better at this, right? Not really. CXO Advisory Group tracks the accuracy of finance gurus and pegs the percentage of correct forecasts at about 46%. You might as well ask the groundhog.

The tradition of a weather prescient rodent dates to Germany in the Middle Ages and has roots in the Christian celebration of Candlemas. Most European cultures have sayings about the weather on that day predicting the length of winter. For instance, "If Candlemas Day be bright and clear, there'll be two winters in the year" or "If Candlemas is mild and pure, winter will be long for sure." The extrapolation is that a nice day means more winter ahead, while a cloudy one would mean mild weather to come. Readers will immediately recognize and be wary of such statements using rhyme as reason. If not, review History 101, The Problem with Poets.[148]

The Germans introduced the idea of an animal seeing his shadow being the predictive event. They believed when a bear saw his shadow at Candlemas, he would knock off and

148 Traditionally forty days after Christmas, Candlemas is also half way between the winter and spring solstices, making for a good time to reflect on how much longer the cold months will last and when it might be time to prepare for planting.

nap for another six weeks. German immigrants to Pennsylvania had few bears to tempt out of their dens and were smart enough to pick on someone smaller. The ubiquitous groundhog got the job and everlasting fame for "predicting" the course of winter. Inferring one event from another, i.e. more winter based on a shadow, seems quaint to the twenty-first century ear. Yet, as human beings we are still natural extrapolators looking for easy patterns that allow us to skip most critical thought and reach a conclusion quickly. We will ask for and take counsel from just about anyone. Which is too bad, because there are obvious drawbacks to having a ravenous, sleep deprived squirrel predict your weather and planting season.

How You'll Be Tested...

From now until marmots fly, you will hear end of year predictions about stock markets, interest rates, and economic data in financial news outlets of varying reliability. Some will even come from pundits with a cultish following and a list of previous accomplishments that infer a degree of authority in their predictions. And if you hear something often enough, or if the prediction verifies your opinion anyway, you'll be more likely to follow through with some action designed to take advantage of the prediction. Buyer beware.

To save yourself from throwing good money down the proverbial woodchuck hole, ask some questions first. Are these gurus truly as good as perceived at making predictions? What kind of track record do they have? Can you actually make money acting on these prophecies? When has it worked in the past? Has the prognosticator made bets on this information with his or her own money? Digging deeper can be exhausting. So, if you are considering altering your investments based on a prediction of one data point or another, you may want to sleep on that decision for a while. Indeed, feel free to put the idea into permanent hibernation. Following a bad guess can mean being out in the cold a lot longer than six weeks.

EXTRA CREDIT

SEE IT AGAIN (AND AGAIN): I'll get right to it, because you know it is coming. You can't talk about Groundhog Day and not tell people to see *Groundhog Day (1993)*. That is like talking about baseball and ignoring the World Series. Bill Murray may have become a movie star battling gophers, but he isn't bad versus the groundhog either. He plays a weatherman who relives the same day over and over, to which we can all relate. Then he gets it right and can move on with his life, which only happens in the movies.

GO WHOLE HOG: Of course, the movie has an excellent supporting cast including a couple of stand-ins for Punxsutawney Phil. But Phil isn't the only one hogging the weatherman duties around the country. Get the details on Phil and his cousins, including Shubencadie Sam and Staten Island Chuck here: http://www.history.com/news/beyond-punxsutawney-meet-the-other-groundhogs.

GET HIP, MAN: Alas, the poor weatherman has been the subject of jokes for generations. But George Carlin at least invented one that got his forecasts right: "Al Sleet, here and tonight's forecast? Dark. Continued dark tonight, turning to partly light in the morning." See, it's not that hard! Probably not as hard as getting through this entire bit from *George Carlin: Again! (1978)* while only using one of the seven words you can't say on television: https://www.youtube.com/watch?v=MGzPMjnkoPE.

GET RULED OUT: Feeling your inner guru stirring and want to try your hand at forecasting? Fine. The Harvard Business Review presents six rules for making a forecast at: https://hbr.org/2007/07/six-rules-for-effective-forecasting. Invoke rule number six immediately and "know when to **not** make a forecast." Like now.

SEEK SOME STATUS: Maybe sleep deprivation has more to do with the unreliability of forecasts. Regardless, the extra rest won't hurt you. And this New York Times article demonstrating that sleep is the new status symbol, might help you gear up with the new gadgets your friends will envy. You are feeling *very* sleepy at: https://www.nytimes.com/2017/04/08/fashion/sleep-tips-and-tools.html.

Rough Ride Rewrite
Theodore Roosevelt & Asset Allocation

1898 AD

R emember when politicians could unite people? Me
neither. But looking uphill into the face of a determined
foe, a future President rewrote history by mixing men
with different skills, experience, and backgrounds to create
a winning combination.

ILLUSTRATED WEEKLY NEWSPAPER

Est. 1867   July 1st, 1898   Price 6d

Cuban Catastrophe!

Numerous Casualties During
Hopeless Attack
Rough Riders Repulsed
Colonel Roosevelt Slain

—On the road to Santiago:

> *American forces suffered a great disaster here today,*
> *one which will surely change the direction of the cur-*

rent war against Spain. After a march of eight miles in the torrid tropical heat, our brave fighting men emerged from a path still strewn with sugar refining cauldrons at a place dubbed Kettle Hill. Artillery fire soon began on the heights, where Spanish troops in numbers unknown were dug in to well-prepared works. Their repeating rifles, firing eight times for every American volley, began to take a toll on units massing on the road near and in the high grass along the San Juan River.

Then, when it seemed that caution and common sense might carry the day, instead of withdrawing in good order, American fighting men emerged from cover to the whizz and whine of bullets, making their way upward and forward. On a normal day, it might take a man around twenty minutes to scale Kettle Hill and perhaps half an hour for its neighbor, San Juan Hill. But it would take far longer on this July day, with packs, ammunition and rifles weighing down every soldier in the malarial heat.

To be sure, unit cohesion had disappeared on the hill as men fell while their compatriots pushed on. Eventually a mixture of platoons held fast under a withering fire, unable to move up or down the hill without being wiped out. With the Spanish holding the high ground and their own reserve units clogging the roads behind, there was now no opportunity to withdraw.

It was a hopeless attack on Kettle Hill, with numerous casualties, seemingly among them Colonel Roosevelt, lately of the Navy Department, who seemed to lead part of the attack with a maniacal grin. He was singled out for Spanish bullets by the spectacles *he continued to wear throughout, whose reflection in the sun made him a tempting target for sharpshooters. The Colonel seemed to be assembling a patchwork of his own Rough Riders, who were a patchwork to begin with, and combining them with elements of the Buffalo Soldiers of the 10th Cavalry. This hodge-podge of units could not hope to stand up to the disciplined Spaniards and bogged down within sight of their works. I fear they will lay there, in sight of their objective, eternally.*[149,150]

This was not a glorious march with bands playing and bayonets glimmering in the sun. There was no order, no regularity to the units and they came on under withering fire to be slaughtered. The disjointed affair carries with it the feel of a classic military blunder.

---

149 Theodore Roosevelt's journey to the head of the Rough Riders began with a double tragedy: the death of his wife and mother on the same day, in the same house. The anguish drove him westward to clear his mind and rebuild his spirit. He landed in the Dakotas where he made his way as a gentleman rancher. The Harvard graduate and New York Assemblyman encountered some tough characters and earned their respect the hard way, including a bar brawl where he knocked one loudmouth out cold for calling him "four eyes." Returning to New York, Roosevelt authored several books, became Police Commissioner of New York and continued to visit the rough and tumble west for hunting and relaxation. When war came, he assembled men from east and west into the 1st U.S. Volunteer Cavalry, known as the Rough Riders.

150 The 10th Cavalry was one of the original segregated army units stationed in the west in the post-Civil War period. The troops and their sister units (9th, 24th and 25th) were all black units established by Congress and originally deployed against the Plains and Southwestern Indian tribes. Native Americans called them "Buffalo Soldiers" during those Indian Wars from 1866–1890, allegedly because of their curly black hair like a bison's. The 10th was reactivated and integrated in 1958 and remains in service today. The last Buffalo Soldier, Sgt. Mark Matthews died in 2005 at the age of one-hundred-eleven. He is buried in Arlington National Cemetery.

Patrick Huey

The author jumped. "What the hell!" He exclaimed as the world around him seemed to rip, a great tearing sound engulfing the field, as if the world itself were parting at the seams. A rhythmic punching of metal echoed between the two hills. He watched, round after round of seemingly endless ammunition slamming into the Spanish trenches. The newspaperman took to his pencil again.[151]

> *The new Gatling guns made their combat debut, but in keeping with the theme, their awesome power came too late to save the offensive or the men now on San Juan Hill.*

And suddenly, a miracle. The lines of dead soldiers, not dead at all, began to rise and crawl forward again as the killing fire from the crest of the hill slackened. He watched in fascination, as the Colonel, quite alive and waving his hat, rallied men forward and then disappeared over the rise. The writer, sighed and lit his cigar, they made some fine ones there in Cuba, and slowly set it to his original dispatch, catching it afire. When it had turned to ash, he began anew.

---

151 The Gatling machine gun saw limited service in the American Civil War and was notoriously absent from the field at Little Big Horn, where General Custer opted to keep them out of his main force. Action in Cuba demonstrated that the 400–700 rounds per minute, depending on the model, might have helped change that outcome.

ILLUSTRATED WEEKLY NEWSPAPER

Est. 1849   July 1st, 1898   Price 6d

Success at San Juan!

Americans Endure to Carry the Day
Colonel Roosevelt A Hero
The Disparate Desperately Rally

—*On the road to Santiago:*

> *American grit, determination and teamwork have won the day here. Under heavy fire from entrenched Spanish forces, Colonel Theodore Roosevelt managed to rally men from various units pinned down on Kettle Hill.*

He glanced up where fragments of the army had united and moved forward, engaging the Spaniards in a running battle that included brutal hand-to-hand fighting. Finally, the block house where the Spanish had headquartered was overrun and the retreat was on, spilling down Kettle Hill and onto nearby San Juan Hill. The entire length of the San Juan heights, now in American hands.

> *Colonel Roosevelt displayed no fear, looking as if he was carved from stone throughout the melee. When it was time to move on the entrenched positions, he rallied his own Rough Riders, an often rag tag assortment of western roughnecks and ranchers alongside eastern-educated college boys and Native Americans. Interspersed were the Buffalo Soldiers of the 10th Cavalry, the famous regiment of African Americans*

formed after the Civil War. At his urging, these hopelessly confused units coalesced into an unstoppable fighting force that carried the day that moved inexorably forward, cheering the Colonel to victory as they overwhelmed the defenders. Colonel Roosevelt clearly proved that a proper mix of talents, creeds and colors can be a strength in the face of even the longest odds. It seems today that diversity overcame adversity.[152]

The talents of disparate people were needed to carry the day on the San Juan Heights and Theodore Roosevelt was the right man to bring them together. When war with Spain had come, he put together a group of volunteers drawing on his own diverse past. He enlisted cowboys and college men; beat cops and scam artists; blue-blooded politicians and Native Americans. The distinct mix of the group was its strength, with natural administrators standing side-by-side with bare-knuckle fighters. For Teddy Roosevelt, all that mattered was that the blend worked. He was a master of **Asset Allocation**, putting the right talent to the right task. So, when it came time to bring other units together and make it work in a tough situation, perhaps no one in America was more prepared.[153]

152 Years later, Roosevelt would literally be carved in stone, part of the monument at Mount Rushmore. And though he held many offices afterward including Governor of New York, Vice President, and President of the United Sates, Roosevelt always preferred to be called Colonel. He was awarded the posthumous Medal of Honor in 2001 for his actions in Cuba.
153 Most reports after the battle indicated that a member of the 10th Cavalry, Sgt. George Berry, was the first to the summit. But black soldier's participation was minimized by much of the press at the time, a reflection of racial

── DIVIDE AND CONQUER ──

Research by Vanguard shows that the broad strategic mixture of your assets will determine the spectrum of your returns. This decision will explain about 88% of your future up and down movements. But there is also a lot more to allocation than just picking a mix of stocks and bonds.

A properly constructed portfolio will also allocate in as many as three other ways:

- *Sub-asset allocation: A bit of exposure everywhere (small, large, foreign, etc.) minimizes the impact of weaker areas and your risk of missing out.*

- *Active or passive allocation: Passive indexing give you broad diversification, while active strategies can provide flexibility, tax advantages and outperformance during some market cycles.*

- *Taxable or tax advantaged allocation: If you have different tax treatments for your accounts, they may need to hold different investments.*

Bottom line: investors need to construct disciplined portfolios that weigh risks *and* returns to meet their previously defined goals and objectives.

Take a lesson from Teddy and be prepared to lead your own team when the ride gets roughest. A proper allocation of elements working toward a common goal will keep you from making news for all the wrong reasons.

---

attitudes in the Jim Crow era. Roosevelt was certainly not immune to such issues, despite his reputation for inclusiveness on the battlefield. After inviting Booker T. Washington to dine at the White House in 1901, the backlash from politicians and press was so severe that he never invited another African American to do so during his two terms. Indeed, no President did for another three decades.

How You'll Be Tested...

Investors must decide how their assets will work together and toward what goal. But many omit that step, often looking only at historical performance when making their decision to invest. Maybe you will be tempted to skip the important stage of determining a mix you can thrive with and attack the market without a plan. Please don't. You'll only to be lured into hasty changes when your accounts come under fire.

Make a stronger whole by recruiting those with different and necessary talents. Choose your **asset allocation**. Stocks, bonds, real estate, large cap, small cap, foreign, emerging markets, high yield, tax advantaged; like New York cops and North Dakota cowboys, these assets don't have much in common, but they *can* work well together when properly led. Teddy Roosevelt did an admirable job of selecting and training his Rough Riders to work together, but was fortunate, dare I say lucky, to find other units like the 10th Cavalry that would follow him. In the world of investments, there is no reason for you to leave a properly allocated portfolio to chance.

EXTRA CREDIT

SEE THE SHOW: Joe Wiegand served two terms on the student government at the University of Sewanee, Tennessee. Today he is better known as the pre-eminent reenactor of another two-termer, Teddy Roosevelt. Catch this historian actor's hour-long talks and hear the stories of San Juan Hill, his attempted assassination, and dinner with Booker T. Washington from the man himself. Well, sort of. Get the tour schedule at: http://www.teddyrooseveltshow.com/events.

TRI AGAIN: Dive deep into the complex life of one of the most bewildering personalities ever to reach the Presidency. Roosevelt was a bundle of contradictions, so it takes a collection of books to get it right. Behold, the Theodore Roosevelt Trilogy Bundle by Edmund Morris. *The Rise of Theodore Roosevelt (1979), Theodore Rex (2001),* and *Colonel Roosevelt* (2010) divide Roosevelt's life into thirds and tackle each in detail. Environmentalist and big game hunter; big stick diplomat and Nobel Peace Prize winner; one percenter and trust buster; the Colonel's whole life seems a paradox. But don't judge. No one likes a critic, for it is not the critic who counts: http://www.theodore-roosevelt.com/trsorbonnespeech.html.

ADD A FOURTH: Not enough Teddy? Sail on with *The River of Doubt, Theodore Roosevelt's Darkest Journey (2005)* by Candice Millard. After his time in the Dakotas, Roosevelt thought himself an outdoorsman capable of traveling anywhere on earth. The Amazon jungle laughed and then tried to kill him. A good reminder to be aware of our own limitations, though I think I've done a good job of reminding you about many of those out over the last couple hundred pages.

GET IT STRAIGHT: You probably won't confuse Teddy Roosevelt with Benjamin Franklin, though historian David McCullough doesn't call Americans historically illiterate without reason (http://www.americanthinker.com/articles/2010/12/historical_illiteracy.html). But the difference between diversification and asset allocation might be a bit fuzzier. Check out: https://www.youtube.com/watch?v=BK9KmpgjEFw and clear this up once and for all.

MIX IT UP: Use an interactive tool to adjust asset mixes and see how much risk and return they offered historically at: https://www.portfoliovisualizer.com/backtest-asset-class-allocation. Spend some time with sub-allocation decisions as well. Note that even a perfect back-tested portfolio is still backward looking, and the future could be totally different. Which is where this ubiquitous warning comes form: past performance is not a guarantee of future returns.

WORK IT: Clever journalists referred to 2015 as "the year nothing worked" and promptly declared asset allocation dead. See an example here: https://www.bloomberg.com/news/articles/2015-12-28/the-year-nothing-worked-stocks-bonds-cash-go-nowhere-in-2015. Financial writers should tear up more of their drafts, including this one. The article notes that "the idea behind asset allocation is simple, when one market struggles, it's OK because an investor can *jump* into another that is thriving. Not so in 2015." Right, except that isn't the idea of asset allocation AT ALL. Other than that, the story is accurate.

Salt of the Earth
(The Pilot Episode)
Patillo Higgins & Cyclical Sectors

1901 AD

The making and breaking of oil fortunes produces must see prime time viewing. While you've probably never heard of Patillo Higgins and his Texas sized booms and busts, his life was a television script too good to be true… almost. Partner, even I can't make this stuff up.

———

<Fade In, theme music plays>

A man in dusty dungarees and boots stands on a low hill above a long coastal plain and sweeps the horizon with his lone arm. He wears a boxy pleated jacket that has seen better days and a flat straw boaters hat. "My name is Pattillo Higgins, and I'm looking for oil in Texas. I've gone boom and I've gone bust, but you expect that in this business. And before I'm done everything will be bigger in Texas, including the betrayals."

Scene One: \<Flashback\> A montage begins with a young boy in a small town in the post-Civil-War period. He leaves school in the fourth grade and begins working for his father making guns. But he ignores authority and habitually makes trouble. As a teenager, we see him shot in the arm by a sheriff's deputy during a brawl, but he escapes a murder charge claiming self-defense. Young and uneducated, he drifts into logging camps managing to cut trees with one arm but drinks to excess at night. Finally, at age twenty, he meets a preacher, and as we fade out we see the same one-armed, young man, cleaned up and going to church.

\<Cross Fade\>: Higgins, the one-armed man, is sitting at a desk in a bank.

Higgins: You know, we use a lot of oil and gas to light the large spaces in our factories. Just imagine how much easier it would be to get this energy source locally.

Banker: Sir, the Higgins Manufacturing Company is a treasured account here. But oil? In Texas? Mr. Higgins...I'm not so sure. Tell me again about this Spindletop Hill you keep mentioning.[154]

Higgins: It's a lovely high promontory, with a dense pine forest to the north that you could smell when the wind was right.[155]

---

154 To date, Pennsylvania led the nation in the production of petroleum, used in the late nineteenth century in lamps and various lubricants. It was a nice, quiet industry with a limited production that substituted well for whale oil. Nobody got obscenely wealthy and no one went broke. Heavy combustion engines ran on coal. But changes in technology, including the automobile, were right around the corner.

155 When the wind wasn't right, it was possible for storm surges and floods to wrack the lowlands as they had the previous fall when the Great Galveston Hurricane had come ashore and killed tens of thousands.

Banker: Go on…

Higgins: And I believe it to be what is known as a salt dome. You see, Beaumont sits in a humid subtropical zone some thirty miles inland from the Gulf. The occasional floods we get allow all that water to dredge salt out of the lower strata of rocks. It creates an impermeable pocket of minerals, and often oil.[156]

Banker: You really think so?

Higgins: Read your history. Stories have circulated since the Conquistadors about a black, tar like, substance used to waterproof their boots. And the local tribes used something similar as an aid to digestion. But I wouldn't much recommend the latter.

Banker: Mr. Higgins, this would be your fourth attempt to drill there. I'm sorry, but without a partner who can bear some of this risk with you, we would have to decline your loan.

<Fade out>

Scene Two: <Fade in> A montage runs of Higgins desperately placing ads nationwide for someone to partner with him. <Cross fade> Higgins is standing with another man on Spindeltop Hill.

Higgins: I need a partner. Someone to help secure the financing to drill down deeper. There is oil here; I know it in my heart.

Lucas (w/Austrian accent): Yes, a full heart and an empty bank account are a frustration for any man of vision.

---

156 Higgins was an amateur geologist, engineer, and designer.

If we can get down to five hundred feet or so on your budget, will that be sufficient?

They shake hands smiling <cross fade> Another montage ensues showing drilling operations.

———

Scene Three: <Fade In> Lucas and another clearly wealthy man sit in an opulent office.

Man: I hear they are deriding Higgins, calling him the Prophet of Spindeltop, while they sneer at his ideas. He is the biggest little fool in Texas. Why should we keep him around?

Lucas: Because he is right. There is oil there. We just have to keep drilling. We need more money Mr. Mellon, but it will be the investment of a lifetime. And you are not a man to miss such an opportunity.

Mellon: No, no, I suppose I am not. But we do it without Higgins. Sign this and we can get drilling again in a few days. But if he is involved in any capacity financially, then there is not a red cent for the project.

Lucas: But this is his dream.

Mellon: Not if he can't finance it. Finish this thing Lucas. <Cut>

———

Scene Four: <Fade in>A gusher is raining oil over Spindeltop Hill. Higgins is making his way through the chaos on the hill to a wooden building where he slams open the door to confront Lucas.[157]

---

157 On January 10, 1901, a great plume of oil erupted from the drilling rigs

Higgins: Bastard. How could you? You took all of this away from me? I saw the papers, you wrote me out.

Lucas: I had no choice.

<Higgins draws a pistol>

Higgins: Maybe not. But I have a choice, don't I? Right now, that choice seems to be putting a bullet in your brain or in your gut so that you suffer.

<Higgins cocks the pistol>.

Lucas: No...

<Cut as a shot is fired>[158]

Scene Five: <Fade in> Higgins holds the smoking gun, but as we pan out it is clearly pointed at a hole in the floor.

Lucas: Why did you shoot?

Higgins: I was hoping it would wake me up. And that this would all be a dream.[159]

Lucas: It's no dream. You were right along. I'm sorry Higgins. I couldn't do it any other way.

Higgins drops the gun and walks stunned through the door, making his way again through the rain of oil, dodging

and ran for nine days uncontrolled until it was capped to produce tens of thousands of usable barrels per day. A new age of energy had dawned. If not for a one-armed amateur geologist, everything would be bigger in Pennsylvania instead of Texas. But the prophet of Spindletop, would see none of the profits. And any chance of JR Ewing being a character in the primetime drama *Pittsburgh* instead of *Dallas* blew sky high.

158 There is no record of how Higgins actually took the news that he'd been written out. He did sue, but no threats were made that survive in the historical record.

159 In that other show about the Texas oil industry, *Dallas* (1978–1991), the entire ninth season was revealed to be a dream. But Patillo Higgins was no Bobby Ewing.

Patrick Huey

workmen and supplies. He flashes back again on the chaos of his earlier life and how he turned it all around. When he is out of the gusher, the sun begins to come out. And as he looks up, he is smiling.

<Fade out>

The End? Hardly. The life of Patillo Higgins could fuel a season or series of a primetime drama just like Dallas did. This being America, he sued Lucas to recover money owed, settling out of court for the usual: an undisclosed sum. But his reputation in the petroleum industry was saved and he founded Higgins Oil & Fuel, continuing to speculate with land leases around Texas. He was bought out once and formed another firm to continue exploring the salt dome formations. He remained a maverick for the next fifty years, sometimes a millionaire, and just as often feuding with investors over financing new wells. And his personal affairs were equally, well, interesting. A bachelor for most of his life he married a woman he had originally adopted once she turned eighteen. Though he changed his life dramatically from his early days, he was still seemingly unable to separate from booms, busts, and scandals.

Higgins' volatile life and career demonstrate the cycles that can occur chasing a dream. The industry he helped found is similarly volatile, showcasing the up and down nature of many **Cyclical Sectors**, those who endure severe up and down periods and are leading indicators of economic growth or decline. We learned in History 201 that economies endure four cycles, evolving in a predictable pattern, though with wide variances in timing. Some sectors, such as energy, follow these patterns closely. Fuel prices fall when demand drops, as fewer people drive to work or alter their summer travel plans because their incomes are dropping. Contrast that with consumer goods like soap or pharmaceuticals, which don't see a drop off in usage just because the economy is bad. Consumers don't forego showering or taking their meds. At least the ones you want to do business, have a drink, or sit in church with.

How You'll Be Tested...

Why is it important to understand what is cyclical and what is not? Because it helps to diversify and maintain an appropriate asset allocation. Perhaps during a particular period of growth, you might be tempted to hold a portfolio that is overloaded with cyclical companies with long dry periods and occasional gushers.

While patience might pay off, most of us aren't like oil speculators with big hats, dusty boots, and seemingly endless supplies of capital and patience. Conversely, holding too defensive of a portfolio might not provide enough long-term growth. Don't fight with one hand if you don't need to. Invest in **cyclicals** and defensive sectors for a more diversified approach and better overall script to your financial life.

EXTRA CREDIT

GIVE IT A SHOT: *Dallas (1978–1991)* ushered in, or "gushered" in, the genre of the primetime soap opera and popularized the cliffhanger ending to each season. You can buy the entire collection of fourteen seasons and three reunion movies for about $170. Too rich for your blood? Settle for an official "I Shot JR" tee shirt celebrating the episode that defined cliffhangers. Available at http://www.cafepress.com/+i-shot-jr+gifts for less than the cost of a barrel of oil. At least today.

HAVE A GREAT DAY: I may have to rename History 301, a tribute to Daniel Day Lewis. After recommending his turn as Abraham Lincoln, I now urge you to consider another of his Oscar winning performances. *There Will be Blood (2007)* is billed as "a story of family, religion, hatred, oil, and madness, focusing on a turn-of-the-century prospector in the early days of the business." That might sound familiar, though the screenplay is adapted from an Upton Sinclair novel set in Southern California. One notices that there are more than a few half-crazed oil speculators in the world about whom to write.[160]

BE CRUDE: Make as much money as you possibly can while speculating in the crude oil market for the next ten years without getting off your couch. Try the Oil Trader simulation at: http://wilcoxen.maxwell.insightworks.com/pages/237.html. Borrow money to get started and hopefully pay it back when your bets on where the cycle is heading pay off. As Pattillo Higgins can attest, sometimes they don't pay off. Then the bank will come calling, and if you don't have cash to pay interest on your loans, it is game over. But

---

160   I could also recant my recommendation from Lesson Three to read *The Last of the Mohicans* and instead urge you to see the 1992 film adaptation instead, starring Daniel Day-Lewis as Hawkeye.

just like Higgins, after a quick refresh you can start again and be back at it in no time.

GO CYCLING: Investopedia has a quick recap of discretionary, non-durable stocks, also known as cyclicals: https://www. youtube.com/watch?v=41DKeOcdhAM. The website's take is that there are some upsides to cyclicals but forecasting and market timing are hard. You can't say I haven't (repeatedly) warned you.

GET LOST: If you find yourself traveling near, Pithole City, Pennsylvania, your mapping app is probably on the fritz. Nevertheless, take some time to visit the spot where the petroleum industry got its start, nearby at Titusville and Drake's Well, the world's first commercial oil rig: https://www.drakewell.org/. Pithole City is the town that grew up with the Pennsylvania oil country in the 1860s when hundreds of barrels bubbled to the surface and sold for $8 apiece. More wells and more oil followed with a predictable outcome. Oil prices plummeted, people went broke and the town failed. Today it is a ghost town and a reminder of the cycle of boom and bust. Perhaps Pithole residents relocated up the road to Pleasantville. Wouldn't you?

HISTORY 401

Modern America, the New Normal & Financial Advice

"You know what the trouble about real life is? There's no danger music."
−JIM CAREY, THE CABLE GUY

"How many of you have self-help books? Okay that's your first problem. You can't help yourself, because your self sucks!"
−BILLY BOB THORTON, SCHOOL FOR SCOUNDRELS

"You're your problem…and you're also your solution."
−MELISSA MCCARTHY, BRIDESMAIDS

"Screws fall out all the time, the world is an imperfect place."
−JUD NELSON, THE BREAKFAST CLUB

"Now, you listen to me…if you're not a part of the solution, you're a part of the problem."
− BRUCE WILLIS, DIE HARD

"Constantly talking isn't necessarily communicating."

—CHARLIE KAUFMAN

"Life's better with company. Everybody needs a co-pilot."

—GEORGE CLOONEY, UP IN THE AIR

"The first principle is that you must not fool yourself and you are the easiest person to fool."

— RICHARD P. FEYNMAN

LESSON ONE: Life in the Fast Lane

Louis Schwitzer & Attention Fragmentation

1909 AD

LESSON TWO: Being Frank

Francis Albert Sinatra & Informational
Reflexivity

1915AD

LESSON THREE: A Proud Papa

Ernest Hemingway & Financial Journalism

1926 AD

LESSON FOUR: My Way or the Conway

Harold Jenkins & The Prosaic Preparation
Paradox

1933AD

LESSON FIVE: All the Kingsmen

Rock-n-Roll & Biased Information Processing

1963AD

LESSON SIX: Raising the Bar

Dick Fosbury & Expert Bias

1968 AD

LESSON SEVEN: To Boldly Go

Lenard Nimoy & Television Personality Bias

Stardate 346915.243–271406.614

LESSON EIGHT: Strike That
Rich Gedman & Economic Estimates
1986 AD

LESSON NINE: You Can Be Serious
The Australian Open & Emotional
 Performance
1990 AD

LESSON TEN: About Nothing
Seinfeld & Contrarianism
1999 AD

LESSON ELEVEN: The First Degree
Kevin Bacon & Investment Fraud
2009

Life in the Fast Lane
Louis Schwitzer & Attention Fragmentation

1909 AD

S peed kills. Sometimes literally. And sometimes it is just our productivity that crashes and burns.

Faster! Go faster! They're gaining on us! He screamed at his machine straining against the wind. Sweat was running in rivulets down his angular face as he drove hard, willing himself to get away. The smell of tar and gasoline were in his nostrils, and he vaguely heard the grinding of his teeth over that of the gears.

He stomped his foot on the accelerator, then did it again emphasizing the clang of metal as it struck the floor. The chase was on, but he was going as fast as he could. *Come on*, he urged. *Come on*.

The driver hunched forward, willing any remaining speed out of the machine. *I have to lose them in the turn. They are not taking this away from me.* He heard the pistons clanging inside the motor, hammering away as it reached the unfathomable speed of nearly sixty miles an hour. He entered the left-hand turn too fast and felt the car start to careen, the back wheels slipping. Then overcorrecting, the outside wheels became airborne.

Dreamlike, in slow motion, he saw a man in pantaloons and slouch hat watch him go by. The man stood open-mouthed and gaping as the car, like a squat half-barrel laid on its side and set on wheels, whizzed by partially airborne. Then, the man was gone, and the driver eased off the wheel and downshifted. The car regained traction, accelerating hard again as the road straightened. From behind, he heard the pursuers drumming out of the turn. Sirens wailed.

He shifted again, running flat out, and the Stoddard-Dayton automobile with the Rutenber engine finally began to open the distance on the pursuers. He couldn't see them, but the drumming of their four-cylinder engines faded slowly as he lurched ahead. It was over. A wide toothy grin appeared on his face under a film of grease.

Then he ventured a look behind him and braked abruptly to a stop. The man he had seen standing on the outside of the final turn was down in a pile. A crowd had gathered and the sirens started up again.

My God. Did I do that?

The driver's name was Louis Schwitzer, an engineer by trade and now a champion automobile racer. He had crossed the finish line ahead of his pursuers and won the first automobile race at the new Indianapolis Motor Speedway. Twelve thousand onlookers had been treated to a racing extravaganza and the novelty of motor cars going around in left-hand circles, twice. It was all over in less than six minutes. Schwitzer's average speed of just over 59MPH was enough to win the race. But he left a pock marked track and rubble spewed grandstands in his wake. The sirens came for several injured spectators who got an unexpectedly up-close look at the track surface as it hurtled toward them.[161]

Racing would continue that day after Schwitzer's win, culminating in a 250-mile event where the race leader was temporarily blinded because a loose rock hit him in the face, smashing his goggles. Winners included racing immortals like Louis Chevrolet and Ray Harroun. Losers included the two drivers, two mechanics, and two onlookers who were critically injured. The nascent American Automobile Association (AAA) threatened to cancel the next day of racing and boycott future events at Indy.[162]

Technology was changing quickly at the dawn of the twentieth century and old ways of doing things couldn't stand up to the new speed of life. The track had been con-

---

161 Schwitzer was another engineer who had emigrated to America from Austria. He is remembered each year in Indianapolis with the presentation of the Louis Schwitzer Award for excellence in motorsports engineering. Presented annually since 1967, the award honors the winner of the first race at the Speedway and provides a $10,000 cash prize for advances in performance, safety, and efficiency of race cars or support equipment.

162 In those days, AAA was equally concerned with racing and touring automobiles and they got what they wanted, improvements to the track. Harroun would go on to win the inaugural Indianapolis 500 in 1911. In the early days of racing, mechanics rode with their drivers, providing on the fly repairs and monitoring traffic behind them. In a five-mile race like Schwitzer's there was no need, but over longer distances it was deemed necessary. Harroun, however, won the first 500-mile race in a single seat vehicle with a novel way of looking behind him: a rearview mirror.

structed with two inches of gravel, a layer of limestone, and a combination of tar and oil covered in stone chips and crushed rock. It was built over the course of a few months by hundreds of manual laborers with an assist from a fleet of mules. The method would not have been out of place had Roman engineers appeared and unrolled scrolls detailing the work to be done. And it obviously could not stand up to the prevailing speeds of the latest motor vehicles. Advances in engine construction brought more brawn and tracks made with mule power were destined for the dustbin of history, just like that Empire in Rome.[163]

When technology progresses and speeds increase, old components break down. In the twenty-first century, sixty miles an hour won't win you anything but a middle finger while driving in the passing lane. Today computers and powerful earth movers build roads to withstand that kind of stress. Meanwhile, we stand by open-mouthed as other things, such as instant data and constant feedback, change at high speed. How can a brain tens of thousands of evolutionary years old keep up? Quite simply, it can't. It too breaks into

---

163 The solution was around 3.2 million bricks laid in sand and kept together with mortar. Indianapolis Motor Speedway reopened in December 1909 and became known as The Brickyard. It would grow considerably over the years not just in length but in size and stature. One hundred years after the inaugural two-lapper, twenty-five thousand fans had seats for the expanded race with an additional fifty thousand spots available on the infield. That turf inside of the famous track could hold Churchill Downs, Yankee Stadium, the Rose Bowl and the Roman Coliseum inside of its expansive two hundred and fifty-three acres. Fans got what they wanted: more, bigger, and faster races with speeds topping out at over two hundred miles per hour.

fragments. Researchers call it **Attention Fragmentation (AF)**—short bursts of brainpower dedicated to a multitude of quickly shifting endeavors. We know it as multi-tasking, a quaint expression meant to make it sound as if it makes us more efficient and is good for us, ignoring the rubble we leave behind. Whatever you call it, AF is like racing an Indy car. It creates high levels of anxiety, is highly addictive, and tends to run you around in circles at great peril. **Attention fragmentation** even has its own version of AAA:

- **Anxiety**: Multi-taskers tend to have full tanks of stress hormones, lower job satisfaction, and scratched and dented personal relationships.
- **Addiction**: Ever struggled with the urge to check your phone when a message arrives, even when you know you shouldn't? Say, while driving? Information and socialization are addictive. But seriously, put it down and get out of the left lane.
- **Adeptness**: While making us nervous and dependent, AF kills productivity in two ways. First, constantly telling your brain to shift between tasks is awfully inefficient. Unfortunately, our brains still can't tell us to perform two actions concurrently. Instead, each task is handled individually by a separate neural path. Performing disparate duties requires the brain to stop, clear out the rules for one process and start up the new one. This is like restarting a car every time you want to shift gears. Which seems like good way to lose a race. Indeed, completing tasks in parallel, instead of individually and sequentially, can take up to thirty percent longer. Second, AF results in a higher rate of error. Mistakes nearly triple when working with numerical problems and switching between tasks.

Given the potential for error, there is no room for multitasking while caring for financial and investment matters. You must be willing to strap in and dedicate time to work solely on your financial plan and investments. Or get a good team behind you to do some of those tasks. Your choice, but trying to do it all may end up costing you quite a bit.

How You'll Be Tested...

So, do you want to make potentially life altering financial decisions while racing to your kid's soccer game, posting photos to Instagram, and answering those leftover work emails? Pay attention here! For an investor planning on going the distance with his or her investments, it is important to know your limitations. On top of mental biases and a general lack of knowledge about economics and markets, modern life piles on a bunch of distractions. If you aren't equipped to deal with them, your race to the checkered flag might end up a cautionary tale.

Modern racing teams have numerous jobs to make it all work competitively. People specialize in areas that help a driver focus on the task at hand and maintain a competitive edge. Think about teaming up with someone to focus *your* efforts and plan for success. If you can't invest your money with both hands firmly on the wheel, you shouldn't be driving.

EXTRA CREDIT

GO INDY: Follow all the racing news from IMS on their Facebook page. As if you need something more to do while fiddling with your smartphone: www.facebook.com/IndianapolisMotorSpeedway/.

CATCH A THIEF: Bad news, someone is stealing from you. Good news, they will be easy to catch. Author Dave Crenshaw offers a demonstration of the larcenous nature of multi-tasking and how it pilfers your productivity. Learn how to stop fragmenting your attention and stealing from yourself. Get back your most precious possession, time. Do your exercise at: www.davecrenshaw.com/myth-of-multitasking-exercise/.

BE GRAPHIC: Don't believe me about how fast things have moved in the last century? How about just the last thirty years? For a refresher, try Atari's Pole Position to get your racing fix and wax nostalgic for 8-bit pixelated graphics: www.2600online.com/poleposition.html.

CATCH LIGHTNING: I don't often use Disney movies to prove my point. Okay, I have a young son so, the truth is, I often use Disney movies to prove my point. But there is no better lecture on the dangers of going it alone when you are distracted by fame and fortune than the one in the animated movie *Cars (2006)*:

> **Strip "The King" Weathers:** *Hey, buddy. You're one gutsy racer.*
> **Lightning Mcqueen:** *Oh, hey, Mr. The King.*
> **Strip "The King" Weathers:** *You got more talent in one lug nut than a lot of cars has got in their whole body.*
> **Lightning Mcqueen:** *Really? Oh, that...*
> **Strip "The King" Weathers:** *But you're stupid.*
> **Lightning Mcqueen:** *Excuse me?*
> **Strip "The King" Weathers:** *This ain't a one-man deal, kid. You need to wise up and get a good crew chief and a good team. You ain't gonna win unless you got good folks behind you.*

Sure, it's essentially the same lesson learned by Tom Cruise in *Days of Thunder (1990)* and Will Farrell in *Talladega Nights: The Legend of Ricky Bobby (2006)*. But in this case, it's a real racing legend giving the talking-to. Strip Weathers is voiced by NASCAR Hall of Famer Richard Petty.

GO TEAM: "According to the Northwestern Mutual 2017 Planning and Progress study, 68% of people with a financial advisor feel very financially secure, compared to 36% of those without an advisor." In the words of Strip Weathers (above), wise up and get a good team: www.fa-mag.com/news/security-comes-with-an-advisor-32980.html.

Being Frank

Francis Albert Sinatra & Informational Reflexivity

1915 AD

You may be tempted to believe those in the know and blindly follow their lead. But if you want more than three coins in your fountain someday, you'll need something other than that sort of witchcraft. Like making a decent high ball, you'll need to mix in a wide band of opinions to make things ring-a-ding-ding.

"Dolly, Dolly stay with me!" The doctor pleaded.

Delirious with pain, sweat pooling beneath her prone body in the kitchen of her Hoboken home, she could only answer with a scream. Periodic spasms of pain wracked her wiry body.

"Dolore!" The young immigrant girl screamed in her native tongue, arching her back. She had been in labor for a long time and could only get out the word for "pain" before crumpling back the floor.

"Soffre molto!" Added her mother, ringing her hands as she watched. Then she translated for the doctor: "She's in a lot of pain."

"I know, it's almost over." Faced with delivering an unusually large baby who couldn't be maneuvered without aid, the doctor turned for his forceps and began to work. It seemed to take a long time and the tiny room felt stifling.[164]

Heaving with exertion the doctor grunted: "There he is. It's a boy." There was no joy in his voice. The baby was still, without breath or vital signs and the doctor knew there was no hope for him. But Dolly had to be saved.[165]

Her own mother looked on, again wringing her hands and perhaps remembered giving birth back in Genoa. Grandma decided not to give up and let that baby go from here to eternity just yet. Snatching the lifeless boy, she turned to the basin to run cold water over him. When it had little effect, she slapped his back and was rewarded with a gasp. The boy spluttered, cried and then began breathing on his own. The Sinatra home had a miracle baby who was alive, though physically scarred by the ordeal of birth. Francis Albert Sinatra already knew that luck would be a lady, in this case his grandmother, Rosa Garavents.[166]

164 The baby would weigh in at thirteen-pounds, a seemingly absurd figure for any child (and mother), no less a kid that would go through most of his life being called skinny.

165 Dolly was a contentious figure in her son's life. She was a powerful woman behind the scenes in local politics. Using her linguistic skills, she translated during court proceedings for recent Italian immigrants, which earned her the position of Ward Leader within the Democratic party. She was also a midwife who allegedly performed illegal abortions and later a saloon keeper during prohibition. Her contentious relationship with her son began early and continued for the rest of her life.

166 The boy would be called Martin after his father, at least until his bap-

Certainly, the best was yet to come for Frank, but his face forever bore the scars of a difficult childbirth. Neighborhood kids called him Scarface, and he would always avoid being photographed from his left side. When he turned twenty-one, that was a very good year. Discovered as a singer, he became a member of the Hoboken Four. Later he landed a gig at the Rustic Cabin in Englewood Cliffs New Jersey, which broadcast his shows on New York's WNEW. Big band leader Harry James discovered him there in 1939, and the skinny kid with big ears crooned his way out of Hoboken to become a mega star, called simply The Voice. It was the beginning of a career that spanned the next six decades and made songs like Fly Me to the Moon and New York, New York standards at Vegas lounges and karaoke bars across the world.

The Voice matured and morphed into the Chairman of the Board and then Old Blue Eyes. Through it all, there was certainly doubt, including at least two suicide attempts, real or feigned depending on the source, and several high-profile marriages and break-ups. There were mob ties, loose or tight, again depending on the source, voice problems, legal problems, and confrontations with the media. There were smash hits and total flubs, two Academy Awards, and a "retirement" in 1971 that led to one thousand more shows. And there was his death two years after his last performance, an ailing man with heart problems, bladder cancer, and battling mild dementia. Born in a Hoboken kitchen, he lived to sing among the stars. Tributes at his death predictably

---

tism. There, the priest would accidentally call him Francis, his godfather's name. Dolly chose to stick with the latter believing it a good omen.

were set to one of his most revered recordings: *My Way*.[167,168]

But, here is the kick in the head, Sinatra reportedly loathed *My Way*. Yes, he viewed the song that put him back in the Billboard Charts in 1968 and became a staple at his numerous retirement concerts as "self-serving" and "self-indulgent." Which should be evident from the title alone. Perhaps, especially later in life, he also thought it hypocritical to sing so confidently when he was really a tortured soul. Regardless, he felt that he had to stick with it because it was expected of him. So, the Chairman poured himself an extra finger of Jack Daniels and belted out *My Way* as the crowds went bonkers from LA to Yonkers.

Sinatra's reliance on a song he loathed is an interesting commentary on what is known as **Informational Reflexivity**. Humans, famous or otherwise, look to others for cues on

---

167 Sinatra's career hit the skids during and after World War II. Medically unfit for service due to a punctured eardrum suffered at birth, his popularity with GIs returning from war paled in comparison to how popular he was with the girls they left behind. His recording career was on the rocks and his life in shambles. His first attempt at suicide was interrupted by his sometime wife, Ava Gardner. But a turn at acting led to an Academy Award for Best Supporting Actor in 1953, thanks in part to Gardner's help in landing the role. Reinvigorated, he signed with Capitol Records and produced a string of hits. He and Gardner parted like strangers in the night in 1954. Another Academy Award followed for *The Man with the Golden Arm*. And in 1959 Sinatra and Dean Martin appeared together at the Sands in Las Vegas, giving rise to the Rat Pack.

168 My Way, written for Frank by Paul Anka, reached number 27 on the Billboard Charts in America, while in Britain it spent the next seventy-five weeks on the charts, a record that still stands. It remains, according to the Guardian, the most popular song at British funerals.

how to behave socially. Most people want to fit in, though Frank may be unique in singing a song called *My Way* while attempting to do so. But he, like most of us, stick with something because it is associated with positive experiences and reinforcement.

Financial expert opinions can also fall victim to **informational reflexivity**. Researchers have noted that otherwise knowledgeable authorities tend to reflect current opinion even if they have data of their own that contradicts such beliefs. They subconsciously conform to the group, especially over time, as ideas become more and more entrenched. They may hate *My Way*, but they too feel they must sing it to be relevant. It is important to carefully consider expert opinions and get more than one point of view. After all, had his own grandmother taken the doctor's expertise for granted, Old Blue Eyes would never have crooned a single note.

How You'll Be Tested…

Sinatra isn't the only one hitting highs and lows, markets clearly do it too. And when authorities on finance form opinions about them while unknowingly taking cues from public opinion, a feedback loop is established. If we believe things are great, then many experts will confirm these feelings. That experts agree with us must mean things are even better than originally thought. When that happens, you might think: time to double down, baby!

─ GREENSPAN ON C-SPAN ─

Two years before Sinatra went to the great boardroom in the sky, markets were raging and everyone, experts and amateurs alike, was caught up in it. Hot tech stock tips were available from taxi drivers, grocery clerks, and your mother-in-law. Average investors had access to the Internet which stimulated their interest. They were buying what they thought they knew. Meanwhile journalists were calling the focus on companies being profitable "quaint" and anointing the head of an unprofitable e-retailer, a possible "New Age Edison." Experts welcomed a new economy where growth trumped profitability. Harvard Business School consultants urged traditional corporations to ditch their brick and mortar businesses and "tired ways."

Head of the Federal Reserve, Alan Greenspan, stepped to the microphone at the Hilton Hotel in Washington DC and, on live TV, coined a phrase that nicely summed it all up, **informational reflexivity**. Okay, he actually said "irrational exuberance", a more memorable catchphrase for a television audience. Unfortunately, though, when it was broadcast to the world it was on C-SPAN, which meant no one was watching.

Keep this in mind: Old Blue Eyes died in 1998 while tech stocks were booming and experts were promoting a "new economy" where growth was boundless. Two years later, tech stocks cratered. Can you say, riding high in April… shot down in May? Well, that's life. Rolling the dice based on the prevailing opinion, even if experts are singing the same tune, does not mean you'll be swinging easy on the Street of Dreams. Find someone who will wade through all that noise and keep you from jumping on a runaway bandwagon, someone to tell you, *listen here pally, nice and easy does it every time.*

EXTRA CREDIT:

BE A RAT: Lauren Bacall dubbed her husband Humphrey Bogart's Vegas friends "a goddamn rat pack." With Bogey's death, Sinatra and company carried on the name, at least in the media, and the tradition of cavorting in the desert. Members like Frank, Dean Martin, Sammy Davis Jr., and Joey Bishop would appear unannounced at each-others shows, yucking it up with topped-off high balls and off-color jokes. For a taste check out Sammy, Dean, and Frank at a charity show in St. Louis. No Joey Bishop? No problem for the Pack. Johnny Carson fills in admirably: https://www.youtube.com/watch?v=Cx2xd1q6bJs. Yep, *that* Johnny Carson.

GET SWINGING: What would the soundtrack to a Sinatra retrospective sound like? Well it might sound a lot like *Songs for Swinging Lovers* (1956) or *Come Fly with Me* (1957). Or perhaps a live performance like *The Main Event* (1974) from Madison Square Garden? *My Way* is only featured on the last of those. Heck, go *All the Way* and listen to all three.

GET SIRIUS: Satellite radio subscribers can tune in to Channel 71, Siriusly Sinatra and hear the Chairmen all day and night. Three days a week, his daughter Nancy plays her favorites. But it's not just Frank here, the American standard songbook is open to all comers including Tony Bennett, Bobby Darin, and Nat King Cole.

GET JACKED: Frank was known to imbibe a bit and Jack Daniels was his beverage of choice. With a special bottling in 2015, you can help Jack celebrate Frank's 100th year for about $179. Blended from one hundred hand-selected barrels, this whiskey is like Frank, mellow and refined with a hard edge that shows itself late at night. Take a shot at: www.jackdaniels.com/en-us/whiskey/limited/sinatra-century. Not a tippler? You have Frank's eternal pity, because when you wake up in the morning that's the best you're going to feel all day.

GET BACK: A bit of music and video whet your whistle for more? Then get your black tie and tails or that strapless number in the back of your closet ready to go. It's time to head for the desert in a time machine set for 1963. The Rat Pack is Back, baby! Or, at least, some passable parodies: www.ratpackisback.com/. The live show at the Tuscany Suites & Casino in beautiful Las Vegas will have you swilling champagne cocktails and humming One for My Baby 'til quarter to three.

BE POETIC: Pick up a copy of *Sinatra's Century: One Hundred Notes on the Man and His World (2015)*, By David Lehman. The poet and literary critic offers a note for each year on the 100th anniversary of the birth of Old Blue Eyes. Is one hundred too many notes? Not for me, I can't get enough of Frank. And not for Lehman who once published an anthology of poems culled from his writing a poem a day *for five years*. That may seem excessive, but hey, he did it his way.

A Proud Papa

Ernest Hemingway & Financial Journalism

1926 AD

E rnest Hemingway worked for over a year writing and
revising *The Sun Also Rises*, but today's financial writers
don't have nearly that kind of time to perfect their own
narrative. A two-step process will help investors decide if
any news story should stop them from running with the
bulls.

The fiesta had ended badly. It had begun brilliantly but
ended badly. Flaming and sparking, the fiesta ran white hot,
spitting and hissing until it faded to nothing. The writer
thought of this while drinking black coffee and watching
workers gather spent fireworks in the square in the late
morning. The cafés were putting out the good furniture
that had been gathered up and stored for seven days during
the fiesta. The coffee was strong and helped him keep the
general feeling of lousiness at bay.

The morning ended, and afternoon came on. His friend Bill came down and met him in the café. They ordered shrimps and beer while shop owners swept the streets. The town felt cooler now that the rains and the crowds had come and gone.

"Fella, that was some fiesta." Bill's face had a weary, parchment look to it.

"Some good, some not."

"Well, the bulls were excellent."

He nodded. "Yes, the bulls were very good." He did not really feel it, but he said it anyway.

"Quite right. I say, that Ordonez fellow was wonderful to see." Bill was from Michigan and as American as apple pie. But a few weeks with the English and he'd taken up their speech. He liked the bullfighter named Ordonez.[169]

"Wonderful. I may just write about that."

"About the bulls?"

"About all of it."

Bill was quiet for a time. He ordered more beer from the waiter. "All of it?"

"Yes."

"Well, how would it go? Give me the draft version if you please. Let's talk it through."

"Well, a man living in Paris and his friend from the States take a trip to Pamplona for the festival of San Fermin to watch the bull fights."

"And then?"

---

169 Cayetano Ordóñez was a young matador from Ronda who would serve as the model for a character named Pedro Romero. Ordóñez fought his last bull in 1942 and founded a family dynasty. His grandsons are toreros still working the bullrings of Spain and appearing in magazines with the likes of Penélope Cruz.

"They are joined by some English ex-pats and the man is in love with one of them."

"And then?"

"Well, she is engaged to one of the Englishmen, but has had an affair with another man on the trip. Everyone drinks too much and there is a big row. The end."

"What about the fishing?"

"Yes, I'll write about that too. They fish the Irati river and teach the trout a hell of a lesson."

"Well, that about sums it up. Tough sell for your publisher, though. Too life-like. No one will believe it."

"You bum."

"Must not be daunted, though. Write it anyway and see what happens. Secret to my considerable success? I was never daunted."

Ernest Hemingway was not daunted. He turned his sojourn to Spain featuring Bill Smith from Michigan and a mishmash of other ex-patriots into *The Sun Also Rises*. The novel propelled him to stardom and made him the premier writer for what became known as the Lost Generation.[170]

Hemingway's style became legendary for being long on dialogue and short on adjectives, adverbs and the semicolon. Having learned his craft as a journalist with the Kansas City Star, he credited their style guide for helping him to focus and not be overly wordy. The result was spare, direct prose. He got quickly to the question: "*and then?*" And only

---

170 Born between 1883 and 1900, members of the Lost Generation came of age during the global cataclysm of World War I. Author Gertrude Stein is thought to have coined the phrase, telling Hemingway who had driven a Red Cross ambulance during the war: "That's what you all are...all of you young people who served in the war. You are a lost generation."

stopped when the tale was told.[171]

Hemingway was also known to be a tireless and fanatical revisionist, rewriting, reworking, and stripping out unnecessary prose. He began his book immediately after the festival in July of 1925 and had the first working manuscript by the end of the fall. His editor was sorry, but "it is almost unpublishable." In May 1926, Hemingway would again refocus, stripping out detail and delete the first sixteen pages. By August, after another trip to Pamplona, he finished the proofs for the novel in Paris for publication in the fall of 1926.

FIT TO PRINT

Criticism of financial journalism isn't new. According to researchers, "superficiality" and a low "level of training and skills" are longstanding complaints. In other words, "they don't have the time and the opportunity and perhaps the education" necessary to do in-depth reporting.

Since the invention of the Internet, the number of financial media outlets has exploded. But more hasn't turned out to be better, leading to overblown analysis of everything and bias toward the excitement of frequent transactions, market timing, and conjecture.

---

171 Hemingway first visited the Festival of San Fermin in Pamplona with his wife Hadley Richardson in 1923 while a correspondent for the Toronto Star. They returned several times including the 1925 Holiday where they were joined by Bill Smith, Harold Loeb, the Lady Twysden (aka Mary Duff Stirling), Donald Ogden Stewart, and Pat Guthrie. Twysden, Loeb, and Guthrie inspired the characters Brett Ashley, Robert Cohn, and Mike Campbell in *The Sun Also Rises*. Hemingway would fall for Twysden and quarrel with Loeb just as Jake Barnes did in the novel. Upon publication Hadley would ask for a divorce and Hemingway would, presumably out of guilt, give her the royalties from the book.

Who needs researchers? In my experience, pessimism pervades because "if it bleeds, it leads." Trading is encouraged, and boring plans to buy-and-hold lose air time to stimulating trading strategies of dubious value. Forecasting substitutes for news to fill air time. Short-term performance is emphasized instead of planning, saving, and investing. All of this is good for advertisers, not investors.

Today, journalists face more pressure to publish quickly than Ernest "Papa" Hemingway ever did. In a 24-hour digital news cycle there is very little time to rework and revise. Hence, we get a lot of information, usually without the full plot or context. Finance journalists usually aren't going to ask the important question "...and then?" They will leave you, or me, to fish for it. Take, for instance, the following examples:

> *There is a pattern emerging here: A Google Trends search shows the last time interest in the VIX was this high was August 2011, when tumult in Washington over the debt ceiling sent markets tumbling.[172] —Wall Street Journal Moneybeat, May 17, 2017*

---

172 VIX is the ticker symbol for the Chicago Board Options Exchange (CBOE) Volatility Index. It uses the volume of contracts meant to protect from stock market downside as a measurement of the potential for short-term market swings.

A sharp and sudden sell-off for US financial stocks helped push the S&P 500 down more than 1% for the first time since October and provided fresh momentum to the recent rally in Treasuries—adding pressure on the dollar. Wall Street grabbed the headlines as the S&P 500 sank 1.2% to 2,344, with the financial sub-index 2.5% lower. The last time that the US equity benchmark closed more than 1% lower was on October 11, 2016. —Financial Times, March 21, 2017

Volatility thrashed investors left and right in 2015. The three big concerns this year were falling oil prices, China's economic slowdown and the seemingly never-ending speculation about when the Federal Reserve would raise interest rates. Greece's debt crisis, the European Central Bank's stimulus plan and fears of a broader slowdown in emerging markets kept investors on their toes, too. The new year couldn't come soon enough for many investors. U.S. markets finished 2015 mostly in the red: The Dow was down 2.2%. The S&P 500 ended the year down 0.7%. It was the worst year for those two indexes since markets collapsed in 2008. —CNN Money, December 31, 2015.

Based on the tone of such articles, you'd assume that bad things ensued. But, I say chap, you'd be bloody wrong. Here is how to read financial news à la Hemingway:

1) Strip out the extraneous information.

2) Ask yourself: "And then...?"

Strip Out Extraneous Information	And then....?
Interest in the VIX hasn't been this high since August 2011.	From August of 2011 until the article appeared on May 17, 2017, the S&P500 returned over 79%.
The S&P 500 sank 1.2%, the most since October 11, 2016.	From October 11, 2016–March 21, 2017 the S&P 500 was up 8.34%.
The Dow and S&P 500 had their worst years since 2008.	From year end 2008 through year end 2015, the Dow Jones Industrial Average rose 104% and the S&P 500 jumped 134%.

Many financial stories imply that bad things happened the last time a particular event occurred. Often, that is bull.

How You'll Be Tested...

Investors tend to follow quite a bit of financial journalism, usually without asking hard questions about the reliability, point of view and experience of those writing it. Heck, with most stories, if it all turned out the same the next time around, like Hemingway and his friends, we'd all have a lot to drink about. No, it won't turn out *exactly* the same. There will be plenty of regret, awkward moments, and morning-after hangovers. But knowing the full story should keep you from feeling daunted by every storyline in the financial news.

The papers will have headlines. They will be bad headlines, but not terrible headlines. But they could be fine stories and, with a little work, great ones. And afterward, the bull (market) is often excellent. Papa would be proud.

EXTRA CREDIT

HAVE A FEAST: *The Sun Also Rises* can be a controversial work. For more of 1920s Paris without the uproar, try *A Moveable Feast (1964)*. Legend has it that in the 1950s Hemingway was sitting at the Ritz Bar in Paris when the manager informed him they had some trunks in storage with his name on them. They contained notebooks he presumed lost from his days living with Hadley and running with the other authors of the Lost Generation. He was revising these notes until his death and they were published posthumously. You don't have to go to Paris to enjoy the book, but it wouldn't hurt either.

HAVE ONE, AND ANOTHER: Philp Greene is a cocktail historian. Not sure how I missed out on that career track, but I'll go on holding a grudge against my high school guidance counselor. Greene's *To Have and Have Another: A Hemingway Cocktail Companion (2012)* is part bartender's guide, part literary history, and a worthy accompaniment to a Mojito or Papa Doble. Papa had a complicated relationship with alcohol, featuring it like a character in most of his books, but suffering from liver problems and diabetes later in life. For Ernest, the answer was never at the bottom of the glass. But who cared if you couldn't remember the question?

STAY UP LATE: Rent *Midnight in Paris* (2011). Owen Wilson stars in the screenplay originally titled "The Lost Generation" about a writer seeking inspiration in Paris and only finding it by traveling back in time. It is an adaptation of a Woody Allen standup skit from the 1960s where he recalls anecdotes from 1920s Paris and ends each with the punchline "...and Hemingway punched me in the mouth." F. Scott Fitzgerald, Hemingway, Gertrude Stein, Pablo Picasso, T.S. Eliot, and Cole Porter make appearances. But no one gets pummeled by Papa.

GET IN THE RING: It turns out that Hemingway wasn't the only American aficionado of the bull ring. Sportswriter Bruce Schoenfeld's *The Last Serious Thing: A Season at the Bullfights (1992)* introduces us to a crew of expats that not even the great author could make up, including an American matador who Papa once sponsored in his quest for acceptance, if not greatness.

WRITE ERNESTLY: Utilize the Hemingway Editor app to highlight and then rid yourself of adverbs, the passive voice, and dull, complicated words: www.hemingwayapp.com/desktop.html. Surely the Nobel Prize in Literature (the Swedish Prize as Ernest called it when he won in 1954) will follow.

JOIN THE CIRCUS: Michael Palin began his career with Monty Python's Flying Circus and the English comedian is still flying everywhere. As a travel writer and documentary filmmaker he's crisscrossed the world from pole to pole, Himalayan Mountains to Sahara Desert. His 1999 documentary *Michael Palin's Hemingway Adventure* globetrots to the late author's haunts in Spain, Chicago, Paris, Italy, Africa, Key West, Cuba, and Idaho. Clips from the show are available on YouTube at the BBC Worldwide Channel. For a travel timeline, book recommendations, and an occasional recipe, check out the show's website: www.pbs.org/hemingwayadventure/.

My Way or the Conway
Harold Jenkins & The Prosaic Preparation Paradox

1933–1993 AD

Yes, prior planning does prevent poor performance
though the maxim is a lot like a supporting musician.
It is worn out, usually ignored, and deserving of more
of your respect.

The truck-stop west of Memphis smelled of bacon and
industrial strength cleaner and was not far, geographi-
cally or metaphorically, from a place called Greasy Corner.
Dishes rattled, and pots clanged as patrons ate, drank, and
smoked their way through the morning hours. An unctuous
smog hung over the tables as Harold Jenkins lit a cigarette
and said "So there it is, I'm leaving. It's over and I'm heading home." The older, grayer, and heavier man sitting across
from him looked briefly like he'd eaten a bad egg. He tried
to speak, but was interrupted by the waitress materializing

from the miasma.[173]

"Coffee?" she drawled. As with the vehicles at the diesel pumps outside, it wasn't the years that had been unkind to her, but the miles.

"No thank you darlin'. I believe I've had enough for two breakfasts." Jenkins smiled. She returned it dutifully and moved on to the rest of her rounds, her eyes lingering a fraction of second longer than necessary. Jenkins felt his smile fade. He was used to the kind of attention that flattered, but never seemed to last.

The older man was jabbing a finger as he spoke. "Damn it Harold, you are an established musician, and this is no time to quit. You've built a solid résumé here. A lot of guys would sell their souls for a chance at your success."

"That's a nice compliment. Thank you." Harold knew he was right, but inside his heart there was a hollowness he'd have trouble explaining, so he didn't try. Harold Jenkins was an established musician without a record deal, fans, or a name that anyone outside of three bars in Memphis would recognize. It just wasn't enough. "This isn't your failure, it's mine. You've been a good manager and I thank you for giving me a shot."

The man smiled sadly and paid the bill. He'd seen it before, the business chewing up good musicians and spitting them out like the gristle on a cheap steak. But this one had some real talent. It was just a shame. "Take care of yourself, kid," he mumbled and left the table, headed for

173 Greasy Corner, Arkansas, is an unincorporated town in St. Francis County about forty miles from Memphis. The name is the result of a restaurant and automobile repair shop located in the same building. The town is often featured in lists of unusual place names.

the bathroom and then back to town to find more meat for the grinder.

Jenkins sat and stared for a bit at the traffic moving along the new highway outside, one that would eventually overlap the famous Route 66 and stretch all the way to California. For now, like him, it went nowhere except back to Arkansas. He sighed. "Elvis. Johnny Cash. Jerry Lee Lewis... Harold Jenkins?" No, that wasn't going to do. He'd been working in Memphis for years, developing his musical style and sitting in on recording sessions at Sun Studios with the likes of those giants. But *he* was still a nobody.[174]

From a pocket, Jenkins pulled out a regional map, tracing lines back and forth across two states and mentally planning his trip home. He felt a figure looming over him and looked up to see his manager returned for one last try.

"Okay, what you need is a new start, I get that. But not at home. Where the blazes would you go anyway?" He bent over the map and traced a rough thumbnail over the westward highway. "Conway?" It was just north of Pine Bluff and a few hours drive from where they sat. "Hell, why not keep running from your problems? Head to Texas. Why not... Twitty?" That town was a full day's drive and four hundred and seventy miles away from Conway.

Jenkins sat confused for a moment, then it hit him like heartburn after the biscuit and gravy special. And he knew he was saved. He snapped his fingers in triumph. "That's it."

"It is? Wait. What?" [175]

---

174 Jenkins was born in Mississippi, but his family moved to Helena, Arkansas by the time he was ten when he wrote his first song and fronted a blues band two years later.

175 Dropped by Sun and Mercury Records, Twitty signed with MGM but

Jenkins beamed. "Elvis, Jerry Lee Lewis, Johnny Cash… Conway Twitty. Come on, let's get back to the studio." He had what he was looking for and would never be a nobody again. Heading for the door he spun the waitress around and planted a smacking kiss on her cheek. The patrons cheered, she blushed, and the rest, as they say, is history.[176]

The newly dubbed Conway Twitty executed his name change and a new plan for fame and glory. He found success on the rock stations of the late 1950s, but his bluesy purr lent itself well to rock-and-roll or country music and his conversion to the latter in 1965 would propel him to national stardom. His1968 hit *Next in Line* was the first of fifty releases to reach number one. They included his most famous hit *Hello Darlin'* and a series of duets with Loretta Lynn. Life was good. Which, in the typical country music song, is where things go wrong. Twitty suffered gastral pains during a show in 1993, not merely the emotional pains for which country musicians are famous. An aneurysm opened in his stomach and he didn't make it through surgery,

---

needed a name to catch the eye of disc jockeys. MGM released a record called *I'll Try* that flopped. Twitty quit the business in despair. But *I'll Try* had a "B Side" called *It's Only Make Believe* that began getting air play in Columbus, Ohio. *It's Only Make Believe* is about a man who convinces himself the woman he loves returns those feelings, but alas it isn't so. The result is a combination of blues and doo wop that fits just fine on a greatest hits compilation alongside his country hits. It made him an overnight sensation and sold over eight million copies.

176 Or at least, a History Lesson. Music had saved Harold Jenkins from his first disappointment in life and came close to becoming his second. His first love and initial disappointment in life was baseball. His career was cut short when he was drafted twice, once by the Philadelphia Phillies and once by the United States Army. The latter was an offer he couldn't refuse. He'd fallen back on his music, developing a style playing at foreign bases and enlisted clubs.

going to the great recording studio in the sky at the age of fifty-nine. Conway Twitty left behind a gruff baritone, four children, and this oft repeated counsel: "Listen to advice, but follow your heart."[177]

Perhaps he should have let his music do the talking. Following your heart is a nice sentiment, but we should consider the source. When Twitty took good advice, made plans, and executed them, he became a star. When he followed his heart, he got divorced. Yes, Conway Twitty never lacked for female attention, and it led him to follow that heart and say "Hello Darlin'" four times, twice to the same woman. Sure, that is fairly normal in the lives of the rich and famous, but after each of those three trips down the matrimonial aisle, he neglected to plan for his ultimate demise and update his will.

The result is as predictable as a country music chorus: heartbreak, angry ex-wives, disinherited children, and an estate at public auction. He ignored the truism that prior planning prevents poor performance, perhaps because it was too simple, too mundane, too Harold Jenkins. Welcome to what I call the **Prosaic Preparation Paradox,** where the

---

177 Occasionally Twitty's blues-rock fusion style was mistaken for Elvis Presley's, a compliment he didn't mind a bit, and his concerts were famous for their lack of chit chat or banter between songs. But Twitty was no aloof artist. "I do talk," he said, "but the communication is through my music." Someone was receiving whatever he was sending. His number one singles generated millions of dollars and helped build a country music and entertainment compound in Tennessee called Twitty City. It was liquidated at auction after his death.

simpler the tasks, the less likely we are to do them, especially when we perceive our life becoming more complicated. When we hit the big time, we focus on the ostentatious issues and let the mundane ones slip through the cracks. For Conway, plain old planning might have saved seven years of legal battles and an estate sale. It might have been worth it to save those gold records and rhinestone suits.

—— LEGIONS OF DOOM ——

Generals, politicians and other strategists demonstrate a host of cognitive biases in their decision making that lead them to prepare for the last war instead of the next one. For example, the French built the Maginot Line to defend against Germany's World War I army, only to have their motorized offspring drive around it.

Today, among military leaders, the fear of "fighting the last war" is soundly ingrained. So, it leads to what some have called the preparation paradox, where if you believe that you will inevitably prepare for the *last* war, you'll feel that any effort at change is ultimately doomed and do nothing.

We see this thinking outside of the military too. Many of us fear that if we prepare or plan for things like retirement, we will be readying ourselves for the wrong thing and thus we take no action. Ironically, the way to protect yourself it is to plan *more*. Plan early, plan often, and share your plans with someone else. Get feedback and clarify what you don't know. That will give you a fighting chance.

How You'll Be Tested...

Investors are also people, which means they usually have lives that need tending. Are you so busy or distracted with your own career and family that financial planning is a forgotten B side? If so, and you are convinced you are doing everything right, *that* is only make believe. For your own good, it might be time to reinvent yourself.

If you want your financial life to make sense now and after the music begins to fade, you better mind the five Ps and get planning for your own hits. Put a blueprint in place you can live, and even die, with. I don't care what your name is, you don't get to number one without putting in the work. And if you can't do it solo, then make it a duet.

EXTRA CREDIT:

BECOME A LEACH: When you do things right, you accumulate wealth, earn the adoration of fawning fans, and are featured on *Lifestyle of the Rich and Famous*. Watch Robin Leach meet Harold Jenkins at: www.youtube.com/watch?v=uitTxQfm6Oo.

GO ON TOUR: Twitty City is now a Christian music center known as Trinity City. Until a few years ago, you could still tour Conway's estate. The tours have ended, mostly because of lack of demand, but you can still get your own here, courtesy of Google Maps: www./goo.gl/maps/g1MnBe68jQn.

GET LIT: One thing that hasn't changed under new ownership is the million bulb Holiday extravaganza. Be one of the visitors to drive through and say Merry Christmas

Conway: www.cityseeker.com/nashville-tn/390055-trinity-music-city-usa.

GO P: There are several variations on the theme of the five Ps. Practitioners use up to seven or eight Ps. Sometimes *Proper* Prior Planning is the key. And sometimes Poor Planning is described with another P, which is a synonym for pee. Confused? Find enlightenment and get updates on (where else?) Facebook at: www.facebook.com/The-Seven-Ps-Proper-Prior-Planning-Prevents-Piss-Poor-Per-formance-279919480824/.

GO COUNTRY: I admit, I'm not much of country music fan, but I had to sit down and write this song in honor of Conway:

> *Kicking back in a smoky diner*
> *Crazy for thinking that my love could hold you*
> *Riding low, heading for the state line*
> *I'm crazy, crazy for feeling so blue*

Complete crap? Jeez, everyone's a critic. But thanks to the Internet (I guess), everyone can now write lyrics.

> *Give it a try*
> *Can you do better than I?*
> *Write a western music song…*
> *Turn the country tune generator on:*
> www.songlyricsgenerator.com/step1.php.

LAWYER UP: When you do things wrong, your family takes to the courts, spends your money, and then sells all your stuff to pay for it. But at least your name is immortalized in this book, various news articles and this web-TV episode: www.videos.howstuffworks.com/investigation-discovery/49420-the-will-battle-for-conway-twittys-money-video.htm.

LAWYER UP (PT.2): Want to properly prepare for your curtain call? Find an Estate Planning Attorney to get you ready for the inevitable, keep you out of the newspapers, and save your family from themselves: www.lawyers.com/estate-planning/find-law-firms-by-location/.

All the Kingsmen

Rock-n-Roll & Biased Information Processing

1963 AD

You know that friend who belts out the wrong lyrics to most songs, and nothing you can say will convince her to stop saying "Hold me closer, Tony Danza" instead of "tiny dancer?" Well, it's only rock-and-roll, right? Hardly.

"Well, the recorders are running, and time is money," Jack said to no one in particular. He glanced around the ten-by-ten room strewn with percussion equipment, keyboards, and amplifiers and then up at the microphone suspended from the ceiling. It was steamy in the confined space, as rain was drumming down outside of Northwestern Recorders. Jack was feeling the vibe, soaking in the aura of the small recording studio in southwest Portland, Oregon. This was the place that had launched the careers of local legends like Jimmie Rodgers who was born across the river in Camas and had recorded his 1957 smash hit *Honeycomb* where Jack now stood. And it was the launching pad to stardom for Johnny Ray, whose flamboyant style and mannerisms propelled *Little White Cloud That Cried* to sell over 2 million records.

"Hey guys, why don't I sing it instead of just doing an instrumental?" Lynn, Mike, Bob, and Dan gave a collective shrug. Jack grinned. *Rock-and-roll!*

Dan opened on the keyboard with two bars in *A Major*. Then Bob on the bass and Lynn on drums, joined the rhythm guitar in a sort of calypso rock romp. Nine seconds in, Jack stepped to the suspended microphone and made history of his own belting out mushy lyrics for another minute then screaming "Okay let's give it to 'em right now!" as Mike kicked in with the lead guitar solo. Finally, Jack brought it home with a new, less intelligible verse and a few more reprises of the chorus. Originally a Jamaican ballad, the song told the story of a sailor returning to his island home for his special lady. And it was all over in two minutes and twenty seconds.

It was done in one take and the Saturday morning session cost all of $36. But whether it was the small space at a cheap price, the angle of the single microphone, or the result of Jack's recent dental work, the vocals were audible, but not totally comprehensible. Yet it had to be good enough, given they had split the cost themselves and couldn't afford another session.

Luckily, the Kingsmen's version of *Louie, Louie* was good if not perfect and it was destined to be great, if not a little bit controversial. In spite (or because) of the controversy, the record sold over twelve million copies and turned up in at least as many fraternity parties over the ensuing five decades.[178]

You see, success usually comes with a certain amount of scrutiny and the unintelligible lines concerned parents who heard and believed rumors about their content. As the song made its way to number two on the Billboard charts, rumors began to circulate that the lyrics were obscene. Of course, this only added to the allure of the song as it made its way toward becoming a cult classic, the mushy vocals making it wildly popular with teenagers who reveled in rebellion.[179]

Letters began accumulating on the desk of Attorney General Robert Kennedy asking the Justice Department to investigate if the Kingsmen were in violation of the Interstate Transportation of Obscene Material Law. One parent noted that in trying to decipher the jumble of words, they'd determined that the content was "so filthy that I can-not (sic) enclose them in this letter. I would like to see these people, the 'artists', the Record company and the promoters prosecuted to the full extent of the law...these morons have gone too far. How can we stamp out this menace?" Meanwhile an alternate set of lyrics was making the rounds at colleges and high schools, as students took artistic license.

---

178 Who knew that those A Major notes would become the most famous and recognizable opening in the history of rock and roll? *Louie, Louie* was converted to rock rhythms in 1955 and covered numerous times by artists of pop, rock, and rhythm and blues. Indeed, Paul Revere and the Raiders would record the song at Northwestern just a week later, leading them to become the first rock-and-roll band to sign with Columbia Records. .

179 *Louie, Louie* would go on to become a Rolling Stone Top 500 hit of all time. But the original lineup wouldn't last. Creative differences led Jack to go his own way shortly after the song was released.

A second letter to J Edgar Hoover accused the record of an auditory illusion whereby listeners could hear one of two sets of lyrics, a clean version and an obscene one. "Is there perhaps a subliminal type of perversion involved?" the writer bemoaned.

Enter the FBI, who subjected the recording to every test known to them at that time. They attempted to match lyrics transcribed by parents when playing the 45RPM record at 33RPM. An FBI memorandum from 1965 notes that "the phonetic qualities of this recording are such that a listener possessing the "phony" lyrics could imagine them to be genuine." In other words, people are going to hear what they want to hear. An eventual four hundred and fifty-five-page report concurred, noting that whether slowed down or sped up, the original lyrics were "unintelligible at any speed." Jack always maintained that he knew the lyrics perfectly well, hadn't slurred or mumbled, and was not one for pornography in any form.[180]

From time to time, we are all guilty of **Biased Information Processing**. That is, ignoring information that doesn't conform to our beliefs or desires. A cousin of confirmation bias, **biased information processing** has us not merely seeking confirming information, but actively ignoring data that contradicts our opinions. How is that for progress? Mentally, we've rocked and rolled our way back to the stone age.

---

180 A 45 at 33RPM? Trust me this makes a certain amount of sense to anyone over forty.

Focusing on information that reinforces your ideas isn't just for annoying parents or Federal agencies. Psychologists studying depression note that there are a series of factors that predispose or make some more vulnerable to melancholy and hopelessness than others.

One factor may be an "information processing paradigm" biased toward negativity. "Individuals who are depressed misinterpret facts and experiences in a negative fashion, limiting their focus to the negative aspects of situations, thus feeling hopeless about the future." In other words, if you are among the estimated one-third of the population suffering from depression, you only hear what you *don't* want to hear. There is a bit of a chicken and egg argument over cognitive functioning for depressed individuals. Which comes first, the depression or the negativity? The evidence seems to point toward the latter, cognitive issues making us more vulnerable. (Which shouldn't surprise readers who started with History 101.) Luckily, for some, treatment may be as simple as helping improve their recall of positive events.

How You'll Be Tested...

When your political party is out of power, are you one to bemoan the general state of the world, including your portfolio? Even if things are going well? Investors, like outraged parents, typically hear what they want to hear. This means subliminally tuning out information that doesn't conform with their professed investment style, aversion to risk or even their political beliefs.[181]

How do we stamp out this menace? Most great bands need a little creative friction to make their best and most enduring music. Your investment plan needs that, too. So, talk it over with someone who doesn't agree with your style or even your politics. If you tend to be a pessimist, seek advice from a specialist who is as positive as you are negative and as calculating as you are emotional. At the very least you'll hear some things you didn't think of before and make your plans more intelligible and less garbled. Adding someone with a new perspective to your ensemble might just lead you to the performance of a lifetime.

EXTRA CREDIT:

TAKE A NEW YORK MINUTE: The New Yorker has an excellent expose on *Why Facts Don't Change Our Minds* at: www.newyorker.com/magazine/2017/02/27/why-facts-dont-change-our-minds. Usually we are most concerned with having facts at hand to win an argument which isn't a great vibe for thinking clearly. When assessing a problem, your first take might not be the best one.

TALK ABOUT IT: Julia Galef is co-founder of the Center for Applied Rationality, trying to help people make better, more reasonable decisions. In her TED Talk, Galef asks: "What do you most yearn for? Do you yearn to defend your own beliefs, or do you yearn to see the world as clearly as you

---

181 For the record, politics and investing go together about as well as the notes in a 3rd inversion of a major 7 chord. Music theorists describe that as particularly harsh and discordant, creating a jarring lack of harmony.

possibly can?" For most, the answer is the former and Galef traces the motivations for such behavior using "a compelling history lesson from nineteenth-century France." A history lesson to teach psychology? An idea whose time has come. Available at: www.ted.com/talks/julia_galef_why_you_ think_you_re_right_even_if_you_re_wrong?language=en.

EXPOSE YOURSELF: Eli Pariser is the author of *The Filter Bubble (2012)* about how personalized search engines might be limiting our exposure to novel ideas. When companies like Google tailor your experience on the web, you are less likely to "get exposed to information that could challenge or broaden our worldview." Pick up the book or check out his TED Talk at www.ted.com/talks/eli_pariser_beware_ online_filter_bubbles. Be sure to follow the link and not look for it through a search engine, or you may not get there.

OPEN THE BUREAU: Lest you think the FBI involvement with the Kingsmen is the stuff of my imagination, the entire FBI study of *Louie, Louie* is available online at: www.vault.fbi. gov/louie-louie-the-song/louie-louie-the-song/view. The file opens in February of 1964, just a few months after the Kennedy assassination. You would think they had better, more pressing things to investigate, but the historical record doesn't lie.

GO TO COURT: Stop making up excuses to skip jury duty and watch a live trial. The decisions we all make are a lot like the battle between prosecution and defense. The facts you seek, and the ones you ignore, depend on which side you represent. And we aren't just talking about petty crimes and misdemeanors. Associate Justice of the Supreme Court William O. Douglas was, to his credit, at least aware of his bias during the longest tenure in the court's history (1939–1975). "At the constitutional level where we work, 90 percent of any decision is emotional. *The rational part of us supplies the reasons for supporting our predilections.*" That kind of honesty couldn't help but make him controversial, so read up on his biography at: www.biography.com/people/william-o-douglas-9278209.

PLEDGE DELTA: Filmed not far from Portland, at the University of Oregon, *Animal House (1978)* has even more incomprehensible singing of *Louie Louie* and the kind of life advice that everyone agrees with. Like this: "Fat drunk and stupid is no way to go through life son." Why watch it? Why not?!

Raising the Bar
Dick Fosbury & Expert Bias

1968 AD

How high can you go in your life's quest for greatness? Pretty far, if you can learn from the expertise of someone who doesn't think you are completely nuts.

The freshman took a deep breath and then launched himself forward. *Speed*, he thought, *be fast*. At a dead sprint, he planted his right foot, turned his shoulders from the padded landing area, and arched his back. *Soar*, he thought, *be weightless*. The rest of the Oregon State track team winced. Someone giggled at the ridiculous spectacle as the young kid's legs spasmed upward when it seemed he'd collide and topple either the cross bar or the entire structure it rested on. Then, with a slapping sound he hit the padded mat like a wet noodle and glanced upward. The bar still rested on the standards where it was braced.

"Fosbury! Fosbury, what in the *hell* was that?" Coach Berny Wagner stood with his hands on his hips and his face contorted in perturbed astonishment.

"Coach?" asked his young freshman high jumper.

"Yes, I am the coach." Wagner barked. "At least until someone sees you trying that ridiculous high jump experiment of yours and fires me for putting you in danger, or merely having bad taste."

"But I've been using it since high school and I think it works. I think I'm jumping higher."

"Son, this isn't high school. You think there is some shortcut to competing in the Pacific Ten Conference? The only shortcut you found is one to mediocrity. Plan A is to use the established techniques to avoid killing yourself. There is no Plan B. And there is no turning your back to the bar. My god, that had all the athletic grace of a fish falling into a boat."

"Yes sir," mumbled Fosbury and shuffled off to try again with a more traditional technique.

An hour later, the freshman had come nowhere close to the six-and-a-half-foot bar he'd been practicing with using his own method. Wagner ambled over to the high jump pit with a look that was hard to figure. "Ah," he began awkwardly. "Fosbury, we need to talk."

"Sure coach? What's up?"

"Well...you are. We did some newfangled video analysis stuff on your jumps and, well, you weren't just barely clearing the six and half foot bar with your...flop thing."

"I wasn't?"

"No. Your last jump, best we can tell, you cleared it by a few inches." Coach Berny Wagner was convinced. "So, this is the end of Plan A. Got it? Plan B is now in full effect. Keep flopping, Fosbury, and we will both hopefully live with the consequences."[182]

---

182 Before the flop, high jumpers had varying ways of going over the bar while moving forward including the scissor kick and western roll. As a youngster, Fosbury found that he was pretty average at every technique but his own. The physics of the flop allowed him to run faster and convert more potential energy into upward motion. Using the technique at Medford High School in Oregon, Fosbury earned his partial college scholarship sight unseen because his jump numbers were compelling. But when Wagner actually saw it, he tried to steer him back to orthodoxy, mostly because he grew tired of the jokes. One suspects the staff at the rival University of Oregon may have been particularly contemptuous.

Dick Fosbury survived and thrived. The next year, as a sophomore, he cleared six-feet-ten-inches to set the Oregon State University record. As news of the technique got out, athletic experts said it looked ugly, ungainly, or like someone slipping off the back of a truck in a rainstorm. But Fosbury kept soaring higher. The experts doubled down on their critiques, thinking he was insane and fearing that the consequences of his style could be disastrous. Such a corkscrew motion at full speed would lead to misfortune, and they envisioned an entire generation of participants "wiped out" due to debilitating injuries. Anyone following this Fosbury fellow was obviously a fool.

At the Mexico City Olympics in 1968, medical teams stood by, ready for the worst when the American with the new jumping style toed the start line. The crowd of 86,000 at the Estadio Olímpico Universitario held a collective breath. White shorts flapping in the thin Mexico City air, his blue clad torso emblazoned with USA in block letters, Fosbury soared over the bar at over seven-feet-and-four-inches. It was easy to see who had the last laugh on his way to collect his gold medal. The story of the Fosbury Flop is about one man ignoring the noise to find a better way onward and upward. Dick Fosbury invented a new way to jump high, stuck with it through intense criticism and created the only successful flop known to man.[183,184]

But it is also the tale of experts losing their impartiality and getting carried away in their critiques of a young student athlete with a novel idea. This is a common manifestation of **Expert Bias,** the process where those supposedly in the know lose the ability to relate. Asked the same questions day after day, the professional authority on sports eventually abandons empathy and concludes that non-experts have ulterior motives or are just plain stupid. Sportswriters and critics had seen thousands of high jumpers and that act of repetition made them sure of the fact that facing the bar was the only way to jump over it.

---

183 After setting the American record at the 1968 Olympics, Fosbury won his second straight NCAA title. Within a few years his soaring technique had become commonplace. Since 1980, no one using any other method has held the world record in the high jump.

184 His triumph is also a rare example of getting past both our physical *and* mental barriers. Studies have shown that certain areas of the brain usually used in decision-making tasks, shut down when confronted with expert opinions. What if Fosbury had turned off when told how reckless and foolish he was? Perhaps they would have had to change the name of the event to the moderately lofty jump. But that wouldn't sell many Wheaties boxes.

How to Successfully Flop
Four steps to soaring with expert advice.

1. Start on the right (or left) foot…	2. Build up some momentum…	3. Kick your feet up…	4. Check the tapes…
High jumpers refer to their run up to the bar as "the J" because of the shape of their path. To arrive at the bar on the plant foot, the approach must be choreographed starting with which foot starts the sequence.	Fosbury Floppers stand tall throughout their approach, keeping a sprinter's posture until the "penultimate" or second to last step. Then they transition that momentum upward by driving high with their hands and shoulders.	Although most of the forward momentum of a high jumper is converted upward, there is still some forward momentum that carries them toward the bar. Kicking their feet and tucking their chin helps avoid it as they soar over.	Elite jumpers know there is always some defect in technique that keeps them from going higher. No practice session is over until the tapes are reviewed, the flaws identified and a plan to correct them is put in place.
Investors must start on the right foot with an expert source of advice. Have a frank discussion about your investment philosophy, goals, and expectations. Feeling talked down to? Sprint in the opposite direction.	Do your homework and ask a lot of questions. Don't like the answers? Plan B is to begin the process again with someone else.	Don't be afraid to stand up for yourself. But once you've cleared the bar, relax and put your feet up. You've hired someone to help you, let her do the job.	Relaxed doesn't mean asleep at the wheel. Periodic reviews and Q&A sessions ensure you continue to improve your relationship and the quality of advice. Has something gone wrong? Jump back to step one or two and start again.

How You'll Be Tested...

If you picked up this book, you are probably open to advice and expert opinion. Unfortunately, some day, you may find that your chosen advisor doesn't think much of your intelligence. Listen, it is okay, even preferable, to disagree. Why work with someone you agree with all the time? Without creative tension, there is no creativity. But if healthy discourse devolves into patronizing, condescending, or ignoring, it is time to move on.

Whether you are hurtling over a bar, or merely taking on financial hurdles, you can't get objective advice from someone who is so confident of his own opinion that he becomes derisive of yours. You simply can't get unbiased advice from someone who has crossed over that line.

EXTRA CREDIT

LAUSANNE UP: You won't get a medal for visiting the Olympic museum in Lausanne Switzerland, but you will get an up-close view of the current world record in the high jump. Visitors enter through a fountain enclosed walkway that leads you under an up-to-date bar. Emphasis on going under the bar as the walkway is concrete, not padded. Plan a trip at: www.olympic.org/museum.

FEEL THE BURN: Before the *Tonight Show*, Jimmy Fallon only worked once a week as a cast member with Saturday Night Live. One of his more beloved skits, missing since he left in 2004 was Nick Burns, aka, Your Company's Computer Guy. Computers repaired with condescension? Servers serviced with snootiness? Uh, you're *welcome*. Live from New York, it's Saturday Night Live: www.nbc.com/saturday-night-live/video/nick-burns-your-companys-computer-guy/n11268.

JUMP UP: Want to float like Fosbury? Learn the details of the modern high jump on WikiHow and practice your technique at: www.wikihow.com/High-Jump-Using-the-Fosbury-Flop. Author's Note: Not liable for injuries or embarrassment while flopping onto your couch cushions.

JUMP AROUND: Can't get enough high jump action? Okay, two quick videos, then get outside and get some exercise, will you? Get inspired on YouTube's Olympic Channel: www.youtube.com/user/olympic.

You love history, right? Trick question. Get an added dose of the high jump past and present in ninety seconds at: www.youtube.com/watch?v=-OtkrNq1fZg.

Dick Fosbury never thought he'd be a champion and he wasn't even trying to be. He was the worst high jumper on his high school team and developed his technique to survive. Good coaching and mental toughness took him higher than he ever expected. The lesson seems obvious, but are worth repeating here: www.youtube.com/watch?v=gGqQXDkpgss.

JUMP IN LINE: Visit the DMV. It is a place notorious for insane amounts of bureaucracy, the kind which most people can master if only given enough time. You don't have that time. The person on the other side of the service window does. Knowing that the folks there are merely exhibiting expert bias and aren't really evil might improve your experience. Or, it might not.

To Boldly Go

Lenard Nimoy & Television Personality Bias

Stardate 346913.600–271404.971

I f you haven't figured it out by now, even smart people do illogical things. Believing too much of what you see on TV will quickly get you typecast as the typical human, taking shortcuts and failing basic logic.

"Spock, analysis?"

He arched an eyebrow. "Analysis?"

"Yes, Spock. We need your insight."

"Insight?" Electronics whirred and beeped in the background. The computers, it seemed, were also waiting on him.

"Yes, your Vulcan logic." Everyone stood by breathlessly expecting him to have some very sound advice. He didn't, so he did the logical thing; he nodded a lot.

"Vulcan logic, yes. Of course." He glanced around the room full of engineers and electrical equipment and vaguely wondered if someone couldn't get him out of here. *I need a transporter. Beam me up!*

"Damn it man," someone barked, "what does your pointy-eared, cold-blooded rationality tell you?"

Wow, these life forms are getting restless, he thought. *Interesting.* The nodding didn't seem to satisfy anyone. They were still looking to him and expecting some sort of advice. *Very interesting. Perhaps a ruse will work?* He flashed the Vulcan salute, a palm out with splayed middle and ring fingers and said: "Keep it up and you'll live long and prosper."

It did work. The tension melted like a warp drive missing its dilithium crystals, the crowd nodding enthusiastically and dispersing back to desks piled high with scientific looking print outs. Lenard Nimoy touched his round ears and then shook his very human head. The Cal Tech students, each with a brilliant young mind, had been looking for words of scientific wisdom from a man with a Master's Degrees in Education. Talk about alien pursuits.[185]

Nimoy was no dummy, but though he had three Emmy nominations for playing the Vulcan Science Officer of the USS Enterprise, he also was *not* Spock. The second son of Jewish Ukrainian immigrants, Nimoy grew up in tenement housing in tough economic times with a love of the theatre. In high school, he acted in community college productions and moved to California to join the Pasadena Playhouse at

---

185 Nimoy related something close to this incident in a New York Times interview: "I had an embarrassing experience once, many years ago. I was invited to go to Cal Tech and was introduced to a number of very brilliant young people who were working on interesting projects. They walked me through, and they would say we're doing this and we're doing that, and we're trying to figure out why this is happening. And then they'd say to me, "What do you think?" Expecting me to have some very sound advice. And I would nod very quietly and very sagely I would say, "You're on the right track."

age eighteen. He served in the army, drove cabs, and poured sodas waiting for his big break. It came in a strange package with alien ears, arched eyebrows, and a bowl-cut hairdo. Star Trek would last just three seasons, but Leonard Nimoy's Vulcan, and his salutary greeting would become a cultural phenomenon. The show became wildly popular in syndication and led to a series of films, Star Trek conventions, several spin-off series, and a rebooted movie franchise.[186]

For forty-seven years Lenard Nimoy portrayed Spock, which isn't bad for a guy whose previous acting jobs lasted, at most, two weeks. Of course, the curse of any actor with strong character identification is being typecast. Nimoy struggled at first with his alter ego, publishing the book *I Am Not Spock* in 1979 and originally opting out of the Star Trek movie. He was tired of putting on the pointy ears and faking the science. He desperately desired to pursue other artistic endeavors such as photography and poetry. After reluctantly joining the movie cast, Spock was killed in the second Star Trek movie. But Nimoy was coming to terms with his fame and, perhaps, his fortune. What better way to fund other pursuits than cashing in at the theatre every

186 The Vulcan salute originated with a Jewish Orthodox religious festival full of pageantry and tradition where, as a boy, Nimoy had been told to close his eyes during a particular blessing. In Depression-Era Boston, one didn't choose lightly to disobey one's parents. But eight-year-old boys are curious, mischievous, and disobedient in any era, religion, or language. And so, as the priests began their blessing, a sort of discordant chant, the congregation averted their eyes; except for Nimoy. He saw the priests with their hands stretched out as if hugging the congregation, but with a twist: their palms were out and their fingers split, mimicking a letter in the Hebrew alphabet that stood for the Almighty. The image and the memory would stick with him for a very long time. And if Trekkies over the years knew they were giving each other a terrestrial religious blessing, no one seemed to mind.

couple of years? For the third movie, he returned as a reborn Spock and continued his role while also directing the next two films. In 1995, he wrote the second volume of his autobiography: *I Am Spock*. No, there isn't much logic to changing your mind like that, but as his day at Cal Tech illustrates, Nimoy was all too human.[187]

TRUST BUSTERS

Humankind's search for non-traditional media characters to trust makes some sense. Dare we say, it is logical? That is because confidence in conventional mass media news outlets has been on the decline.

American viewers have largely given up on their usual sources of journalism when seeking someone "to report the news fully, accurately, and fairly." The percentage of those having a "great deal or fair amount of trust" in the media dove to its lowest level in Gallup polling history at 32% in 2016. And it's been falling steadily for years, not just during divisive elections.

Yet another mental shortcut for our species is known as **Television Personality Bias.** It means we tend to give more credence to those we've seen on television or the big screen, regardless of their actual expertise. Researchers have shown that television viewers maintain a "para-social" relationship

---

187 He would continue to revisit the character in various Star Trek formats until the 2013 film, *Into Darkness*. The role was his last. He died in 2015 at the age of 83.

with characters they view, often placing them somewhere above mere acquaintances but slightly below real friends on a relationship scale. While kind of disturbing, and more than a little sad, without that kind of bias no one at a technical school would give a Tribble for the opinion of someone with a liberal arts degree.

When we hear the opinion of someone we see often on television, we are predisposed to lend it a greater weight than a total stranger. Even though A) the television personality *is* a total stranger and B) we have no idea of his actual level of knowledge about, well, anything! Analysis, Spock? Fascinating, as this seems a form of tribal instinct, ceding decision-making to a person or persons whom the tribe elevates and allows to speak in front of it. Highly illogical, of course. But, to borrow a quote from Star Trek IV, who ever said the human race was logical?

How You'll Be Tested...

Throughout my career, I've heard investors say things like: "I follow the guy on CNBC who writes all the books and he had to have done something right to get there." You may feel similarly about someone you watch or listen to regularly while having little idea about her actual background, expertise, or education. Face it, the only qualification you seem to care about is that she is on television. Seriously, if your idea of investment research is calling in to talk mutual funds with Suze, I invite you to step up and receive your Vulcan nerve pinch.

Contemplating following advice from mass media

sources? Sorry, but in most cases, it is way too general because they don't know you. And you don't know them. At all. If Leonard Nimoy were really Spock, he never would have released the album *Highly Illogical* featuring such embarrassments as *The Ballad of Bilbo Baggins*. And if anyone on television was actually great at investing, they wouldn't need side projects either. Understand all this and prosper so that you can afford to live long.

EXTRA CREDIT

BOLDLY GO LISTEN: Don't take my word for it, lest you think I exaggerate or deal unfairly with Leonard's gratuitous ventures, just you try to make it through all two minutes and twenty seconds of the music video *The Ballad of Bilbo Baggins* at: www.youtube.com/watch?v=AGF5ROpjRAU. In mere seconds, you'll be wishing someone would put one of those creatures from Star Trek II (www.youtube.com/watch?v=3i42Smtbmeg) in your ear, just to drown out the sound.

MIND MELD: There is occasional controversy about other biases among those on television. Those who study such things found that a change from dispassionate reporting to "humorous and hostile" styles (Hannity, The Daily Show etc.) has increased the amount of bias perceived by viewers. Read *Political Interviews: Examining Perceived Media Bias and Effects Across TV Entertainment Formats* at http://ijoc.org/index.php/ijoc/article/viewFile/1932/863. It seems that style matters. Say it with me in your best Vulcan monotone: fascinating.

LIVE LONG: Dr. John Day's *The Longevity Plan* (2017) will have you exploring the outer reaches of a normal lifespan if you cut out processed foods and sugars, and decrease your stress. Other tips include smiling more and making time to play. Set Phasers to fun!

AND PROSPER: Thomas Stanley and William Danko's *The Millionaire Next Door: The Surprising Secrets of America's Wealthy (1996)* offers to make those golden years of yours a little more, you know, golden. Spoiler alert: spend less, save more, invest well. Engage Warp Factor 'thrive'!

KEEP ON TREKKING: The Enterprise travels on in two web series, *Star Trek Continues* and *Star Trek Phase 2*, that logically shouldn't exist, yet here they are:

www.startrekcontinues.com/episodes.html.

www.youtube.com/user/startrekphase2DE.

And CBS recently launched *Star Trek: Discovery* on its streaming platform. Discovery takes place about a decade before the crew of the Enterprise set off on the original five-year mission, which turned into almost half a century. This franchise has more lives than Spock.

GAME THE SYSTEM: Seeking new life forms? Check out www.startrek.com/games for a full supply of games, apps, and even emojis. Or choose from the best Trek themed games of all time: www.metacritic.com/feature/best-and-worst-star-trek-videogames. Of course, if you are spending too many hours in other worlds via your computer or game system, you don't need to get new life forms. You need to get a life.

DON'T BE A KLINGON: A bit harsh, you say? Well, Captain Kirk himself agrees and is even more harsh when he confronts conventioneers and urges them to "get a life" and "grow the hell up." Beam yourself in to Evil Kirk's rant courtesy of Saturday Night Live at: www.nbc.com/saturday-night-live/video/trekkies/n9511?snl=1. At least take some of his advice and move out of your parents' basement.

Strike That

Rich Gedman & Economic Estimates

1986 AD

B aseball fans are bonkers about statistics. But even the craziest ones know that you still have to play the game to see what happens.

For Rich Gedman the voices in his head started as a child. But not in the horror movie nor the crazy uncle sort of way.

One ball and two strikes to Gedman. He swings and drives it to center field...

As a kid, Rich always had a radio program in his head, calling the play-by-play at the local park or sandlot. There he'd hit a host of game winners and even won a few World Series, something his local club, the Red Sox, hadn't done in anyone's memory. Signed as a free agent by those same Sox, he worked his way up through the organization in the minor leagues, catching the first nine innings of the longest professional game on record between Pawtucket and Rochester, a thirty-three-inning affair. When he finally got his call up to the big leagues, he made his first appearance pinch hitting for future Hall of Famer, Carl Yastrzemski. Maybe he wasn't all that gifted, but there was still plenty to talk about.[188]

… Way Back. Gone. And Boston wins the pennant!

As a professional, at age twenty-seven, he was still a kid at heart, and though he would never admit it, the broadcasters were still there, along with the chill of spring baseball in his bones and the smell of sweat and leather mixed with popcorn and grilling hot dogs. Early in the 1986 season, Gedman and his announcing crew were optimistic that this was their year to go all the way. The signs were good, even if it was only April.

Welcome back to Fenway Park on a brisk night in Boston where the wind is blowing in over the Green Monster and we are on the verge of history. Red Sox catcher Rich Gedman calling a gem of a game for his young pitcher, and keeping our stats guys in the truck busy looking up all kinds of records tonight.

The Red Sox catcher and his hurler started the game by striking out six batters through the first three innings and blowing through this Seattle lineup like an angry Nor'easter. Had it not been for Mariners' shortstop Spike Owen's lazy single in the fourth, we'd be talking about a no-hit bid. Instead, we've flirted with the record books in other ways including the all-time consecutive strikeout record, broken up by that same pesky Spike Owen. And now the Major League record for putouts by a catcher seems ready to fall.[189]

---

188 Gedman grew up in Worcester, Massachusetts and his Wikipedia page notes, not unkindly, that he was not "classically athletic" and was never drafted.

189 Putouts by a catcher (PO2 in baseball scorekeeping shorthand) are

Yep, hardly your average night at the ballpark. Top of the ninth now, and in steps the left fielder Phil Bradley. Bradley is...

"...a career .290 hitter. Not bad Phil, but off to a slow start this season, eh? Batting just .230 this spring. And 0 for 3 tonight. That won't help the stat line one bit. They must be nuts in that dugout of yours. I mean, have you had a homerun in either of the Reagan administrations? Have you run out of pinch hitters on that bench?"

Bradley said nothing and patiently watched as Gedman's pitcher wound, delivered, and missed high with his first offering. Then the batter stepped out of the box, stretching a bit to release the tension.

"Yep, better get loose. Long walk back to the dugout, could pull something on a night like this," Gedman gloated. He had a bachelor's degree in bull and a master's in mind games. And all his skill was on display.

But the next pitch missed as well and suddenly it was two balls and no strikes. The score was 3–1, and the truth was the Mariners didn't need a homerun. They needed a baserunner. If someone could get on base, it would bring the Designated Hitter, Gorman Thomas, to the plate with a chance to tie the game with one swing of the bat. Thomas had led the league in strikeouts a couple of times, statistics which Gedman had shared with him during his at bat, back in the seventh inning. Thomas had listened, smiled, and then launched a souvenir into the stands, reminding

recorded when catching a ball for an out, tagging a runner, forcing an out, or catching a third strike.
Tom Seaver still holds the Major League record of ten straight strikeouts set in 1970. The Red Sox record of seventeen strikeouts was set by Bill Monbouquette in 1961.

Gedman as he crossed home that he'd also led the league in Home Runs twice.

Phil Bradley knew what he had to do to get the game into Thomas's hands. That might finally silence the Red Sox catcher. So, Bradley patiently took the next pitch as well, trying to work the count and earn a walk. It thumped home for a strike.

Gedman tossed the ball back to his pitcher and said earnestly: "Phil, why don't we salvage a little something positive out of this? Let's get you in the record books, too. What do you say? No need to be a hero after all." Bradley sighed then stepped in and watched the next pitch as well, again a fastball for a called strike.

"That's it Phil, nice night to be a spectator. Just relax and watch the game. Maybe we can get you a bag of peanuts and a beer." Now, the count at 2–2, the fans came to their feet and made all the noise they could, sensing the record about to fall. It was early in the season and the empty seats outnumbered the paid customers by a two-to-one margin. But they had all moved to surround the infield and they made enough noise to set the hairs on the back of Gedman's neck on end. This is what you lived for as a baseball player. One moment, a record on the line, history in the making.

Bradley stepped into the batter's box slowly, deliberately. *He feels it too*, Gedman thought, *good*. The Red Sox pitcher went into his wind up and the crowd came to its feet. Gedman saw the ball, perfect and white silhouetted against night sky as it left his hand, hurling toward home plate. Then it was gone. *Gone? Did he hit it out? Maybe we really are cursed*. But, again, Bradley hadn't swung. With adrenaline pulsing though his body, Gedman hadn't noticed the ball as it pounded into his mitt with a muffled thump, for strike three.[190]

And there it is, number twenty! Phil Bradley struck out without a single swing of the bat and there is a new Major League Baseball record for put outs by a catcher. Rich Gedman has done it! What a gritty performance by a true professional! What a night for baseball.

Rich Gedman still holds the Major League Baseball record for put outs by a catcher. Oh, and Gedman's pitcher, a future all-star named Roger Clemens, also set a record that night with 20 strikeouts. But pitchers get all the press, and this was Gedman's story, at least in *his* mind.

Now, imagine if Gedman (or Clemens if you must) had his record-breaking game called off after three innings and the rest of it statistically determined by the trends of the first third of the game. It would have drastically changed the box score. Gedman would have just eighteen putouts. He only had six through the first three innings which extrapolates

---

190 The Curse of the Bambino was, at the time, a sixty-six-year-old superstition amongst the Red Sox faithful that they had been hexed during the offseason in 1920 when they sold Babe (The Bambino) Ruth's contract to the Yankees. Before that the Sox had won five World Series and were widely considered the cream of the crop in professional baseball. After the trade they just got creamed, going decades without sniffing a league championship. The Sox, who would acquire that pest Spike Owen in a mid-season trade, would go on to the World Series in the 1986 season losing in seven games to the Miracle Mets. Poised to close out the series in game six, a ground ball squirted through Bill Buckner's legs at First Base to extend the series, the curse and the agony for nearly two more decades.

to eighteen over the course of a full game. (Clemens would have thrown a perfect game as he didn't give up a hit until the fourth inning, but the strikeout and putout records would have stayed at nineteen. He'd have also earned a "no-decision" as the game remained a 0–0 tie. I suppose they would have to go to extra statistical innings to sort out a winner. And I have no idea how *that* would work.)[191]

The Advance Estimate						
Boston Red Sox	IP	H	R	ER	BB	SO
Clemens (ND)	3.0	0	0	0	0	6
Stat Analysis	6.0	0	0	0	0	12
Totals:	9.0	0	0	0	0	18

PO2: 18

And if the game had been called two-thirds of the way through, Gedman would have twenty-one putouts (And Clemens would have logged twenty-one strikeouts.) Still tied, they'd again earn a no-decision. Fortunately, baseball is a game of nine innings. Gedman set the record. (Clemens did, too.) *And* they won the game.

---

191 The previous record of nineteen strikeouts happened three times and was a fraternity of Major League pitching royalty: Steve Carlton, Tom Seaver and Nolan Ryan. Twenty strikeouts would happen three more times, once by Clemens himself, still the only player to do it on two occasions. Gedman's mark has been tied since, but 20 is still the record for putouts by a catcher in a regulation nine-inning game. As of this writing, Clemens has not been nominated to the Hall of Fame due to accusations that he used performance enhancing drugs later in his career.

Boston Red Sox	IP	H	R	ER	BB	SO
Clemens (ND)	6.0	0	0	0	0	14
Stat Analysis	3.0	0	0	0	0	7
Totals:	9.0	0	0	0	0	21

PO2: 21

The details matter. Yet many economic statistics are published based on the presumption that one-third of the data is enough to predict all of it. For instance, Gross Domestic Product (GDP), the market value of goods and services produced within the country, is used to measure our overall economic growth or contraction. Three estimates are provided each quarter for GDP, the advance estimate only containing data for the first month while the other two are inferred using statistical means. Other terms for inferring using statistics include guessing and speculating. Likewise, after two months, the third month is extrapolated, and the first estimate struck from the record. Even after the quarter concludes, there are revisions years later due to data that is deduced at first and replaced later with real figures.

The Real Box Score

Boston Red Sox	IP	H	R	ER	BB	SO
Clemens (W)	9.0	3	1	1	0	20
Totals:	9.0	3	1	1	0	20

PO2: 20

So, GDP is both closely watched *and* subject to significant revisions, not a great combination. In the US, GDP averages a 3% rate of growth. Revisions of up to 1.5% are common, or half of the original number. Like Gedman and his pitcher, the economy may have gotten better as the game went on. Or it may have gotten worse. Quite often we have no idea based solely on statistical sampling.

How You'll Be Tested...

Investors aren't always known for their patience *or* their understanding of how government statistics work. And maybe the voices will get in your head. They will tell you that this or that statistic is the one that will be the difference between the minor leagues and the big show. But no single data point is going to make you great, or conversely, make you a goat. Let's go up to the booth for more...

Folks, most statistics are subject to revision. Sometime big ones. So, someone needs to make sure you get the full story before you swing for the fences. That is what teammates are for, to get you in position to succeed and make the right calls together.

Listen up rookie, if you want to avoid having to work extra innings toward your financial goals, ask yourself one question: How deep is your bench?

EXTRA CREDIT

GO DEEP: Think I'm kidding about baseball fans and numbers? Check out: www.baseball-reference.com/bullpen/ for eighty-thousand pages of records, stats, and minutiae. Seeing all of it likely takes longer than a twi-night double header.

JOIN THE TRIBE: Best baseball movie ever is up for debate. In fact, you can do that here: www.bleacherreport.com/ articles/1604919-ranking-the-top-25-baseball-movies-of-all-time. But there is no debate about the best trash-talking catcher or best play-by-play man in such a movie. Tom Berenger (Jake Taylor) and Bob Uecker (Harry Doyle) take those honors in *Major League (1989)*. A team of misfits comes back to play for the pennant, though we find out in the sequel that they fail in their bid to capture the World Series. Enjoy as any Cleveland sports fan would, knowing that, in the end, your team will fall short.

TUNE IN: Want to step to the plate with your own broadcast crew in your head? Check out www.//archive.org/details/classicmlb-baseballradio for classic radio broadcasts from the 1934 All Star Game to the 1973 World Series. Gather around the radio (or Bluetooth enabled device) with your favorite crazy uncle.

CARTOON IN: Check out all the government collected data from The Bureau of Economic Analysis at www.bea.gov/ index.htm. Then watch an animated feature from the BEA on "Why Old GDP Numbers Change" available at: www. youtube.com/watch?v=3vxh9B8xAiI. The early numbers weren't wrong, they claim, it's just that business people and policy makers demand quick answers. If they wait, the later numbers are better. If we can sit through a four-hour baseball game, we should have that kind of patience.

TAKE IN THE TRASH: In reality, Rich Gedman wasn't known for trash talking any more than other catchers at the MLB level. But if he wanted to get some pointers, this is a good place to start: www.askmen.com/money/how_to_300/378_how_to.html. Note that we will not be held responsible for what happens if you actually follow some of this advice at the company softball game.

GET TO FIRST BASE: Want to know the basics of baseball scorekeeping? Here is a hint: the casual fan doesn't track "putouts by the catcher," only the statisticians do. For more tips, visit: www.mlb.mlb.com/mlb/official_info/baseball_basics/keeping_score.jsp.

KEEP IT WEIRD: Portland, Oregon is known for having things be just a little outside the lines of normality. So, a 1970s minor-league team with no Major League Baseball affiliation was unique enough to be a perfect fit. Actor Kurt Russel's father brought a band of misfits to town and won more than a few games, as well as hearts and minds. Watch a preview here: www.youtube.com/watch?v=RA76b5Hhvxg and check out the full Netflix documentary for the hairier side of the minors. I mean, literally hairy. It was the 70s, after all.

You Can Be Serious

The Australian Open & Emotional Performance

1990 AD

Athletes attempt to use emotions as a weapon to get an edge. This might work sometimes, but over a long career they are better off shutting their traps and staying in the game.

Mock....mock....mock. The sound of the tennis balls battering about in the Melbourne sun was trance inducing. It was a hot, hazy day in Australia, roasting waves rising from the hard court that seemed to be melting into a green ooze. It had slowed play, balls seemingly sticking to the court. *Mock...mock.* And then it stopped, the players went to their chairs and slathered on sunscreen.

After a towel and some water, the American player stood and ambled to the baseline. There, three feet from the lineswoman he stared menacingly at her, bouncing tennis balls onto the face of his racquet, a sour expression on his sun crisped face. Clearly, he disagreed with at least one of her line calls.

"Code violation, unsportsmanlike conduct, warning mister McEnroe," the chair umpire admonished. Johnny Mac was known to use confrontation and emotion like other players used graphite and oversized racquet heads, pushing the boundaries to legally gain an advantage. Or mostly legally.

Hoots and whistles rained down from the crowd. John McEnroe was a divisive force among fans and players, using his temper as a weapon, psyching himself up, getting his adrenaline going and distracting his opponents. He was good at it too, winning seventy-seven ATP singles titles, and spending one hundred and seventy weeks at #1 in the world. He was also widely recognized as the greatest doubles player of all time. But in the twilight of his career, with his skills on the wane, McEnroe was turning to his confrontational abilities more often, seeking a slight edge to break an opponent's concentration and allow him to blast a winner or deliver a smashing overhead. And occasionally, he'd do the opposite, expending his own energy in futile rage that ended in an implosion, rather than an explosion.

McEnroe's verbal barrage was mercifully brief this time and play resumed at its drowsy pace. *Mock.... mock... mock.* As it was wont to do, Mac's play improved a bit when the haze of battle cleared. But the invigorating effect was brief, and the day continued to be a long one. Games passed, until they were deep in the fourth set, with McEnroe serving to even it at three games all. If he failed, it would mean a decisive fifth set and at least forty more minutes on the blazing court.

With the game tied at deuce, McEnroe's first service smacked harmlessly into the net. But his second was true and the two players traded tentative groundstrokes, even more lethargic than the past couple of hours. Then McEnroe floated an easy forehand toward the far sideline. The ball, gleaming and golden kept arcing away, landing eight inches outside the sideline.

McEnroe, unimpressed, delivered heavy retribution to his racquet. It crashed into the conveniently placed court surface. It crumpled. The entire stadium heard the frame give up its always tenuous grip on useful life. Thus, did it die a horrible death, mangled and cooking in the midday sun.

"Code violation, racquet abuse, point penalty Mr. McEnroe," came the announcement. Unfortunately, that penalty came after he had lost the deuce point, giving the game to Mac's opponent.

McEnroe's chin set like quick drying cement. He charged the chair like an angry wombat and exploded into a tirade about the unfairness of it all. This went on for some minutes while tournament referees tried to calm the situation. Things relaxed a bit as he turned from the chair, ready, it seemed, to resume play.

"EXPLETIVE!" Storming back to the baseline McEnroe, uttered one, perhaps two profanities that caused truck drivers to swoon and longshoremen to blush across Australia. They might have rhymed, given the right Aussie accent, with the word 'mock'.[192]

---

192 In reality, the microphones on court didn't pick up the exact words. But Ken Farrar, the tournament referee that day, didn't need any amplification. He refused to specify what the magic words were, but he did say that had anyone heard what he did, they would've defaulted McEnroe from the match

"Code Violation, Default Mr. McEnroe. Game, set, match." And thus, on a sweltering day Down Under the Super Brat became the first player disqualified from a modern Grand Slam tennis match. Once a legend of the game, by the 1990 Australian Open, Mac was struggling to maintain his form and hoping for one last good season, perhaps one last Grand Slam title. It was the only reason he'd come to Australia, a tournament he usually skipped. Unfortunately, the heat or the jet lag caused him to be somewhat inattentive to the rules. He thought it took *four* code violations to receive a default and had neglected a rule change that went into effect late the prior year. Little did he know how hard it is to win tournaments where you are defaulted in the fourth round.[193]

Athletes often tap into **Emotions** in an effort to enhance their **Performance**. Even negative emotions, such as anger or hostility, can increase your intensity and motivation. This was obviously McEnroe's intent in Australia and elsewhere. But lingering too often in the emotional zone can lead to muscle tension and a loss of coordination. In time, that hurts performance more than it helps. With further set-

---

too. After the temper tantrum and default, he would never be ranked in the Top 10 in the world again.

193 McEnroe did not use his notorious catch phrase: "You cannot be serious!" Later in life, he would be expected to use the line at least once in exhibition matches or the fans didn't feel like they were getting the full Johnny Mac experience. "They're disappointed," he said. "And so that's sort of a weird dynamic, to put it mildly—that I'm actually getting paid extra for things I used to get fined for." Seriously.

backs, anger and passion can devolve into despair or even hopelessness; the kind of emotions that certainly keep you from performing your best. Or performing at all if you are tossed out of the tournament. So, take a tip from The Brat and calm the (expletive) down. That's right, years later, a mellower McEnroe eschewed his conflict-driven approach believing that any distraction to his opponent or motivation he gained was far outweighed by the bitterness he fostered and the energy he wasted.

— BLOOD, SWEAT AND EARS —

McEnroe isn't the only athlete to learn the hard way that emotions are difficult to harness and disqualification doesn't lead to winning ways. Six years later a former Heavyweight champion named Mike Tyson was determined to show off his boxing abilities, and not just his infamous punching, against Evander Holyfield.

Frustrated by Holyfield's clutching and grabbing, the challenger resorted to old tactics, opting to go toe-to-toe for long periods of time. And then something in him snapped. To begin the third round, Tyson charged out and landed a series of punches that seemed only to annoy Holyfield, who again smothered him against the ropes. So, Tyson bit him on the ear drawing blood and losing a point on the judge's cards. It was only the third round and all hell was breaking loose. Then Tyson bit him again just as the round ended. A chunk of upper ear joined the blood and sweat in the ring.

The MGM Grand went berserk with each fighter's camp charging the ring. Tyson was disqualified, a new career low for a man whose early career had been a cringe inducing highlight reel of first round knock outs that led him to the heavyweight championship when he was just nineteen. Yes, Tyson would regret the bites, but regrets are about the only things that come cheaply in Las Vegas.

How You'll Be Tested...

Investors are always looking for an edge. Perhaps, even after all I've written, you'll try to use your emotions to gain an advantage. When agitated by something you'll sell, buying back (you say) when you feel calmer. If you are scoring at home, that is a decision you need to get right under emotional duress. Code violation! I don't care if your aggravation is chafing like those miniature white tennis shorts they wore in the early 90s, studies show emotion-based investors struggle mightily with their own performance, usually getting both decisions wrong. They trail *all asset classes* and *even inflation* over the past thirty years. Why? Because they use emotions as buy and sell signals. Managing things by yourself and your impassioned strategy can't even beat inflation? Sounds like it is game, set, and match for that plan.

When you reach your own break point, emotions don't add to your performance, they smash it like a weak overhead lob. Frustrating? Sure, break all the inanimate objects you desire, but find someone to remind you of the rules when necessary. And the first rule is to take the heat without letting your passions prevail.

EXTRA CREDIT

MEET MAC: One of the greatest compliments ever paid to John McEnroe was whenever someone called him an artist. Anyone who knows tennis and has seen him hit a drop volley understands. His election to the Hall of Fame in 1999 was a no brainer despite his temperament. See the website for a further portrait of the artist: www.tennisfame.com/hall-of-famers/inductees/john-mcenroe/.

MORE MAC: For a recap of young McEnroe's larger than life 1980 season, pick up Matthew Cronin's *Epic* (2011). The 1980 Wimbledon final ended with twenty-one-year-old McEnroe's defeat by his idol, Bjorn Borg, and is often considered the greatest tennis match ever played. McEnroe got his revenge later that summer in what is considered the greatest U.S. Open final ever. Gone were wooden racquets and a country club stodginess. Rock-and-roll tennis was born.

THE MOST MAC: Still think emotions might help win the day from time to time? Time to get serious. McEnroe disagrees, though he is a bit more polite about it these days. He writes in his autobiography, *Serious* (2003), that calming down would have helped his performance.

GO UGLY EARLY: Brad Gilbert was never called an artist, and his record against McEnroe was a dismal 1–13 all time. Nevertheless, Gilbert perfected the art of hanging around and turned the skill into a career that included twenty career titles and a perennial ranking among the top ten in the world. His book, *Winning Ugly (2013)*, teaches us to fall out of love with how things look and focus on the result. Gilbert, in his own words, has a lesson for tennis, investing, and life: "The perfect match is finding a way to win that match." For the CliffsNotes, try this article: www.espn.com/sports/tennis/columns/story?columnist=drucker_joel&id=5402752.

CONSIDER THE OPTIONS: The narrator of this piece from OptionAlpha.com, sure sounds serene: www.youtube.com/watch?v=Ykrz9IMfWrc. But have no doubt, his strategy of identifying and trading on fourteen different emotional stages would make a younger McEnroe proud. And probably confused. McEnroe didn't have more than three emotions. Ever. Keep in mind with emotion-based trading, it doesn't really matter how YOU feel, it matters how all the other players, billions of them, feel. And you don't get to know that. Ever.

GET SERVED: Need to brush up on your forehand and backhand without leaving the couch? Grab a copy of EA Sports Grand Slam Tennis 2 to play against over twenty legendary pros including the cover boy, Johnny Mac himself. With the computer calling the lines, what could possibly go wrong?

LEND ME YOUR EARS: Need more proof that such emotions are fleeting? Mike Tyson and Evander Holyfield would reconcile, even become friendly. Indeed, as this video shows, Holyfield was presented for induction to the Nevada Boxing Hall of Fame by none other than Mike Tyson: www.youtube.com/watch?v=Yr39FAwbO2Q.

About Nothing
Seinfeld & Contrarianism

1998 AD

T hree may have been company in television land of
earlier decades, but it was Seinfeld's foursome who
ruled the 90s. Of their many memorable episodes,
who can forget the one about a contest to see who could
go the longest without…without, ah…well that is beyond
the scope of this course. However, one of their other most
memorable episodes explains why doing the opposite won't
always win you an award and something more mundane
might be smarter.[194]

Jerry and Larry slunk from their yellow New York cab and
ducked into Tom's Restaurant. Outside traffic edged noisily
along Broadway and college kids from nearby Columbia

---

194 *The Contest* was the 51st episode and aired in the show's fourth season.
It would win a Primetime Emmy Award for Outstanding Individual
Achievement in Writing in a Comedy Series by using a topic unsuitable for
prime time television and never naming it. I won't name it either in hopes
that similar accolades will follow.

University stood in loose groups discussing incredibly important topics.

Inside, ensconced in a fake leather booth that smelled like chicken salad, the two comedians were downcast and overdressed. Suits made them uncomfortable. And by suits they meant the network executives that had gathered around them like carrion birds in their wood paneled board room at NBC headquarters.

"Well, they said they liked it. In general. They said it's smart and different." Larry was trying not to allow their enthusiasm to be curbed.

"Smart and different? What, like Rain Man?"

"No, not *that* smart. Good movie though. Had some funny moments."

"But they also said it is a little too New York, and a little too Jewish." Jerry pointed out.

"Rain Man?"

"No, our pilot."

"Ouch" said Larry nodding. "Not good." [195]

"No, it could have been worse," said Jerry. "He could have actually killed us instead of just ending our professional lives. So, there's that."

The waitress came and chased away their banter, mumbling something that might have been a question. When

---

195 Warren Littlefield, the second in command of NBC's entertainment division, had been relatively positive. Division head Brandon Tartikoff though had made the "too New York, too Jewish" comment. Presumably Tartikoff knew of what he spoke being a Jewish New Yorker himself. Audiences who screened the pilot show agreed with Tartikoff, asking for funnier sketches from a more diverse cast. Dejected, the pair of New York humorists were dismissed to reconsider their situation comedy about a standup comic who found inspiration in the lunacy of his friends and family.

they looked confused, she pointed to the pitcher of coffee she carried and they nodded.

"Soft-talker," Larry noted when she'd gone.

"You see her hands?" Jerry asked.

"No, I was busy figuring out how to drown myself in a pitcher of coffee. Or poison myself licking envelopes. Why?"

"Man hands. Woman's body, hands of a man."

They drank coffee for a bit in silence.

"Does that look like Keith Hernandez to you?" Larry asked.

"From the Mets? The guy at the counter in that puffy pirate shirt? Couldn't be."

"No, I guess not. Got any script ideas?"

Jerry sighed. "One, but it is for later. After we've established the neurotic who lives with his parents as completely pathetic, we do an episode where he does everything opposite of his instincts and becomes a total success. Gets the girl, a job working for the Yankees. That sort of thing. At least for an episode."

"I don't like it." Larry said shaking his head.

"What's the deal with that? Why not?"

"Too New York. Too Jewish." Larry was grinning.

Jerry threw up his hands. "Serenity...serenity now!" [196,197]

---

196 Though the original pilot fared poorly, executives remained excited by the writing and, for perhaps the last time in television history, quality won out. Given a stronger supporting cast, the show did well with the young male adult demographic and the critics. It was renewed for a second season and within three years it was part of NBC's vaunted Thursday night lineup and cracked the top five in the Nielsen ratings where it would stay for the entirety of its run.

197 Tom's Restaurant's exterior became the fictional Monk's Café in the show. The chance to sit in the first booth on each episode, filmed on a

But serenity remained elusive for Jerry Seinfeld and Larry David, co-creators of *The Seinfeld Chronicles*. Months of rework by NBC writers and executives kept them busy. In the end, *Seinfeld* (the show) dropped the *Chronicles*, took production funds from a cancelled Bob Hope special and rolled out five episodes in 1990. Seinfeld (the character) kept his portly and bald best friend George and mysterious and gravitationally challenged neighbor Kramer, from the pilot. He added an ex-girlfriend who was rhythmically deficient, named Elaine, to round out the craziness taking place in an apartment on Manhattan's Upper West Side. The writing *was* different. *And* smart. The plots were simple, exploring mundane aspect of life that everyone related to like waiting in line, looking for a parking place, or what to do with the remaining chip after you've dipped and taken a bite. And the characters never learned anything from their misadventures. Everyone remained indifferent and sometimes callous, never seeming to grow or become a better person. It was so close to real life that diverse audiences not hailing from New York still fell in love with it.[198]

---

soundstage, was auctioned off for charity. The cashier at Monk's appears in 101 of 180 Seinfeld episodes, more than any other character outside the main quartet.

198 Seinfeld (the comedian) had only one rule for the show's scripts: "No learning and no hugging." According to the book Total Television, "Not since *The Adventures of Ozzie and Harriet* has a sitcom been less truly plot-driven." And George Constanza, agrees: "I think I can sum the show up for you in one word: nothing." The formula worked. Indeed, the Seinfeld vernacular remains a part of popular culture to this day. E! named the series

By season five it was time for that episode titled *The Opposite*. George realizes that: *"Every decision I've made in my entire life has been wrong. My life is the complete opposite of everything I want it to be."* Jerry notes that if everything he did was wrong, then the opposite would have been right. Hilarity ensues.[199]

This is **Contrarianism**—doing the opposite of what others and perhaps your own instincts tell you to do, the antithesis of herd-like behavior. It can be an attractive option, especially if you have a more than healthy fear of groupthink and conventional wisdom. But blind contrarianism isn't a foolproof plan either and any success can be fleeting. George eventually loses his job and his fiancée and moves back in with his parents. Contrarians, like the rest of us, are still prone to bad episodes where they learn nothing and have no one to hug at the end. Instead of outright hostility to the norm, try a bit of callous indifference. Of course, if you choose to ignore the cautionary tale of George Costanza…well then, no soup for you![200]

---

the "number one reason the 90s ruled," due to catchphrases like man-hands, double-dipping, soft-talker, serenity now, puffy pirate shirt, and re-gifter.

199 George becomes, if not a better person, at least a more successful one for a few episodes. Elaine, meanwhile becomes a de facto George, losing her job and her boyfriend and facing eviction from her apartment for accidentally buzzing a jewel thief past the security door. At the end of the episode, George is up and Elaine is down, but Jerry remains blissfully the same. Life goes on. Good thing Jerry had a diverse group of friends to help balance out their ups and downs. So, I'm thinking, hey…diversification works!

200 Seinfeld aired its last episode in 1998 to a record audience of over seventy-six million people. The episode features a trial where the main four characters are accused of violating Good Samaritan Laws. During sentencing, Judge Arthur Vandelay opines: "I do not know how, or under what circumstances the four of you found each other, but your callous indifference and utter disregard for everything that is good and decent has rocked the

THE CONSTANT CONTRARIAN

Contrarianism can devolve from a difference of opinion to a way of life. After all, any fool can follow the party line, but by not doing so, aren't you then indicating that you are nobody's fool? Think about it this way: if a ten-year-old child could understand an issue and agrees with the widely-held view, doesn't that mean the intelligence of the consensus group is that of a ten-year-old? So, why not continually take a contrarian view and show how smart you are?

Biologists study this process, known as signaling, in ours and other species. Humans provide all kinds of cues to others to relay information. Some signals are more genuine than others. As with most signals and shortcuts to rational thought, this one is, shall we say, problematic, because it eschews even basic analysis of the underlying issue. You must be right on the merits, not just because you are supposedly smart. Note that the example of the ten-year-old is a false syllogism. If the group holds an opinion and a child is part of the group, it *does not* follow that the group's opinion is childish. Sorry full-time contrarians, you aren't any smarter just because you hold an alternate view. You may be smarter *and* have such views, but you'll have to do more than just signal that. You'll have to prove it.

very foundation upon which our society is built." But the question remains, if something is about nothing can it ever actually end? Thanks to DVD and syndication, the answer is no.

How You'll Be Tested...

Market swings aren't fun or funny. Which is why you may be tempted by someone's market timing act. They may try to get you to take a contrarian position, to sell out of investments merely because they perceive everyone else is greedy. Or to buy something to be the opposite of timid. Such contrarian instincts are the basis for Warren Buffet's famous investment advice to be fearful when others are greedy and greedy when others are fearful. While famous, this is only part of Buffet's original quote. That is the problem with re-gifting information, there is often something lost in translation. Here is a more complete version from his 2004 Annual Shareholder Letter: *"And if they insist on trying to time their participation in equities, they should try to be fearful when others are greedy and greedy only when others are fearful."* Meaning, you don't have to try to time anything at all. And probably shouldn't. Or, to summarize, yada, yada, yada.

Take my advice and have your own version of The Contest. See how long you can go without touching it. Your properly constructed, long-term portfolio, I mean.

EXTRA CREDIT

HULU LOOP: Seinfeld predates the concept of binge watching, but thanks to Hulu's $160 Million deal for all 180 episodes, you can enjoy it in one glorious four-day bonanza. Maybe the sleep deprivation will make you the ultimate contrarian, the kind who actually likes the final episode.

DISCLAIM THE ACCLAIM: Unemployed after Seinfeld left the air, Larry David was offered a one-hour special on HBO in 1999. That turned in to a nine-season run for *Curb Your Enthusiasm*, which is back in 2017 after a six-year hiatus. A quasi-mockumentary about a fictional version of Larry David, *CYE* gives you the other Seinfeld writer's take on the minutiae and annoyances of everyday life. If it sounds like a familiar formula, it is. And it still works. *Curb Your Enthusiasm* is one of the most highly acclaimed shows on television. Which means nothing to a contrarian.

WORK IT OUT: Want to take home the office NCAA tournament bracket pool? Learn from the 2017 tournament field and USA Today, how to build a contrarian bracket: www. usatoday.com/story/sports/ncaab/tourney/2017/03/15/ contrarian-ncaa-tournament-bracket-tips-march-madness-picks-betting/99214700/. Of course, a true contrarian would have the four lowest seeds moving forward, which the author points out is "stupid." So, at best this seems to be a hybrid strategy. Which is why it might just work. Unfortunately, not in 2017 as the simulation picked only two of the Final Four teams and chose the wrong winner. It also failed to pick several upsets and missed most of the other regional finalists. If that wins your office pool, you might want to update your résumé. No organization can last long with a lack of brainpower like that.

LISTEN TO BUFFETT: No, not the Oracle of Omaha, Jimmy, the Parrothead King. Who better to convince you to have a good time and let the world do what it does without shifting between avarice and anxiety? Does our desire to be contrarian come from ignorance or apathy? He doesn't know, and he doesn't care. And he'd gladly trade all the daily worries for a fruity beverage and a nap on the beach. Waste away at: www.youtube.com/user/jimmybuffett.

GET ALONG LITTLE DOGGY: Learn to be the ultimate contrarian from a talking dog, courtesy of the animated show *Family Guy:* https://en.wikiquote.org/wiki/Family_Guy/Season_9#Excellence_in_Broadcasting. The dog, Brian Griffin, disagrees with everyone to seem smart. But really, he comes out looking smug and overbearing. Well, when you follow the dog, the view never changes.

GATHER THE FAMILY: Festivus was Frank Constanza's (George's father) holiday creation, celebrated on December 23rd. Contrary to other winter holidays it is distinctly non-commercial, religious, or even fun. Gather around the aluminum pole to air your grievances and then pin the head of the household to the ground. I announce my gripes often, a benefit of being a writer. But for those of you who need to get it all off your chest and then deadlift your uncle, the official guides to Festivus are here: www.festivusweb.com/ and here: www.festivusweb.com/festivus-book.htm.

The First Degree
Kevin Bacon & Investment Fraud

2009 AD

For your financial life to have a Hollywood ending, you'll need to steer clear of some bad actors. Using the knowledge accumulated throughout this book, you might avoid starring in a tragic scene.[201]

Emerging from the subway at 81st and Central Park West, the man with the disheveled hair braced himself and wrapped his scarf a little tighter around his neck, gazing at the snow-crusted park. He gasped a little, involuntarily, as the cold invaded his lungs, but it felt good to be out from the subway and walking. Home was but a few blocks away and he was determined to shake off the seemingly ever-present gloom and enjoy the holidays. Snow was drifting in small waves from cherry and cedar trees, muffling the noise of the

---

201 According to a survey, 70% of respondents said that recent events in the industry have made them question the trustworthiness of financial services professionals. We have men named Ponzi and Madoff to thank for much of that.

New York traffic. It was quiet that day, subdued. Yet another reminder of the tough economic times and financial crisis that had engulfed the entire country.

As he turned down to walk between the Museum of Natural History and the line of brownstone buildings dotted by awnings, a few people waved or stared mutely, star struck. He had long ago given up on prosthetics and disguises, finding that fame suited him much better than obscurity. In New York, if you weren't famous, people weren't inclined to be all that nice to you, even during the holidays.[202]

Strolling leisurely he took the long way home, turning right and colliding with a mountain of muscle leaving the wine shop. His breath left him in a gasp, white vapor arcing upward in the frosty air. But he steadied himself and looked up into the face of a large man with a wide forehead and a nose that had been broken at least once.

The man was going to say, *Hey! Watch where you are going moron*, but stopped himself abruptly. "It's you. I know you. From the movies, right?"

All he could do is smile, catch his breath and nod.

"Yeah, yeah. I know you. He was wagging a finger, smiling. "Yeah…Ben Affleck."

"Excuse me? No, no. I'm Kevin…"

"Yeah, yeah," the mountain man cut him off. "I *know* who you are. I'm trying to do that thing where I connect you with another actor in less than six flicks. So, Ben Affleck." He wasn't asking it as a question. He was demanding an answer.

"Ah, that's easy I guess. He was in *Chasing Amy* with

---

202 The route would have taken him past 129 West 81st, Seinfeld's apartment building as depicted in the television show.

Matt Damon. And Matt was in *Ocean's Eleven* with Julia Roberts. And Julia and I were in *Flatliners* together. Three degrees of separation."

"*Chasing Amy*, man that movie sucked! I get you with Matt Damon, but I'd a gone with *Good Will Hunting*."

"Sure, okay. Well, either would work. Same Bacon number."

"Bacon number, that's a good one," he heard the man chuckling. "What if we used *Good Will Hunting* and then connected you and Robin William in that *Hook* movie. Ya know, the one that was kind of like Peter Pan? C'mon, weren't you in that one? You had to be."

"No, you know, you've picked the one movie I'm not actually in."

"Ha, you got that right. Jeez, it's a wonder the unemployment rate ain't higher. Seems like you are the only one working. Ha, get it?"[203]

"I do. I get it. That's very…clever." He shrugged, hunkering down against the wind. "Well, Merry Christmas."

"Hey, yeah. Merry Christmas, Kevin Bacon."

Bacon thought next time he went out he would cover his face with the scarf. [204]

---

203 Unemployment had doubled during the financial crisis and by December 2009, 15.3 million people were out of work. Bacon starred in the aptly titled HBO film *Taking Chance* that year.

204 Bacon's prolific career became part of the national conscience after a 1994 interview in which he claimed, tongue in cheek, to have either worked with everyone in Hollywood or with someone who worked with them. While this wasn't quite true, it spawned a cottage industry of books and Kevin Bacon party games that sought the elusive actor or actress whose path didn't cross Bacon's in less than six degrees. Connecting film icons became more than a party trick, it was a passion for some. Indeed, a website followed where today you can calculate a Bacon number for just about anyone in Hollywood.

"Excuse me, but I couldn't help overhear," said a man who appeared next to him as his boots started to carry him away, crunching through blackened snow on Amsterdam Street. "Did that man say your name is Kevin Bacon?" Bacon turned to look at him, thinking recognition might dawn. But nothing happened. *Has this guy never seen a movie in his life?*

"Yeah, I'm Kevin Bacon." He took a moment to assess the man. *Pasty skin, a bit overweight, probably doesn't get out much.*

"Well, I'm with the State Attorney General's office, Mr. Bacon." *Nope, definitely doesn't get out much.*

"What's this about?" Bacon was a bit wary of scam artists in New York. Because it was, after all, New York.

"Do you know of Madoff securities, sir?"

Bacon shrugged. "Doesn't ring a bell."

"How about Bernie Madoff." Now the bells were ringing. And it wasn't the sound of recognition, but alarm.

"Bernie, yeah. I've got some money with him. I don't really know his firm that well." Bacon conceded warily. "Is there a problem?"

"Are you sure you don't want to sit down?" But Bacon waved him off. "Bernie Madoff was running a Ponzi scheme. I'm sorry, sir but it appears you are directly connected to Mr. Madoff and are a victim of his fraud." He added sheepishly, "I guess you might say *his* Bacon number is one."[205]

---

205 Bacon and his wife Kyra Sedgwick have never revealed how much they lost in the scandal except to say they lost a lot, but not everything. They have chosen to rebuild their finances in a very Bacon way. By working more.

Investment Fraud still happens, even in our cynical and suspicious modern society, though thankfully it is nowhere near as abundant as Kevin Bacon movies. Want to know how to spot some of it? Or at least know when to keep walking? Here is a review of the lessons that might have helped Kevin and thousands of others save their bacon:

Cognitive Biases: Madoff used investor psychology as a weapon against his victims.	• Hot Hand Fallacy: Madoff supposedly had perfect market timing ability, going to 100% cash before market declines in 1998 and 1999. Even if true, it wouldn't mean he was more likely do it again. • Recency Bias: According to one source, a Madoff fund returned 10.5% consistently for 17 years. Investors believed, despite common sense, that such performance would continue to happen. • Confirmation Bias: Clients would call to complain that Madoff promised 18% but they'd gotten 16%. An amended statement showing the promised rate would appear soon after. Investors were looking for information to confirm what a great investment they had made, and avoiding the obvious, nonconforming data. • Bandwagon Effect: Steven Spielberg, Sandy Koufax, Larry King, and John Malkovich all invested with Madoff. Why form your own ideas when others were already sold?
Economic Basics: Madoff's purported returns violated several rules of basic economics.	• Technology: Technology leads to progress and Madoff was a pioneer in electronic trading. Yet no one at his firm had an email account lest it leave an electronic trail. • Business Cycles: Business cycles occurred throughout Madoff's investing history, including recessions in 1991 and 2001. But his funds managed to post positive returns during both periods. How? No one had any idea. He didn't allow outside performance audits.

Investment & Market Basics: Madoff had no bad years. Cue ominous alarm bells.	• Random Walk Theory: Madoff rarely had a negative month, only seven of them in over fourteen years. That kind of consistency is somewhere between suspicious and totally impossible. • Risk v. Reward: During his negative months, he never lost more than 0.55% and never posted back to back negative months. There was seemingly no tradeoff between performance and downside protection. His investors got both high returns and low risk. • Asset Allocation & Diversification: To put all of one's assets in a single fund using a single strategy isn't diversified. Bernie even claimed to have warned his victims not to put all their money in his fund. A proper allocation would have at least limited the losses when he went belly up.
Financial Advice: Madoff's was a new version of an old scheme. Clearly, we haven't learned better since Ponzi lent his name to the scam.	• Attention Fragmentation: Bacon starred in sixteen movies between 2000 and 2007, directing and producing four other projects during that time. Like the rest of us, he had a few other things going on, raising the potential for error. • Informational Reflexivity: Otherwise knowledgeable authorities, such as fund managers, suspected Madoff was subsidizing their performance to pad his numbers. Yet, they continued to invest with him. • Biased Information Processing: Madoff promised 12% to 20% returns for his clients, no matter how the market was moving. Investors believed he was delivering on his promise. Because they wanted to.

How You'll Be Tested...

Sometimes investing is a case of *He Said, She Said* or *Telling Lies in America,* but you can remain *Footloose* and fancy free knowing that market *Tremors* are nothing in *The Big Picture.* Your investments might include *Rails and Ties, Digging to China,* or even an assortment of *Planes, Trains and Automobiles.* And there will be some *Flatliners* and some *Sleepers.* But at the *End of the Line,* despite the *Wild Things* you encounter, you can still end up *Picture Perfect.* Of course, if you are wondering if your advice comes from a *Hollow Man* then you need to consult someone about *Criminal Law.* There are a *Few Good Men* and women out there who can show you *Where the Truth Lies.* Lesson learned: if you aren't getting open and honest advice, and if things are too good to be true, that might require *Enormous Changes at the Last Minute.*[206]

EXTRA CREDIT

STAY UNLISTED: Who else got swindled by Bernie? To borrow a line from the 1986 movie *Top Gun,* "the list is long but distinguished." Of course, *Top Gun* is not a Bacon film, though he is an easy connection to Tom Cruise (*A Few Good Men*). Kelly McGillis and Val Kilmer are only sec-

---

206 A partial list of the Bacon filmography: *He Said, She Said (1991). Telling Lies in America (1997). Footloose (1984). Tremors (1990). The Big Picture (1989). Rails and Ties (2007). Digging to China (1998). Planes, Trains and Automobiles (1987). Flatliners (1990). Sleepers (1996). End of the Line (1987). Wild Things (1998). Picture Perfect (1997). Hollow Man (2000). Criminal Law (1989). A Few Good Men (1992). Where the Truth Lies (2005). Enormous Changes at the Last Minute (1983).*

ondary connections. Anyway, the list includes foreign banks, money managers, Hollywood moguls, hedge funds, and several non-profit organizations. You can view it here: www.wsj.net/public/resources/documents/st_madoff_victims_20081215.html.

UNDERSTAND THE ORIGINAL: Get to know Charles Ponzi, how the schemes that still carry his name work, and how they eventually unravel at: https://money.howstuffworks.com/ponzi-scheme.htm. Unfortunately, these scams happen more frequently than we know and only the large ones make headlines. Madoff was certainly national news as his fraud was the largest, nearly $65 Billion. Hopefully, that's a record that was not made to be broken.

BINGE ON BACON: How long would it take to watch every Kevin Bacon movie ever made? Well, he currently has 84 acting credits to his name, though that may change before this book is printed or even by the time I finish lunch. But working with round numbers, at an average running time of 120 minutes, that would work out to 168 hours. Or seven days without stop. Better order in.

MAKE IT A SNACK: Or, for a much briefer sampling of Bacon's repertoire check out his commercial for the UK's TV service, EE: www.youtube.com/watch?v=fJ1mbOIfTpo. There he parodies his roles in *Hollow Man, Apollo 13, Footloose, A Few Good Men,* and *Friday the 13th.* While none of those movies is a comedy, the commercial gets a few good chuckles. Even after Madoff, Bacon clearly retains a sense of humor.

LISTEN TO BERNIE: It is *still* not a good idea to take advice from Madoff. But listening to him tell his story, contradictions and all, on the phone from a North Carolina prison, is both comical and chilling. Check out the Audible original series *Ponzi Supernova* by journalist Steve Fishman: www.audible.com/mt/ponzisupernova. Note how even Fishman, the skeptical journalist, initially gets duped by Madoff's stories before they begin to unravel. Luckily, Bernie is serving the maximum one-hundred-and-fifty-year sentence, because his skills don't seem to be deteriorating behind bars.

SEE THE WIZARD: Madoff clearly does not deserve to have someone with the stature of Robert De Niro play him in a movie, but he gets it anyway in HBO's *Wizard of Lies*. Then again, it takes a gifted actor to portray another gifted actor: www.hbo.com/movies/the-wizard-of-lies.

BLOW THE WHISTLE: Harry Markopolos is a quantitative analyst and financial fraud investigator (he calls himself the Greek Geek) who reported Madoff to the Securities and Exchange Commission (SEC) in 2000, 2001, and 2005. You can hear his interview with C-Span at: www.c-span.org/video/?292982-1/words-harry-markopolos. The result can best be summed up by the title of his book: *No One Would Listen: A True Financial Thriller (2010).*

AFTERWORD

The Final Exam

Well, here we are. Ready for the final exam. I know if you took the preceding pages seriously, except when I was making jokes, you are fully prepared for it. It will be a practical test, consisting of how you do as an investor for the rest of your life. Make it through your golden years without running out of money and slighting your heirs and we'll call it a passing grade. But hey, no pressure. Here are a few reminders to get you though:

- Your brain is not your ally in this struggle. Indeed, there are days when your own brain will be your worst enemy. Heed the warning signs.
- Economic data is important, and widely misused. Understand the basics and don't waste time on the minutiae.
- Financial markets are large, complex, and ultimately for your benefit if you can be patient and master your self-destructive urges.
- If you still don't feel comfortable taking all of this on by yourself, it is permissible to get help. Hire a financial planner to give you guidance. He or she can't take the test for you, but they can keep you

on track when there is too much work for one person.

If you still need help for the exam, check out HistoryLessonsfortheModernInvestor.com. There you will find updated blog posts, new Extra Credit assignments and updates to links as they change.

Good work. Now, I believe you are ready to make your own history.

NOTES & SOURCES

History 101

LESSON ONE: Living in Babble On

Babylon:
http://www.nationalgeographic.com/archaeology-and-history/
magazine/2017/01-02/babylon-mesopotamia-ancient-city-iraq/

Hammurabi:
http://www.ancient.eu/hammurabi/

The Hanging Gardens:
http://www.ancient.eu/babylon/

Hammurabi's Code Translated:
http://sourcebooks.fordham.edu/halsall/ancient/hamcode.asp

Outcome Bias:
https://hbr.org/2016/09/what-we-miss-when-we-judge-a-decision-
by-the-outcome

Study on Paying for Outcomes of a Coin Flip:
https://link.springer.com/article/10.1007/s40881-016-0023-9

LESSON TWO: Every Dog Has His Day

Thutmose III
https://discoveringegypt.com/ancient-egyptian-kings-queens/
thutmose-iii-the-napoleon-of-ancient-egypt/

https://www.biography.com/people/thutmose-iii-39569

Battle of Meggido:
http://www.reshafim.org.il/ad/egypt/megiddobattle.htm
https://www.thoughtco.com/egypt-battle-of-megiddo-2360877

The Hot Hand:
http://www.investopedia.com/terms/h/hot-hand.asp
https://www.logicallyfallacious.com/tools/lp/Bo/
LogicalFallacies/233/Hot-Hand-Fallacy

Mathematics of a coin flip:
http://www.basic-mathematics.com/coin-toss-probability.html

LESSON THREE: The Problem with Poets

Homer:
http://www.ancient.eu/homer/
https://www.poets.org/poetsorg/poet/homer

Homeric Composition:
http://www.classics.upenn.edu/myth/php/homer/index.
php?page=comp
https://www.poets.org/poetsorg/text/epic-poetic-form

Dactylic Hexameter:
http://www.skidmore.edu/academics/classics/courses/1998fall/
cl202/resource/meter/metintro.html

Rhyme as Reason:
https://www.researchgate.net/publication/12102517_Birds_of_a_
Feather_Flock_Conjointly_Rhyme_as_Reason_in_Aphorisms

Dr. McGlone's Study:
https://www.psychologytoday.com/articles/199809/sounds-true-me

Sell in May Statistics:
> https://www.forbes.com/sites/oppenheimerfunds/2016/05/20/
>   debunking-a-popular-investing-myth-sell-in-may-go-
>   away/#3eff31f46e1a
> https://seekingalpha.com/article/4072942-sell-may-empirical-
>   evidence-market-adage

LESSON FOUR: Questioning the Answers

Socrates:
> https://www.biography.com/people/socrates-9488126
> https://plato.stanford.edu/entries/socrates/index.html

The Socratic Problem:
> http://plato.stanford.edu/entries/socrates/#SocProWhoWasSocRea
> http://plato.stanford.edu/entries/socrates/supplement.html

Anchoring Bias Studies:
> https://youarenotsosmart.com/2010/07/27/anchoring-effect/
> http://psiexp.ss.uci.edu/research/teaching/Tversky_
>   Kahneman_1974.pdf
> Ariely, Dan. Predictably Irrational: The Hidden Forces That Shape
>   Our Decisions. New York: Harper Perennial, 2010.

The Anchoring Effect:
> http://bucks.blogs.nytimes.com/2012/08/27/dont-let-the-original-
>   price-haunt-your-decision-to-sell/?_r=0

LESSON FIVE: The Ancient Chinese Secret

Confucius:
> http://www.iep.utm.edu/confuciu/
> http://www.ancient.eu/Confucius/
> https://plato.stanford.edu/entries/confucius/.

Availability Bias:
http://www.psych2go.net/availability-heuristic-recall-ability-affects-
perception/
http://us.beyondbullsandbears.com/2012/10/05/availability-bias/

Sharks v. Coconuts:
http://kwc.org/mythbusters/2005/07/special_jaws_special_1.html

LESSON SIX: Peripatetic Fits

Aristotle:
http://www.ucmp.berkeley.edu/history/aristotle.html, https://plato.
stanford.edu/entries/aristotle/
http://www.ancient.eu/aristotle/

Syllogisms:
http://www.wikihow.com/Understand-Syllogisms

Illusory Correlations:
http://brainshortcuts.blogspot.com/2010/11/illusory-correlation-
bias.html

Stocks and Oil:
https://www.brookings.edu/blog/ben-bernanke/2016/02/19/the-
relationship-between-stocks-and-oil-prices/

LESSON SEVEN: To Be, or Knot to Be

Alexander:
http://www.biography.com/people/alexander-the-great-
9180468#synopsis&awesm=~oFoetd7gfypVb4
http://www.ancient.eu/Alexander_the_Great/
http://www.historyofmacedonia.org//AncientMacedonia/
AlexandertheGreat.html

Battle of Granicus:
http://www.ancient.eu.com/Battle_of_the_Granicus/

The Gordian Knot:
http://www.history.com/news/ask-history/what-was-the-gordian-knot
http://www.alexander-the-great.co.uk/gordian_knot.htm

Duncker's Experiment:
https://www.futilitycloset.com/2012/04/19/the-candle-problem/
https://en.wikipedia.org/wiki/Candle_problem

LESSON EIGHT: Stuck in the Middle

Assassination of Caesar:
http://www.eyewitnesstohistory.com/caesar2.htm
http://www.telegraph.co.uk/history/12193529/The-Ides-of-March-The-assassination-of-Julius-Caesar-and-how-it-changed-the-world.html
http://www.history.com/this-day-in-history/the-ides-of-march-julius-caesar-is-murdered

Recency Bias:
http://bucks.blogs.nytimes.com/2012/02/13/tomorrows-market-probably-wont-look-anything-like-today/?_r=0
https://www.businesszone.co.uk/hr-glossary/recency-bias

Study on Toddlers and Recency Bias:
https://www.bcs.rochester.edu/people/ckidd/papers/SumnerEtAlCogSci2015.pdf

LESSON NINE: With Friends Like These

Ovid:
http://www.ancient-literature.com/rome_ovid.html

https://www.poets.org/poetsorg/poet/ovid
https://www.biography.com/people/ovid-9430940

Banishment of Ovid:
http://www.pbs.org/empires/romans/empire/ovid.html

Confirmation Bias:
https://explorable.com/confirmation-bias
https://www.forbes.com/sites/peterlazaroff/2016/09/28/
confirmation-bias/#109ffa034b7d
https://www.psychologytoday.com/blog/science-choice/201504/
what-is-confirmation-bias
https://youarenotsosmart.com/2010/06/23/confirmation-bias/.

Wasson's Experiments:
https://www.psychologyinaction.org/psychology-in-
action-1/2012/10/07/classic-psychology-experiments-wason-
selection-task-part-i
http://www.telegraph.co.uk/news/obituaries/1428079/Peter-Wason.
html
https://www.nytimes.com/interactive/2015/07/03/upshot/a-quick-
puzzle-to-test-your-problem-solving.html

Cumberbatch and Doyle:
http://www.imdb.com/title/tt1475582/trivia?ref_=ttcc_ql_1

LESSON TEN: Where There's Smoke, There's Fire

Pliny the Elder:
http://www.livius.org/articles/person/pliny-the-elder/

Pliny the Younger:
http://www.ancient-literature.com/rome_pliny.html

Vesuvius Eruption:
http://www.history.com/this-day-in-history/eruption-of-mount-
vesuvius-begins

https://www.livescience.com/27871-mount-vesuvius-pompeii.html
http://www.eyewitnesstohistory.com/pompeii.htm

RHT:

http://riskhomeostasis.org/about-risk-homeostasis
https://www.ncbi.nlm.nih.gov/pmc/articles/PMC1730348/pdf/
v004p00089.pdf
https://doclib.uhasselt.be/dspace/bitstream/1942/4002/1/
behavioraladaptation.pdf

Thaler and Benartzi Study:

https://www.researchgate.net/publication/227351035_Risk_
Aversion_Or_Myopia_Choices_in_Repeated_Gambles_and_
Retirement_Investments

LESSON ELEVEN: Falling to Pieces

Alexandria:

http://www.ancient.eu/alexandria/

Hypatia:

http://www.smithsonianmag.com/history/hypatia-ancient-
alexandrias-great-female-scholar-10942888/
http://www.ancient.eu/Hypatia_of_Alexandria/

The Bandwagon Effect:

https://www.psychologytoday.com/blog/media-spotlight/201512/
riding-the-bandwagon-effect
https://www.mindtools.com/pages/article/newLDR_82.htm

History 201

LESSON ONE: Exceptions to the Rule

The Middle Ages:
http://www.history.com/topics/middle-ages

The Renaissance:
http://www.history.com/topics/renaissance-art

Creative Destruction:
http://www.econlib.org/library/Enc/CreativeDestruction.html
https://www.aei.org/publication/the-netflix-effect-is-an-excellent-example-of-creative-destruction/

Joseph Schumpeter:
https://vimeo.com/75421736

Destruction of Videotape Rental Jobs:
https://www.bls.gov/data/, data set-All employees, thousands, video tape and disc rental, seasonally adjusted

Roman Empire and Provence:
Caro, Ina. The Road from the Past: Traveling Through History in France. Harcourt Brace & Company, 1996. P 16-31.

LESSON TWO: All the Kings Men

All things Magna Carta:
https://www.bl.uk/magna-carta
https://www.bl.uk/magna-carta/articles/magna-carta-english-translation
http://www.history.com/topics/british-history/magna-carta

Runnymede and Beyond:
http://www.history.com/this-day-in-history/magna-carta-sealed

Property Rights:
http://www.econlib.org/library/Enc/PropertyRights.html
http://www.investopedia.com/terms/p/property_rights.asp

Horne v. Department of Agriculture:
https://www.nytimes.com/2015/06/23/us/politics/supreme-court-sides-with-raisin-farmers-in-property-rights-case.html

LESSON THREE: Building Blocks

Santa Maria Al Fiore:
https://www.museumflorence.com/

Brunelleschi and the Dome:
http://ngm.nationalgeographic.com/2014/02/il-duomo/mueller-text

McDonald's:
http://www.telegraph.co.uk/news/2016/06/29/bunfight-in-florence-over-plans-for-a-new-mcdonalds-in-the-citys/
http://fortune.com/2016/11/08/mcdonalds-sues-florence-italy/

LESSON FOUR: Ratted Out

How to Swear in Italian:
http://icebergproject.co/italian/2015/09/8-swear-words-in-italian-to-add-sass-to-your-vocabulary/

The Plagues:
https://www.cdc.gov/plague/history/index.html

Equilibrium Price:
https://www.khanacademy.org/economics-finance-domain/microeconomics/supply-demand-equilibrium/market-equilibrium-tutorial/a/changes-in-equilibrium-price-and-quantity-the-four-step-process-cnx

Online Retailers and Pricing:
http://benjaminshiller.com/images/First_Degree_PD_Using_Big_Data_Jan_27,_2014.pdf
https://www.theatlantic.com/magazine/archive/2017/05/how-

online-shopping-makes-suckers-of-us-all/521448/
www.amazon.jobs/en/job_categories/economics

Equilibrium of Financial Assets:
Mishkin, Frederic. The Economics of Money, Banking and Financial Markets (11th Edition). Pearson, 2015.

LESSON FIVE: Crowd Control

Agincourt:
http://www.longbow-archers.com/historyagincourt.html
http://www.eyewitnesstohistory.com/agincourt.htm

The Longbow:
http://web.mit.edu/21h.416/www/militarytechnology/longbow.html

Quote on the French:
Neillands, Robin. The Hundred Years War, Routledge, 2002. P. 214.

Frontier Justice:
https://www.gsb.stanford.edu/faculty-research/working-papers/
technological-innovation-resource-allocation-growth
https://www2.deloitte.com/uk/en/pages/finance/articles/
technology-and-people.html

The Production Possibilities Frontier:
http://econperspectives.blogspot.com/2008/04/shifts-of-production-
possibilities.html
http://www.investopedia.com/university/economics/economics2.asp

LESSON SIX: King Me

Battle of Bosworth:
http://www.r3.org/richard-iii-the-battle-of-bosworth/

Richard:
http://www.britroyals.com/kings.asp?id=richard3
https://www.biography.com/people/richard-iii-9457120#recent-news&awesm=~oIHnFmKS8mlFIJ

Quote about Richard:
http://www.historyextra.com/feature/tudors/10-things-you-need-know-about-battle-bosworth

Tudor Propaganda:
https://www.bl.uk/collection-items/richard-iii-portrait-with-overpaint-c-1504-20

Susntein's Research:
https://papers.ssrn.com/sol3/papers.cfm?abstract_id=2752068

Cost Benefit Analysis:
https://www.mindtools.com/pages/article/newTED_08.htm

Henry VII's Rule:
http://www.tudorplace.com.ar/aboutHenryVII.htm

LESSON SEVEN: The Italian Job

Old St. Peter's:
https://churchpop.com/2015/08/03/the-lost-1200-year-old-wonder-a-tour-of-the-old-st-peters-basilica/

Michelangelo Biography:
https://www.michelangelo.org/

The Pieta:
http://www2.fiu.edu/~mirandas/bios1493.htm#Bilheres
http://www.michelangelo.net/pieta/
ItalianRenaissance.org, "Michelangelo's Pieta," in ItalianRenaissance.org, July 23, 2012: http://www.italianrenaissance.org/michelangelos-pieta/.

The Medici:
http://www.historyworld.net/wrldhis/PlainTextHistories.
asp?ParagraphID=hxf

Il Gobbo:
http://www.katz.art/Cristoforo-Solari-Milan-1468-1524-Hercules-
resting-DesktopDefault.aspx?tabid=6&tabindex=5&objectid=2
97081

Photo Taking and Memory:
https://bus.wisc.edu/~/media/bus/knowledge-expertise/academic-
departments/marketing/photo-memory-revision-final.
pdf?la=en
http://bigthink.com/philip-perry/taking-photos-improves-certain-
kinds-of-memories-and-weakens-others

Opportunity Cost:
http://www.investopedia.com/terms/o/opportunitycost.asp
http://www.econlib.org/library/Enc/OpportunityCost.html.

LESSON EIGHT: Upward Facing Dogma

Copernicus:
https://www.biography.com/people/nicolaus-copernicus-9256984

Copernicus and Monetary Theory:
https://mises.org/library/copernicus-and-quantity-theory-money

On Coinage of Money:
http://copernicus.torun.pl/en/archives/money/4/
https://mises.org/library/copernicus-and-quantity-theory-money

Heliocentric Theory:
http://www.nmspacemuseum.org/halloffame/detail.php?id=123
https://www.astronomyclub.xyz/uniform-circular/copernicus-and-
planetary-motions.html

Copernicus Quote:
https://plato.stanford.edu/entries/copernicus/

LESSON NINE: Brave New World

Thomas Morton:
https://patriciahysell.wordpress.com/tag/thomas-morton/
http://www.u-s-history.com/pages/h576.html
http://www.swarthmore.edu/SocSci/bdorsey1/41docs/08-mor.html
Morton, Thomas, New English Canaan, Edited by Jack Dempsey.
John Dempsey, 1999. P-iii.

The First Thing We Do:
Shakespeare, William. Henry VI Part II, Act 4 Scene 2.

The Maypole:
http://www.newenglandhistoricalsociety.com/maypole-infuriated-puritans/

Puritans on Morton:
http://www.bartleby.com/400/prose/24.html

Trade:
http://www.economicsdiscussion.net/international-trade/9-disadvantages-of-international-trade-discussed/1910
https://vittana.org/12-advantages-and-disadvantages-of-international-trade

LESSON TEN: Going Around in Ellipses

Comets:
http://spaceplace.nasa.gov/comet-nucleus/en/

Halley's Comet:
http://www.space.com/19878-halleys-comet.html

Johann Georg Palitzsch:
http://www.messier.seds.org/xtra/Bios/palitzsch.html
https://link.springer.com/referenceworkentry/10.1007
%2F978-0-387-30400-7_1047

Edmond Halley:
http://www-history.mcs.st-anEdmond Halley: d.ac.uk/Biographies/
Halley.html

Business Cycle circa 2006:
https://core.ac.uk/download/pdf/53173378.pdf

NBER Business Cycle Data:
http://www.nber.org/cycles.html

Business Cycle Phases:
http://www.investopedia.com/terms/b/businesscycle.asp
https://www.thebalance.com/what-is-the-business-cycle-3305912

LESSON ELEVEN: Fowl Play

Tegetmeier:
http://friendsofdarwin.com/articles/tegetmeier/

Darwin:
http://darwin-online.org.uk/biography.html

Adaptive Radiation:
https://www.pbs.org/wgbh/evolution/library/01/6/l_016_02.html

Marx Quote:
Marx, Carl. Karl Marx on Society and Social Change: With Selections
by Friedrich Engels. University of Chicago Press, 1973. P.97.

Networking:
Brusoni, Stefano & Prencipe, Andrea & Pavitt, K. (2001). Knowledge
specialization and the boundaries of the firm: why do firms know

more than they make? Administrative Science Quarterly. 46. 597–621-597–621. https://www.jstor.org/stable/3094825?seq=1#page_scan_tab_contents

Specialization and Adam Smith's Pins:
http://www.econlib.org/library/Topics/HighSchool/DivisionofLaborSpecialization.html

LESSON TWELVE: A House of Cards

Gavrilo Princip:
http://www.firstworldwar.com/bio/princip.htm

The Black Hand:
https://net.lib.byu.edu/estu/wwi/comment/blk-hand.html

The Duke's Assassination:
http://www.history.com/this-day-in-history/archduke-franz-ferdinand-assassinated
http://www.history.com/news/the-assassination-of-archduke-franz-ferdinand-100-years-ago
https://www.smithsonianmag.com/history/gavrilo-princips-sandwich-79480741/

Merton's Paper:
http://www.jstor.org/stable/2084615?seq=1#page_scan_tab_contents

History 301

LESSON ONE: New World Disorder

Columbus:
http://www.biography.com/people/christopher-columbus-

9254209#mixed-legacy

First Voyage:
http://www.indepthinfo.com/columbus-christopher/first-voyage.
htm
http://www.eyewitnesstohistory.com/columbus.htm

Persistence:
https://psmag.com/social-justice/be-warned-this-study-may-
encourage-your-child-to-keep-pursuing-that-career-as-a-
stand-up
http://www.brianjlucas.com/uploads/1/8/5/6/18565392/lucas___
nordgren_2015.pdf
https://www.carnegiehall.org/BlogPost.aspx?id=4295022505

Corrections:
http://www.investopedia.com/terms/c/correction.asp

LESSON TWO: A Pilgrim's Lack of Progress

The Mayflower:
Nathaniel Philbrick, *Mayflower*, Viking Books, 2006, Thomas J.
Fleming, *One Small Candle,* Norton & Company, 1963
http://www.plimoth.org/learn/just-kids/homework-help/mayflower-
and-mayflower-compact

Missing Days Data:
JPMorgan Asset Management, Guide to Retirement 2017. Slide 35,
Impact of being out of the market. Data from Bloomberg.

LESSON THREE: A Gage of Randomness

Thomas Gage:
http://militaryhistory.about.com/od/americanrevolutio1/p/gage.
htm

Washington:

http://www.mountvernon.org/george-washington/french-indian-war/ten-facts-about-george-washington-and-the-french-indian-war/

http://www.mountvernon.org/george-washington/french-indian-war/washington-and-the-french-indian-war/

French & Indian War:

http://www.history.com/topics/french-and-indian-war

Malkiel's Walk:

http://www.businessinsider.com/a-random-walk-down-wall-street-summary-2014-9

LESSON FOUR: All About the Benjamins

Ben Franklin:

http://www.history.com/topics/american-revolution/benjamin-franklin, http://www.history.com/this-day-in-history/benjamin-franklin-dies

http://www.publicbookshelf.com/public_html/The_Great_Republic_By_the_Master_Historians_Vol_II/benjaminf_hc.html

Franklin's Diplomacy:

http://www.unc.edu/depts/diplomat/item/2007/0103/sich/sicherman_franklin.html

Diversification:

http://www.investopedia.com/articles/02/111502.asp

http://www.investopedia.com/articles/basics/11/why-should-not-invest-in-what-you-know.asp

http://www.unc.edu/depts/diplomat/item/2007/0103/sich/sicherman_franklin.html

Eggs and Baskets:

http://www.theidioms.com/dont-put-all-your-eggs-in-one-basket/

Optimum Diversification:

http://www.investopedia.com/articles/stocks/11/illusion-of-diversification.asp

http://www.aaii.com/journal/article/how-many-stocks-do-you-need-to-be-diversified-.touch

LESSON FIVE: Going Postal

Wilson Price Hunt:

http://www.3rd1000.com/history3/biography/wphunt.htm

http://www.oregonencyclopedia.org/articles/hunt_wilson_price_1783_1842_/#.VX8bnyHBzRY

John Jacob Astor:

http://www.biography.com/people/john-jacob-astor-9191158#early-life

St. Louis:

https://www.stlouis-mo.gov/archive/history-physical-growth-stlouis/#terr

Econ Words:

https://news.google.com/newspapers?nid=1144&dat=19580313&id=jPoeAAAAIBAJ&sjid=EU4EAAAAIBAJ&pg=7426,4042997

Equity Risk Premium:

http://www.cfapubs.org/doi/pdf/10.2470/rf.v2011.n4.3

http://www.investopedia.com/terms/e/equityriskpremium.asp

JPMorgan Asset Management, Guide to Retirement 2017. Slide 63, Time, Diversification and the Volatility of Returns. Data from Barclays, FactSet, Federal Reserve, Robert Shiller & Ibbotson.

LESSON SIX: On the Money

Father Abraham:
http://www.abrahamlincolnsclassroom.org/abraham-lincoln-in-depth/abraham-lincolns-stories-and-humor/
http://housedivided.dickinson.edu/sites/lincoln/father-abraham/

Salmon P. Chase:
http://www.biography.com/people/salmon-p-chase-38185
http://inventors.about.com/od/mstartinventions/a/money.htm

The Lincoln Administration:
Doris Kearns Goodwin, Team of Rivals, Simon & Schuster, 2005.

History of Money:
http://www.secretservice.gov/money_history.shtml

Keep Digging:
H.W. Brands, *Reagan, The Life,* Anchor Books, 2015.

Plants and Interest:
V. H. BLACKMAN; *The Compound Interest Law and Plant Growth,* Annals of Botany, Volume os-33, Issue 3, 1 July 1919, Pages 353–360, https://doi.org/10.1093/oxfordjournals.aob.a089727

LESSON SEVEN: Shaving Face

Burnside:
www.civilwar.org/education/history/biographies/ambrose-burnside.html?referrer=https://www.google.com/
www.biography.com/people/ambrose-burnside-923221
www.civilwarhome.com/burnbio.html

The Mud March:
www.history.com/this-day-in-history/mud-march-begins
Meade of Gettysburg, Cleaves Freeman, *University of Oklahoma Press, 1960.*
Emotions & decisions: https://scholar.harvard.edu/files/

jenniferlerner/files/annual_review_manuscript_june_16_final.
final_.pdf

https://ppw.kuleuven.be/cscp/documents/mesquita/frijda-
mesquita-1998-the-analysis-of-emotions-dimensions-of-
variation.pdf

LESSON EIGHT: Extrapolation Celebration

The Groundhog:
www.nationalgeographic.com/animals/mammals/g/groundhog/

Groundhog Day:
www.history.com/this-day-in-history/first-groundhog-day

Phils's Predictions:
http://www.syracuse.com/news/index.ssf/2014/01/groundhog_day_
how_welll_does_phils_shadow_predict_spring_in_cny.html
http://www.livescience.com/32974-punxsutawney-phil-weather-
prediction-accuracy.html

Candlemas Sayings:
https://www.netweather.tv/forum/topic/75803-candlemas-day-
saying-2nd-feb/

Guru Grades:
https://www.cxoadvisory.com/gurus/#aggregate,
http://theirrelevantinvestor.com/2015/12/02/can-stock-market-
forecasters-forecast/
Alfred Cowles, *Can Stock Market Forecasters
Forecast? Econometrica*, vol. 1, no. 3, 1933, pp. 309–324. *JSTOR*,
JSTOR, www.jstor.org/stable/1907042.

LESSON NINE: Rough Ride Rewrite

Teddy Roosevelt:

https://www.pbs.org/weta/thewest/people/i_r/roosevelt.htm
https://www.whitehouse.gov/1600/presidents/theodoreroosevelt
http://www.theodore-roosevelt.com/

San Juan Hill:

www.arlingtoncemetery.net/mark-matthews.htm
The Rough Riders Storm San Juan Hill, 1898, EyeWitness to
History, www.eyewitnesstohistory.com/roughriders.htm (2004).

Vanguard Research:

Vanguard's Framework for Constructing Diversified Portfolios,
Vanguard Research, 2013: https://advisors.vanguard.com/iwe/
pdf/ICRPC.pdf.

LESSON TEN: Salt of the Earth

Pattillo Higgins:

Tracé Etienne-Gray, Handbook of Texas Online, "Higgins, Pattillo,"
accessed February 27, 2017, http://www.tshaonline.org/
handbook/online/articles/fhi07
https://aoghs.org/petroleum-pioneers/prophet-of-spindletop/

Spindletop Hill:

http://www.investopedia.com/articles/00/082800.asp

History 401

LESSON ONE: Life in the Fast Lane

IMS History:

http://indymotorspeedway.com/500hist.html
www.history.com/news/history-lists/10-things-you-may-not-know-

about-the-indianapolis-500
http://www.history.com/this-day-in-history/first-race-is-held-at-the-indianapolis-motor-speedway

Attention Fragmentation:
www.npr.org/templates/story/story.php?storyId=95256794
www.mckinsey.com/insights/organization/recovering_from_information_overload

Airline Safety:
www.denverpost.com/2010/02/13/human-error-is-biggest-obstacle-to-100-percent-flight-safety/
www.planecrashinfo.com/cause.htm

LESSON TWO: Being Frank

Francis Albert Sinatra:
http://abcnews.go.com/Entertainment/wireStory/hoboken-celebrates-frank-sinatras-100th-birthday-35729021
http://www.biography.com/people/frank-sinatra-9484810
http://www.wtsp.com/story/news/2015/12/06/frank-sinatra-100th-anniversary-special-sunday-cbs/76888864/
https://www.theguardian.com/music/2015/dec/12/very-long-retirement-frank-sinatra-final-years
http://www.sinatra.com/timeline

My Way:
http://www.dailymail.co.uk/tvshowbiz/article-3353685/The-one-song-Sinatra-hated-Way-odd-facts-Ol-Blue-Eyes-eve-100th-birthday.html
https://www.theguardian.com/uk/2005/nov/17/arts.artsnews1

Reflexivity:
Invested interests? Reflexivity, representation and reporting in financial markets: http://jou.sagepub.com/content/14/2/208.abstract

Greenspan:
https://www.c-span.org/video/?c4517742/greenspan-quote.

Origins of the Crash:
Roger Lowenstein, *The Great Bubble and Its Undoing*. Penguin Books, 2004.

LESSON THREE: A Proud Papa

Papa's Style:
https://www.cliffsnotes.com/literature/h/hemingways-short-stories/critical-essay/hemingways-writing-style

The Sun also Rises:
http://www.literarytraveler.com/articles/fitzgerald-hemingway-and-the-sun-also-rises/

Financial Journalists:
http://odft.nt2.ca/blogue/what-are-financial-journalists-review
http://eprints.lse.ac.uk/28840/1/What%20are%20financial%20journalists%20for%20(LSERO).pdf

LESSON FOUR: My Way or the Conway

Conway Twitty:
http://www.countryweekly.com/magazine/vault/cover-story-we-remember-late-great-conway-twitty-1994
http://conwaytwitty.com/bio
http://www.nytimes.com/1993/06/06/obituaries/conway-twitty-59-dies-on-tour-country-star-had-50-no-1-songs.html & http://people.com/archive/town-without-twitty-vol-42-no-18/

Follow Your Heart:
www.brainyquote.com/quotes/keywords/advice_4.html#FGoRWwylrerCQGdK.99

The Estate:
http://www.estateofdenial.com/2011/11/13/flashback-conway-
twitty-estate-dispute/

The Other Preparation Paradox:
http://keithba.net/fighting-the-last-war
Antulio Joseph Echevarria, *Preparing for One War and Getting
Another,* Strategic Studies Institute, 2010.

LESSON FIVE: All the Kingsmen

Studio History:
http://www.jimmie-rodgers.com/biography/
http://www.nytimes.com/1990/02/26/obituaries/johnnie-ray-63-50-
s-singer-who-hit-no-1-with-a-sob-in-his-voice.html
http://www.historylink.org/File/8946

The Kingsmen:
www.imdb.com/name/nm0969456/bio
www.nydailynews.com/entertainment/music/louis-louie-singer-
jack-ely-dies-article-1.2202725
http://www.history-of-rock.com/kingsmen.htm

Louie, Louie:
https://vault.fbi.gov/louie-louie-the-song/louie-louie-the-song/view

Information Processing:
http://blogs.worldbank.org/publicsphere/i-only-hear-what-i-want-
hear-and-so-do-you
Gotlib, Ian & Krasnoperova, Elena. (1998). Biased Information
Processing as a Vulnerability Factor for Depression. Behavior
Therapy. 29. 603-617. 10.1016/S0005-7894(98)80020-8.

Chords:
http://www.guitarland.com/ChordDiagrams/Frame3.html

LESSON SIX: Raising the Bar

Fosbury:

https://www.youtube.com/watch?v=rX3bCh8v1FE

http://www.gazettetimes.com/news/local/fosbury-takes-track-and-field-to-new-heights/article_17dcc0d8-b6cc-11e3-850a-0019bb2963f4.html

Financial Media:

The Media and Financial Crises: Comparative and Historical Perspectives, Edited by Steve Schifferes, Richard Roberts. Routledge, Aug 27, 2014.

Expert Bias:

http://olivierlacan.com/posts/expert-bias/

https://www.psychologytoday.com/blog/everybody-is-stupid-except-you/201008/the-expertise-bias

https://thoughtrefuse.wordpress.com/2009/04/15/study-supports-expert-bias/

Depression:

https://www.researchgate.net/publication/222771943_Biased_Information_Processing_as_a_Vulnerability_Factor_for_Depression

http://www.personalityresearch.org/papers/allen.html

LESSON SEVEN: To Boldly Go

Stardates:

https://web.cs.sunyit.edu//~rawdinm/Stardate.html

Nimoy:

http://www.nytimes.com/2015/02/27/arts/television/leonard-nimoy-spock-of-star-trek-dies-at-83.html?_r=0

http://www.imdb.com/name/nm0000559/bio?ref_=nm_ov_bth_nm

http://www.cnn.com/2015/02/27/entertainment/feat-obit-leonard-nimoy-spock

https://artsbeat.blogs.nytimes.com/2009/05/08/a-mind-meld-qa-with-leonard-nimoy/

Television:

Television in Society, Arthur Asa Berger, Transaction Publishers, Jan 1, 1987

http://www.cjc-online.ca/index.php/journal/article/view/1096/1002

http://journals.sagepub.com/doi/abs/10.2466/pr0.1985.57.1.263

Mass Media Trust:

http://news.gallup.com/poll/195542/americans-trust-mass-media-sinks-new-low.aspx

LESSON EIGHT: Strike That

4/29/1986:

http://www.baseball-almanac.com/box-scores/boxscore.php?boxid=198604290BOS

http://www.boston.com/sports/baseball/redsox/articles/1986/04/30/clemens_fans_a_record_20/?

https://www.youtube.com/watch?v=5WTM3YBzfxw

https://www.baseball-reference.com/boxes/BOS/BOS198604290.shtml

GDP:

http://bea.gov/newsreleases/national/gdp/gdpnewsrelease.htm

https://fivethirtyeight.com/datalab/the-messy-truth-behind-gdp-data/

LESSON NINE: You Can Be Serious

Down Under:

http://www.nytimes.com/1990/01/22/sports/boom-mcenroe-is-ejected.html

https://www.nytimes.com/2015/01/24/sports/tennis/mcenroe-takes-it-all-in-stride-25-years-after-epic-meltdown-at-australian-open.html

Sports and Emotions:
https://www.psychologytoday.com/blog/the-power-prime/201012/sports-the-power-emotions

Investor Performance:
Oppenheimer Funds, *Compelling Wealth Management Conversations*. Slide 6. What Has the Greatest Impact on Investment Results? 2017.

LESSON TEN: About Nothing

Seinfeld:
http://uproxx.com/tv/10-fascinating-facts-about-the-seinfeld-pilot/2/

Buffett Quote:
http://www.investopedia.com/university/warren-buffett-biography/warren-buffett-most-influential-quotes.asp#ixzz4d27vTUUv

The Opposite:
http://en.wikipedia.org/wiki/The_Opposite

Signaling
http://lesswrong.com/lw/2pv/intellectual_hipsters_and_metacontrarianism/
Signaling Theory: A Review and Assessment, Brian L. Connelly, S. Trevis Certo, R. Duane Ireland and Christopher R. Reutzel, Journal of Management 2011 37: 39

LESSON ELEVEN: The First Degree

Confidence Survey:
> http://www.planadviser.com/Financial-Industry-Scandals-Causing-Consumers-to-Lose-Confidence/

Kevin Norwood Bacon:
> http://www.azcentral.com/thingstodo/celebrities/free/20130203kevin-bacon-uses-public-transport.html
> https://en.wikipedia.org/wiki/Kevin_Bacon_filmography

Madoff:
> http://www.nytimes.com/2009/05/13/business/13madoff.html
> http://www.nytimes.com/interactive/2009/06/29/business/madoff-timeline.html?_r=0
> http://www.wsj.com/articles/SB112966954231272304?alg=y
> http://www.bankrate.com/finance/personal-finance/six-degrees-of-bernie-madoff-1.aspx

Bacon Number:
> http://oracleofbacon.org/help.php

Ponzi:
> http://money.howstuffworks.com/ponzi-scheme6.htm.

> Charles Ponzi didn't invent the idea of creating returns with money from new investors, but his 1920s scam was memorable enough, losing investors $20 million, that his name became synonymous with the ruse.

Made in the USA
Middletown, DE
26 May 2018